THE WISDOM OF
WINSTON
CHURCHILL

WORDS OF WAR AND PEACE

THE WISDOM OF
WINSTON CHURCHILL

WORDS OF WAR AND PEACE

EDITED BY
SEAN LAMB

CONTENTS

INTRODUCTION

Winston Churchill was one of the twentieth century's greatest orators and a Nobel-Prize-winning author. His greatest achievement was leading his country to victory in World War II, where his adversary was another great orator, Adolf Hitler. But Churchill did not fulminate or rant. His great wartime speeches were delivered in measured tones to a hushed House of Commons or by radio broadcast direct to the peoples of the British Empire.

World War II was a terrible conflagration which consumed the lives of over sixty million people. It was a war of bombs and bullets, aircraft and tanks, steel and blood. It was also a war of competing political ideologies – a war of words. And it was with words that Churchill was the acknowledged master.

In a broadcast of 1954, the veteran foreign correspondent, Edward R. Murrow, who had covered the London Blitz for CBS, said of Churchill: "He mobilized the English language and sent it into battle to steady his fellow countrymen and hearten those Europeans upon whom the long dark night of tyranny had descended."

These sentiments were echoed by President John F. Kennedy when he made Winston Churchill an honorary US citizen in 1963. Signing the proclamation, he said: "In the dark days and darker nights when England stood alone – and most men, save Englishmen, despaired of England's life – he mobilized the English language and sent it into battle. The incandescent quality of his words illuminated the courage of his countrymen."

After the attacks on the twin towers of the World Trade Center on 11 September 2001, New York Mayor Rudolph Giuliani drew strength from Churchill's words. He had been reading Roy Jenkins' full-length biography, *Churchill: A Life*, and in the early hours of 12 September, he returned to the passage where Churchill, who had only just become prime minister, shepherded his people through the Battle of Britain by offering them nothing but "blood, toil, tears and sweat".

Churchill's mastery of language is surprising. He had done so poorly at school that his father decided that he was fit for only one career – the Army. Even then, it took him three attempts to pass the entrance exam to the Royal Military College at Sandhurst. However, after graduating in the top twenty in a class of 130, he moved into journalism, covering Cuba's war of independence from Spain for the *Daily Graphic*. On India's north-west frontier and with Lord Kitchener's expeditionary force on the Nile, he saw further service as a soldier and a war correspondent. He wrote books about his experiences, along with a romantic novel called *Savrola*.

During his time in the Army, Churchill embarked on a reading programme to make up for the deficiencies of his education. He resigned his commission to make a living by his pen and enter politics. Losing a by-election at Oldham in 1899, he went to cover the South African War for the *Morning Post*. He quickly won fame for his actions, including a daring escape after being captured by the Boers. Returning to England, he won the parliamentary seat for Oldham in the 1900 election – and made £10,000 from his writing and lecture tours. He wrote the biography of his father, Lord Randolph Churchill, in 1906 and *My African Journey* in 1908.

In the House of Commons, he was acknowledged as the master of debate with the set speech as his forte – despite a speech impediment. Later in life he had his dentures modified to retain his famous slur.

At the outbreak of World War I in August 1914, Churchill was at the Admiralty, but resigned in November 1915 following the failed invasion of Gallipoli. He fought on the Western Front as lieutenant-colonel of the 6th Royal Scots Fusiliers, returning to parliament in June 1916 and the government in July 1917, where he began the development of the tank. As minister of war, he oversaw the Allied invasion of the nascent Soviet Union.

Out of office in the 1920s, he began writing *The World Crisis*, which netted him £20,000. During the General Strike of 1926, he edited the *British Gazette*, a government propaganda sheet. Between 1933 and 1938, he produced a biography of his distinguished ancestor John Churchill, the first Duke of Marlborough, British commander during the War of the Spanish Succession and victor at Blenheim, Ramillies and Oudenaarde.

With the rise of Hitler in Germany, Churchill became a vocal critic of his own government's policy of appeasement. He urged re-armament, particularly the build-up of the Royal Air Force in the face of the threat of the growing German Luftwaffe. When appeasement failed and Britain went to war, Churchill was seen as the only man who could stand up to the Nazi menace.

It has frequently been remarked that his judgment was sometimes erratic, but the power of his oratory rallied the British people at a time when they seemed doomed to lose. Then, when the United States entered World War II in December 1941, he addressed Congress, emphasizing the need for Anglo-American solidarity and citing his own trans-Atlantic heritage: his mother was the New York heiress Jenny Jerome. For him the vital component was not the shared blood, but the shared language. During the war, the British Cabinet set up a committee to develop a simplified form of English that the whole world could embrace.

Although Churchill fell from power in 1945, his command of rhetoric was far from over. He coined the term "Iron Curtain" in a speech in Fulton, Missouri, in 1946, marking the advent of the Cold War. Returning to popular favour, he was Prime Minister once more from 1951 to 1955.

Determined that history would judge him favourably, he wrote *The Second World War* in six volumes between 1948 and 1953. It won him the Nobel Prize for Literature in 1953. Between 1956 and 1958, he wrote *A History of the English-Speaking Peoples*, which again emphasized the importance of language in world politics.

By his death in 1965, he had proved his mastery of both the written and spoken forms of the language – not just in the heavyweight arenas of war and politics. His unique wit and acerbic asides made him one of the most acute observers of the twentieth century.

Nigel Cawthorne

THERE NEVER WILL BE ENOUGH OF EVERYTHING WHILE THE WORLD GOES ON.

The more that is given the more there will be needed.

That is why life is so interesting.

Commons, June 16, 1926

Abundance

The outstanding feature of the twentieth century has been the enormous expansion in the numbers who are given the opportunity to share in the larger and more varied life which in previous periods was reserved for the few and for the very few. This process must continue at an increasing rate. If we are to bring the broad masses of the people in every land to the table of abundance, it can only be by the tireless improvement of all our means of technical production, and by the diffusion in every form of education of an improved quality to scores of millions of men and women.

Massachusetts Institute of Technology, Boston, March 31, 1949

There never will be enough of everything while the world goes on. The more that is given the more there will be needed. That is why life is so interesting.

Commons, June 16, 1926

Abyss, The

For five years I have talked to the House of these matters – not with very great success. I have watched this famous island descending incontinently, recklessly, the stairway which leads to a dark gulf. It is a fine broad stairway at the beginning, but, after a bit, the carpet ends. A little further on there are only flagstones, and, a little further on still, these break beneath your feet.

Commons, March 24, 1938

Academy, Royal

The function of the Royal Academy is, I think, to hold a middle course between tradition and innovation. Without tradition art is a flock of sheep

'I have watched this famous island descending incontinently, recklessly, the stairway which leads to a dark gulf'

without shepherds, and without innovation it is a corpse. It is not the function of the Royal Academy to run wildly after every curious novelty.

Royal Academy Banquet, London, April, 30, 1953

Ace

I am horrified to learn that the Admiralty propose to scrap the five 15-inch battleships of the Royal Sovereign class, one in 1942, one in 1943 and the rest, I suppose, in the following year. The House would hardly gather from the euphemistic phrase the Parliamentary Secretary employed – "replacement" – that these two ships are to be destroyed. That does not tell us what one would expect, that until the new ships are in commission the old ones will be kept in reserve. In other days I used to say that when the ace is out the king is the best card.

Commons, March 16, 1939

Acquisitions, Territorial

We have got all we want in territory, but our claim to be left in undisputed enjoyment of vast and splendid possessions, largely maintained by force, is one which often seems less reasonable to others than to us.

Commons, March 17, 1914

Action

> Where every step is fraught with grave consequences and with real peril to the cause, deliberate and measured action is not merely prudent, but decent.
>
> *Commons, February 22, 1910*

When you embark on a course of restriction or oppression, caution and hesitancy should rightly impose themselves upon you; but when you are embarked upon a course of relief and liberation, advance with courage.

Commons, June 7, 1928

Adenauer, Dr Conrad

Dr Adenauer may well be deemed the wisest German statesman since the days of Bismarck.

Commons, May 11, 1953

I have greatly admired the perseverance, courage, composure and skill with which he has faced the complex, changing, uncertain and unpredictable situations with which he has been ceaselessly confronted.

Commons, May 11, 1953

Adjustment of Ideas

It is in the nice adjustment of the respective ideas of collectivism and individualism that the problem of the world and the solution of that problem lies in the years to come.

Kinnaird Hall, Dundee, May 14, 1908

Advantage in War

Even taking the lowest view of human nature, nations in war do not usually do things which give them no special advantage, and which grievously complicate their own position.

Commons, March 8, 1934

Adversity as a Stimulant

It is idle to say that the threat of adversity is a necessary factor in stimulating self-reliance.

Commons, April 28, 1925

Advice, Devil's

I will avail myself of the avuncular relationship which I hope I may still possess in respect of the Government to put it to the Prime Minister [Mr Neville Chamberlain] personally and even intimately. Has he ever heard of Saint Anthony the Hermit? Saint Anthony the Hermit was much condemned by the Fathers of the Church because he refused to do right when the Devil told him to. My Right Hon Friend should free himself from this irrational inhibition, for we are only at the beginning of our anxieties.

Commons, May 25, 1938

14

'It is idle to say that the threat of adversity is a necessary factor in stimulating self-reliance'

Advice, Expert

I am a Parliamentarian myself, I have always been one. I think that a Minister is entitled to disregard expert advice. What he is not entitled to do is to pretend he is acting upon it, when, in fact, he is acting contrary to it.

Commons, May 7, 1947

Advice on Disarming

If you press a country to reduce its defences beyond its better judgment, and it takes your advice, every obligation you have contracted, however carefully it has been expressed, will be multiplied in force, and you will find your position complicated by fresh obligations of comradeship, honour and compassion which will be brought very prominently to the front when a country which has taken your advice falls into grave jeopardy, perhaps as a result of what you have pressed upon it.

Commons, March 23, 1933

Aerial Defence

In an aerial war the greatest form of defence will undoubtedly be offence.

Commons, March, 21, 1922

I cannot see in the present administration of Germany any assurance that they would be more nice-minded in dealing with a vital and supreme situation than was the Imperial Government of Germany, which was responsible for this procedure being adopted towards France. No, Sir, and we may, within a measurable period of time, in the lifetime of those who are here, if we are not in a proper state of security, be confronted on some occasion with a visit from an ambassador, and may have to give an answer in a very few hours; and if that answer is not satisfactory, within the next

'No one should go forward in this business without realizing the cost and the issues at stake'

few hours the crash of bombs exploding in London and cataracts of masonry and fire and smoke will apprise us of any inadequacy which has been permitted in our aerial defences.

Commons, February 7, 1934

Aeroplane, The Marauding

I wonder that the League of Nations at Geneva does not offer an enormous monetary prize to incite inventors of all countries to discover methods of bringing down the marauding aeroplane.

Commons, June 7, 1935

Aeroplanes, Fragility of

After all, an aeroplane, though a very formidable engine of war, is also a very fragile structure, and an explosive charge no bigger than a small cigar is sufficient to bring down the most powerful aeroplane if it strikes a spar or the propeller: even a bird has been the cause of fatal accidents. Merely to fire at an aeroplane in the air is like trying to shoot a flying duck with a pea-rifle. What must be aimed at is not the hitting of the aeroplane, but the creation of conditions in the air around the aeroplane which are extremely noxious if not destructive to it. For that purpose it is clear that this effect of the shell which is fired should not be momentary.

Commons, June 7, 1935

Aftermath

We meet this afternoon under the shadow of the disasters of last year. It is not the time to bewail the past; it is the time to pay the bill. It is not for me to apportion the blame; my task is only to apportion the burden. I cannot present myself before the Committee in the guise of an impartial judge; I am only the public prosecutor.

Commons, April 11, 1927

Aftermath of War

The problems of the aftermath, the moral and physical exhaustion of the victorious nations, the miserable fate of the conquered, the vast confusion of Europe and Asia, combine to make a sum total of difficulty, which, even if the Allies had preserved their wartime comradeship, would have taxed their resources to the full. Even if we in this island had remained united, as we were in the years of peril, we should have found much to baffle our judgment, and many tasks that were beyond our strength.

Commons, June 5, 1946

Age, The Febrile

We live in such a febrile and sensational age, that even a month or two is enough to make people not merely change their views, but to forget the views and feeling they entertained before.

Commons, October 24, 1935

Age, The Great

We are living in a great age, of which it will always be said that this present generation, in Britain and in the United States, has cast upon them burdens and problems without compare in the history of the world. Under the severest stresses, and under the most hard and searching trials, they have shown themselves not unequal to these problems. On the contrary, they have triumphed over them, and thus cleared the way to the broad advance of mankind to levels they have never yet attained, and to securities of which they never will be deprived.

The Citadel, Quebec, September 16, 1944

Aggressors

They [Hitler and Musolini] cannot pursue their course of aggression without bringing about a general war of measureless devastation. To submit to their encroachments would be to condemn a large portion of mankind to their rule; to resist them, either in peace or war, will be dangerous, painful and hard. There is no use at this stage in concealing these blunt facts from anyone. No one should go forward in this business without realizing plainly both what the cost may be, and what are the issues at stake.

Corn Exchange, Cambridge, May 19, 1939

> ## Agreement
> It is a sort of British idea that when you reach agreement you take the rough with the smooth.
>
> *Commons, February 16, 1948*

Agreements

When an agreement has been reached everyone who is a party to it is bound by it, and previous misgivings and differences of opinion are blotted out and ought not to be referred to. In every walk of life, in every sphere of human activity, this is the invariable rule and it is the only safe and honest rule.

Commons, March 5, 1917

Air Armaments

Air armaments are not expressed merely by the air squadrons in existence or the aeroplanes which have been made; they cannot be considered apart from the capacity to manufacture. If, for instance, there were two countries which each had 1,000 first-line aeroplanes, but one of which had the power to manufacture at the rate of 100 a month and the other at the rate of 1,000 a month, it is perfectly clear that air parity would not exist between those two countries very long.

Commons, May 31, 1935

Air, Conquest of

We have learned to fly. What prodigious changes are involved in that new accomplishment! Man has parted company with his trusty friend the horse and has sailed into the azure with the eagles, eagles being represented by the infernal [loud laughter] – I mean internal – combustion engine. Where, then, are those broad oceans, those vast staring deserts? They are shrinking beneath our very eyes. Even elderly Parliamentarians like myself are forced to acquire a high degree of mobility.

Harvard University, September 6, 1943

Air Defence

Why should we fear the air? We have as good technical knowledge as any country. There is no reason to suppose that we cannot make machines as good as any country. We have – though it may be thought conceited to say so – a particular vein of talent in air piloting which is in advance of that possessed by other countries. There is not the slightest reason to suppose that we are not capable of producing as good results for money put into action as any other country. That being so, I ask the Government to consider profoundly and urgently the whole position of our air defence.

Commons, March 14, 1933

There is a sensible improvement in our means of dealing with German raids upon this island, and a very great measure of security has been given to this country in day-time – and we are glad that the days are lengthening. But now the moonlight periods are also looked forward to by the Royal Air Force as an opportunity for inflicting severe deterrent losses upon the raiders, as well as for striking hard at the enemy in his own territory. The fact that our technical advisers welcome the light – daylight, moonlight, starlight – and that we do not rely for protection on darkness, clouds and mists, as would have been the case some time ago, is pregnant with hope and meaning.

Commons, April 9, 1941

Air Equality

Speeches are made in the country by leading Ministers saying that we have decided that we must have air equality, that we cannot accept anything less. We have not got it. We are already decidedly inferior to Germany, and it must be said, of course to France.

Commons, May 31, 1935

'The fact that our technical advisers welcome the light is pregnant with hope and meaning'

Air Force

Not to have an adequate air force in the present state of the world is to compromise the foundations of national freedom and independence.

Commons, March 14, 1933

Air Parity

Military aircraft and first-line strength are two different categories, I wish, therefore, this afternoon to examine the air power of Great Britain and Germany in both categories – that of military aircraft and that of first-line strength.

Commons, November 28, 1934

Air Potential

The air power of any country cannot be measured by the number of aeroplanes, nor by any of the particular definitions which are given. It must be measured by the number of aeroplanes which can be placed in the air simultaneously and maintained in action month after month. It is dependent not only on the number of organized squadrons, but upon the expansive power of industrial plant.

Commons, March 10, 1936

Air Power

I cannot conceive how, in the present state of Europe and of our position in Europe, we can delay in establishing the principle of having an air force at least as strong as that of any power that can get at us. I think that is a perfectly reasonable thing to do. It would only begin to put us back to the position in which we were brought up. We have lived under the shield of the navy. To have an air force as strong as the air force of France or Germany, whichever is the stronger, ought to be the decision which Parliament should take, and which the National Government should proclaim.

Commons, February 7, 1934

Air Superiority

We are entering upon a period of danger and difficulty. And how do we stand in this long period of danger? There is no doubt that the Germans are superior to us in the air at the present time, and it is my belief that by

'An effort at rearmament ought to be made forthwith, and all the resources of this country should be bent to that task'

the end of the year, unless their rate of construction and development is arrested by some agreement they will be possibly three, and even four, times our strength.

Commons, May 22, 1935

The sole method that is open is for us to regain our old island independence by acquiring that supremacy in the air which we were promised, that security in our air defences which we were assured we had, and thus to make ourselves an island once again. That, in all this grim outlook, shines out as the overwhelming fact. An effort at rearmament, the like of which has not been seen, ought to be made forthwith, and all the resources of this country and all its united strength should be bent to that task.

Commons, October 5, 1938

Air War

There seem to me to be four lines of protection by which we can secure the best chance, and a good chance, of immunity for our people from the perils of air war – a peaceful foreign policy; the convention regulating air warfare; the parity in air power to invest that convention with validity; and, arising out of that parity, a sound system of home defence – in addition to all these other arrangements if they all fail.

Commons, March 8, 1934

Any nation that refused to enter into discussions of a convention to regulate air warfare would consequently be left in a position of grisly isolation, proclaiming its intention deliberately to make war as a scientific and technical operation upon women and children for the terrorization of the civil population.

Commons, March 8, 1934

21

Airships

If war breaks out tomorrow, foreign airships, no doubt, might do a certain amount of mischief and damage before they got smashed up, which would not be very long, but it is foolish to suppose that in their present stage of development they could produce results which would decisively influence the course of events.

Commons, March 26, 1913

Alamein

Two Sundays ago all the bells rang out to celebrate the victory of our desert army at Alamein. Here was a martial episode in British history which deserved a special recognition. But the bells also carried with their clashing joyous peals our thanksgiving that, in spite of all our errors and short-comings, we have been brought nearer to the frontiers of deliverance. We have not reached those frontiers yet, but we are becoming ever more entitled to be sure that the awful perils which might well have blotted out our life and all that we love and cherish will be surmounted, and that we shall be preserved for further service in the vanguard of mankind.

London, November 29, 1942

Alarm

We are told that we must not interfere with the normal course of trade, that we must not alarm the easygoing voter and the public. How thin and paltry these arguments will sound if we are caught a year or two hence, fat, opulent, free-spoken – and defenceless. I do not ask that war conditions should be established in order to execute these programmes. All I ask is that these programmes to which the Government have attached their confidence shall be punctually executed, whatever may be the disturbance of our daily life.

Commons, May 21, 1936

Albania

What has happened to the negotiations with Albania by which we were to have some satisfaction given to us for the murder of 40 British naval men and the grievous injury to many more, by a state we have helped and nourished to the best of our ability? That is not a matter which can be

'How was the Aliens Bill passed? It was introduced to the House of Commons in a tumbril'

ignored or forgotten, because it occurred in time of peace, and cannot be, as it were swept into the vast, confused catalogue of human injuries and wrong deeds which were done on both sides in the course of the great war.

Commons, January 23, 1948

Nearly two years have passed since Albania, which we had helped and nourished during the war, murdered over 40 British sailors by mining our ships in the Corfu Channel. Not the slightest satisfaction has been obtained for the outrage of ingratitude and treachery. I could give you many other instances which prove how British rights and British lives are being disregarded by minor foreign states to a degree never known before in the history of our country.

Luton Hoo, June 26, 1948

Aliens Bill

How was the Aliens Bill passed? It was introduced to the House of Commons in a tumbril. They began debating it on the steps of the scaffold, and before two days had passed in Committee they were hurried to the framework of the guillotine.

Commons, July 31, 1905

Aliens in Britain

I sympathize very strongly with the objection against drawing class distinctions based solely on the possession of money. To draw a distinction between a man who could afford a cabin passage and a man who could only afford a steerage passage was absurd. If a man were a lunatic or an idiot he could come in if he could pay for a cabin passage.

Commons, June 27, 1905

'How perfect is the co-operation between the commanders of the British and American Armies. Nothing like it has ever been seen before among allies'

All-night Sittings

Many objections could be urged against all-night sittings, but the ancestors of present Members had not been afraid to subject themselves to considerable strain and exertion in the interests of public and free discussion.

Commons, March 16, 1905

Alliance against Aggressors

Let us, therefore, do everything in our power to add to our strength and use that strength for the purpose of helping the gathering together of the nations upon the basis of the Covenant of the League. Upon the rock of the Covenant many nations, great and small, are drawing constantly and swiftly together. In spite of the disappointments of the past, in spite of many misgivings, difficulties and ridiculings, that process is continuing, and these nations are welding themselves into what will some day be a formidable yet benignant alliance, pledged to resist wrong-doing and the violence of an aggressor.

Commons, March 4, 1937

Alliance with America

I would turn aside for a moment to emphasize how perfect is the co-operation between the commanders of the British and American Armies. Nothing like it has ever been seen before among allies. No doubt language is a great help, but there is more in it than that. In all previous alliances the staffs have worked with opposite numbers in each department and liaison officers, but in Africa General Eisenhower built up a uniform staff, in which every place was filled with whoever was thought to be the best man, and they all ordered each other about according to their rank, without the slightest regard to what country they belonged to. The same unity and brotherhood is being instituted here throughout the Forces which are gathering in this country, and I cannot doubt that it will be found most serviceable, and unique also in all the history of alliances.

Commons, February 22, 1944

Alliances

When one looks at the disadvantages attaching to alliances, one must not forget how superior are the advantages.

Commons, September 21, 1943

Alternatives

The questions which have to be settled are not always questions between what is good and bad; very often it is a choice between two very terrible alternatives.

Commons, June 10, 1941

Ambassadors

Ambassadors are not sent as compliments but as necessities for ordinary daily use. The more difficult relations are with any country in question, the more necessary it is to have the very highest form of representation on the spot.

Commons, December 10, 1948

Ambitions

At my time of life I have no personal ambitions, no future to provide for. And I feel I can truthfully say that I only wish to do my duty by the whole mass of the nation and of the British Empire as long as I am thought to be of any use for that.

BBC, March 21, 1943

Ambuscade

What fools the Japanese ruling caste were to bring against themselves the mighty, latent war-energies of the great Republic, all for the sake of carrying out a base and squalid ambuscade.

BBC, March 26, 1944

America and Britain

> I have always thought that it ought to be the main end of English state-craft over a long period of years to cultivate good relations with the United States.
>
> *Commons, June 22, 1903*

Undoubtedly this process [fifty American destroyers handed over to Britain] means that these two great organizations of the English-speaking democracies – the British Empire and the United States – will have to be somewhat mixed up together in some of their affairs for mutual and general advantage. For my own part, looking out upon the future, I do not view the process with any misgivings. I could not stop it if I wished – no one can stop it. Like the Mississippi, it just keeps rolling along. Let it roll! Let it roll on in full flood, inexorable, irresistible, benignant, to broader lands and better days.

Commons, August 20, 1940

America and Europe

Twice in my lifetime the long arm of destiny has reached across the oceans and involved the entire life and manhood of the United States in a deadly struggle. There was no use in saying, "We don't want it; we won't have it; our forebears left Europe to avoid these quarrels; we have founded a new world which has no contact with the old." There was no use in that. The long arm reaches out remorselessly, and everyone's existence, environment, and outlook undergo a swift and irresistible change.

Harvard University, September 6, 1943

At this point I must turn to the United States, with whom our fortunes and interests are intertwined. I was sorry that the Hon Member for Nelson and Colne [Mr S Silverman], whom I see in his place, said some weeks ago that they were "shabby moneylenders". That is no service to our country nor is it true. The Americans took little when they emigrated from Europe except what they stood up in and what they had in their souls. They came through, they tamed the wilderness, they became what old John Bright called "a refuge for the oppressed from every land and clime". They have become today the greatest state and power in the world, speaking our own language, cherishing our common law, and pursuing, like our great Dominions, in broad principle, the same ideals.

Commons, October 28, 1947

'Twice in my lifetime the long arm of destiny has reached across the oceans and involved the entire life and manhood of the United States in a deadly struggle'

I must pay my tribute to the United States Army, not only in their valiant and ruthless battle-worthy qualities, but also in the skill of their commanders and the excellence of their supply arrangements. When one remembers that the United States four or five years ago was a peace-loving power, without any great body of troops, munitions, and with only a very small regular army to draw their commanders from, the American achievement is truly amazing. After the intense training they have received for nearly three years, or more than three years in some cases, their divisions are now composed of regular professional soldiers whose military quality is out of all comparison with hurriedly-raised war-time levies.

Commons, September 28, 1944

American Aid

The President and Congress of the United States, having newly fortified themselves by contact with their electors, have solemnly pledged their aid to Britain in this war because they deem our cause just, and because they know their own interests and safety would be endangered if we were destroyed. They are taxing themselves heavily. They have passed great legislation. They have turned a large part of their gigantic industry to making munitions which we need. They have even given us or lent us valuable weapons of their own.

London, April 27, 1941

American Army

There have been many occasions when a powerful state has wished to raise great armies, and with money and time and discipline and loyalty that can be accomplished. Nevertheless the rate at which the small American Army of only a few hundred thousand men, not long before the war, created the mighty force of millions of soldiers, is a wonder in military history.

The Pentagon, Washington, March 9, 1946

American Audiences

At intervals during the last forty years I have addressed scores of great American audiences in almost every part of the Union. I have learnt to admire the courtesy of these audiences; their sense of fair play; their sovereign sense of humour, never minding the joke that is turned against themselves; their earnest, voracious desire to come to the root of the matter, and to be well and truly informed on Old World affairs.

London, June 16, 1941

American Bases

His Majesty's Government are entirely willing to accord defence facilities to the United States on a 99 years' leasehold basis, and we feel sure that our interests no less than theirs, and the interests of the Colonies themselves, and of Canada and Newfoundland, will be served thereby.

Commons, August 20, 1940

'The American eagle sits on his perch, a large, strong bird with formidable beak and claws'

American Eagle

It cannot be in the interest of Russia to go on irritating the United States. There are no people in the world who are so slow to develop hostile feelings against a foreign country as the Americans, and there are no people who, once estranged, are more difficult to win back. The American eagle sits on his perch, a large, strong bird with formidable beak and claws. There he sits motionless, and Mr Gromyko is sent day after day to prod him with a sharp pointed stick – now his neck, now under his wings, now his tail feathers. All the time the eagle keeps quite still. But it would be a great mistake to suppose that nothing is going on inside the breast of the eagle.

Commons, June 5, 1946

American War Effort

When I think of the measureless output of ships, munitions and supplies of all kinds with which the United States has equipped herself and has sustained all the fighting allies in generous measure, and of the mighty war she is conducting, with troops of our Australian and New Zealand Dominions, over the spaces of the Pacific Ocean, this House may indeed salute our sister nation as being at the highest pinnacle of her power and fame.

Commons, September 28, 1944

Amphibious Operations

All large amphibious operations, especially if they require the co-operation of two or more countries, require long months of organization, with refinements and complexities hitherto unknown in war. Bold impulses, impatient desires, and sudden flashes of military instinct cannot hasten the course of events.

Guildhall, London, June 30, 1943

Anger

If I valued the Hon Gentleman's
[Sir J Lonsdale, MP] opinion I might
get angry.

Commons, January 1, 1913

Anglo-American Solidarity

Prodigious hammer-strokes have been needed to bring us together again, or if you will allow me to use other language, I will say that he must indeed have a blind soul who cannot see that some great purpose and design is being worked out here below, of which we have the honour to be the faithful servants. It is not given to us to peer into the mysteries of the future. Still, I avow my hope and faith, sure and inviolate, that in the days to come the British and American peoples will for their own safety and for the good of all walk together side by side in majesty, in justice, and in peace.

Speech to Congress, Washington, December 26, 1941

Anglo-American Unity

It is no exaggeration to say that the future of the whole world and the hopes of a broadening civilization founded upon Christian ethics depend upon the relation between the British Empire or Commonwealth of Nations and the USA. The identity of purpose and persistence of resolve prevailing throughout the English-speaking world will, more than any other single fact, determine the way of life which will be open to the generations and perhaps to the centuries which follow our own.

London, January 9, 1941

Anglo-German Naval Agreement

Under the Anglo-German Agreement no provision was made, as some of us suggested, that old ships should be counted at a lower tonnage than new ships in estimating the tonnage of German naval construction. If we keep the Royal Sovereigns, Germany would be entitled under the Treaty to build two additional battleships in the four-year period in question, and they have asked us to state in advance, as they have a right to ask, what we propose to do. We have promised to scrap or sink the first two Royal Sovereigns, and I presume that there is no hope now of rescuing the others from that imprudent decision.

Commons, March 16, 1939

Anglo-Italian Agreement

The Agreement, of course, has been violated in every material respect by Italy, but I do not feel that anything would be gained by a denouncement with bell, book and candle at this juncture. It certainly represents a sincere, if hitherto unrequited, attempt on the part of Great Britain to dwell on terms of friendship with Italy and with the Italian people in the Mediterranean Sea.

Commons, April 13, 1939

Animals, Sea and Land

It is difficult to make the Russians comprehend all the problems of the sea and of the ocean. We are sea animals, and the United States are to a large extent ocean animals. The Russians are land animals. Happily, we are all three air animals. It is difficult to explain fully all the different characteristics of the war effort of various countries, but I am sure that we made their leaders feel confidence in our loyal and sincere resolve to come to their aid as quickly as possible and in the most effective manner, without regard to the losses or sacrifices involved so long as the contribution was towards victory.

Commons, September 8, 1942

'We are sea animals, and the United States are to a large extent ocean animals. The Russians are land animals'

Antiques

It is important in the legislation of a country to draw a clear distinction between art and luxury, between the work of art – "a thing of beauty and a joy for ever" – and a mere consumable article of indulgence or ostentation.

Commons, April 26, 1926

Anxieties

We have a lot of anxieties, and one cancels out another very often.

Commons, September 22, 1943

Apologies

I have no intention of passing my remaining years in explaining or withdrawing anything I have said in the past, still less in apologizing for it.

Commons, April 21, 1944

Appeasement

Appeasement in itself may be good or bad according to the circumstances. Appeasement from weakness and fear is alike futile and fatal. Appeasement from strength is magnanimous and noble, and might be the surest and perhaps the only path to world peace. When nations or individuals get strong they are often truculent and bullying, but when they are weak they become better mannered. But this is the reverse of what is healthy and wise.

Commons, December 14, 1950

Approaches, Western

Owing to the action of Mr de Valera, so much at variance with the temper and instinct of thousands of Southern Irishmen who hastened to the battle-front to prove their ancient valour, the approaches which the Southern Irish ports and airfields could so easily have guarded were closed

'Appeasement from weakness and fear is alike futile and fatal. Appeasement from strength is magnanimous and noble'

by the hostile aircraft and U-boats. This was indeed a deadly moment in our life, and if it had not been for the loyalty and friendship of Northern Ireland we should have been forced to come to close quarters with Mr de Valera or perish for ever from the earth. However, with a restraint and poise to which, I say, history will find few parallels, His Majesty's Government never laid a violent hand upon them, though at times it would have been quite easy and quite natural, and we left the de Valera government to frolic with the Germans and later with the Japanese representatives to their heart's content.

London, May 13, 1945

Arabian Nights Tales

The United States is a land of free speech; nowhere is speech freer, not even here where we sedulously cultivate it even in its most repulsive forms. But when I see some of the accounts of conversations that I am supposed to have had with the President of the United States, I can only recall a Balfourian phrase at which I laughed many years ago, when he said that the accounts which were given bore no more relation to the actual facts than the wildest tales of the Arabian Nights do to the ordinary incidents of the domestic life in the East.

Commons, September 28, 1944

Argentina during the War

We all feel deep regret and also anxiety, as friends of Argentina, that in this testing time for nations she has not seen fit to take her place with no reserve or qualification upon the side of freedom, and has chosen to dally with the evil, and not only with the evil, but with the losing side. I trust that my remarks will be noted, because this is a very serious war. It is not like some small wars in the past where all could be forgotten and forgiven. Nations

33

must be judged by the part they play. Not only belligerents, but neutrals, will find that their position in the world cannot remain entirely unaffected by the part they have chosen to play in the crisis of the war.

Commons, August 2, 1944

Arguing

No constitutional or democratic principle with which I am acquainted compels a Minister of the Crown to argue. He may be tempted to do so; but he cannot be compelled.

Commons, July 30, 1952

Arguments

The Right Hon and learned Gentleman [The Attorney General, Sir Hartley Shawcross] may shake his head till he shakes it off, but it does not affect the argument.

Commons, July 15, 1948

In the German view, which Herr Hitler shares, a peaceful Germany and Austria were fallen upon in 1914 by a gang of wicked designing nations, headed by Belgium and Serbia, and would have defended herself successfully if only she had not been stabbed in the back by the Jews. Against such opinions it is vain to argue.

London, April 28, 1939

It seems to me – and I have a lengthening experience in the House – that false arguments very rarely pay in debate. [An Hon Member: "You are using them now."] I always try to economize the use of false arguments as much as possible, because false argument is so often detected, and it always repels any listener who is not already a convinced and enthusiastic partisan.

Commons, April 28, 1926

Arithmetic

We shall not allow any prejudice against individual personalities engaged in this conflict [General Strike] to complicate our task. But you cannot ask us to take sides against arithmetic.

Commons, August 31, 1926

'The Right Hon and learned Gentleman may shake his head till he shakes it off, but it does not affect the argument'

Armageddon

When a whole continent is arming feverishly, when mighty nations are laying aside every form of ease and comfort, when scores of millions of men and weapons are being prepared for war, when whole populations are being led forward or driven forward under conditions of exceptional overstrain, when the finances of the proudest dictators are in the most desperate condition, can you be sure that all your programmes so tardily adopted will, in fact, be executed in time?

Commons, March 4, 1937

Armaments

Nobody keeps armaments going for fun. They keep them going for fear.

Commons, November 23, 1945

I am not to be understood to mean that the possibilities of a gigantic war are nearer, but the actual position of Great Britain is much less satisfactory than it was this time twenty years ago, for then at least we had a supreme fleet; nobody could get at us in this island; and we had powerful friends on the Continent of Europe, who were likely to be involved in any quarrel before we were. But today, with our aviation in its present condition, we are in a far worse position. The Disarmament Conference has been carried out year after year ad nauseam. It must no longer delay our taking the necessary measures ourselves.

Commons, July 13, 1934

If you wish for disarmament, it will be necessary to go to the political and economic causes which lie behind the maintenance of armies and navies. There are serious political and economic dangers at the present time, and antagonisms which are by no means assuaged.

Commons, May 13, 1932

It used to be said that armaments depend on policy. It is not always true, but I think that at this juncture it is true to say that policy depends, to a large extent, upon armaments. It is true to say that we have reached a position where the choice of policy is dictated by considerations of defence.

Commons, May 2, 1935

Armaments Race

Let us see what we are doing. It is a general impression that we are overhauling Germany now; that we started late, it is true, but we are making up for lost time, and that every month our relative position will improve. That is a delusion. It is contrary to the truth this year, and probably for many months next year. I am not saying anything which is not known in every country of the world. These matters are thoroughly understood. Germany will be out-stripping us more and more even if our new programmes are accepted, and we shall be worse off at the end of this year than we are now, in spite of all our exertions.

Commons, March 10, 1936

Armed Forces

No satisfactory line of division can really be drawn between the navy and the air, between the air and the army, and between the navy and the army. Every attempt to draw such a line has failed.

Commons, March 21, 1922

Armed Forces

All the three services in modern times have a new common factor which they never had in anything like the same degree until the present century, or, indeed, until after the recent Great War. I mean science and invention. Science and invention are sweeping all before them. The same science applies to all three services alike, and its application must play a large part in all your plans and outlook. Nothing like this was known in the nineteenth century, and in those days the segregation of the services seemed comparatively simple. The Navy, to quote Lord Fisher, was a dismal mystery surrounded by sea-sickness, and had nothing in common, except good conduct, with the barrack square and the red-coated army of those days. The air force did not exist.

Commons, March 21, 1934

'I am all for volunteers who come from some uplifting of the human soul, some spirit arising in the human breast'

Armistice

A quarter of a century ago ... the House, when it heard ... the armistice terms, did not feel inclined for debate or business, but desired to offer thanks to Almighty God, to the Great Power which seems to shape and design the fortunes of nations and the destiny of man; and I therefore ... move "That the House do now attend at the church of St. Margaret, Westminister, to give humble and reverent thanks to Almighty God for our deliverance from the threat of German domination." This is the identical motion which was moved in former times.

Commons, May 8, 1945

Army, British

England, through the character of her people – who did not mind fighting, but detested drill – necessarily had very largely to depend, and her insular position made it possible for her so to do, in great crises, on an army of emergency.

Commons, February 24, 1903

The equipment of our army at the outbreak of war was of the most meagre and deficient character, and the deficiencies made themselves most marked – and still make themselves most marked – in the very type of weapons for which there is the greatest possible demand.

Commons, June 10, 1941

A national army is quite different from an army of volunteers, who were produced largely by the pressure in the economic market. I am all for volunteers who come from some uplifting of the human soul, some spirit arising in the human breast.

Commons, May 6, 1947

> In making an army, three elements
> are necessary – men, weapons and
> money. There must also be time.
>
> *Commons, December 1, 1948*

Standing armies, which abound on the European continent, are not indigenous to the British soil, they do not flourish in our climate, they are not suited to our national character, and though with artificial care and at a huge and disproportionate cost we may cultivate and preserve them, they will after all only be poor, stunted, sickly plants of foreign origin.

Commons, May 13, 1901

The army was not an inanimate substance, it was a living thing. Regiments were not like houses; they could not be pulled down and altered structurally to suit the convenience of the occupier and the caprice of the owner. They were more like plants: they grew slowly if they were to grow strong; they were easily affected by conditions of temperature and soil; and if they were blighted or transplanted they were apt to wither, and then they could only be revived by copious floods of public money.

Commons, August 8, 1904

Army Contractors

If Germany is able to produce in these three years equipment and armament of every kind for its air force and for sixty or seventy divisions of the regular army, how is it that we have been unable to furnish our humble, modest military forces with what is necessary? If you had given the contract to Selfridge or to the Army and Navy Stores, I believe that you would have had the stuff today.

Commons, May 25, 1938

Asquith, Herbert Henry

At forty, with a massive legal record behind him, he was Home Secretary. At fifty he was Prime Minister. He made his way by his distinction in the House of Commons debate, clear-cut, lucid argument, expressed in happy terms with many a glint of humour and flash of repartee, brevity as well as clarity – these were his weapons in those days of lengthy, sonorous harangues. He was no ebullient orator pouring forth his sentimental or passionate appeal. But few there were who could face him in the tense debating of issues, large or small. Here was a man who dealt in reasoned processes, who placed things in their proper scale and relation, who saw the root of the matter and simplified the tale.

Commons, December 6, 1950

Assembly, Feudal

It is not perhaps surprising in a country so fond of tradition, so proud of continuity, as ourselves that a feudal assembly of titled persons, with so long a history and so many famous names, should have survived to exert an influence upon public affairs at the present time. We see how often in England the old forms are reverently preserved after the forces by which they are sustained, and the uses to which they were put, and the dangers against which they were designed, have passed away.

Norwich, July 26, 1909

Assembly, Shape of

There are two main characteristics of the House of Commons which will command the approval and the support of reflective and experienced Members. They will, I have no doubt, sound odd to foreign ears. The first is that its shape should be oblong and not semi-circular. Here is a very potent factor in our political life. The semi-circular assembly, which appeals to political theorists, enables every individual or every group to move round the centre, adopting various shades of pink according as the weather changes.

Commons, October 28, 1943

'We see how often in England
the old forms are
reverently preserved'

Astor, Lady

When the Right Hon Member for Caithness [Sir Archibald Sinclair] dwelt on the point of Russia and emphasized it, I heard a sort of commotion behind me. I heard the Noble Lady the Member for the Sutton Division of Plymouth [Viscountess Astor] express her dislike of any contact with Bolshevik Russia. Where was this dislike when she paid a visit to Soviet Russia with Mr Bernard Shaw? The Noble Lady was treated with great consideration. But the point which the House should notice – it is a very serious point, and I hope I shall be able to put it without any offence – is that the time when she went to Russia and gave all her applause and credit to Russia, was a time when the influence of Russia was deeply detrimental to the interests of this country.

Commons, April 13, 1939

Atlantic Charter

Upon the fraternal association and intimate alignment of policy of the United States and the British Commonwealth and Empire depends, more than on any other factor, the immediate future of the world. If they walk, or if need be march, together in harmony and in accordance with the moral and political conceptions to which the English-speaking peoples have given birth, and which are frequently referred to in the Atlantic Charter, all will be well. If they fall apart and wander astray from the commanding beacon-light of their destiny, there is no end or measure to the miseries and confusion which await modern civilization.

Guildhall, London, June 30, 1943

Atlantic Meeting

This was a meeting [with President Roosevelt] which marks for ever in the pages of history the taking-up by the English-speaking nations, amid all this peril, tumult and confusion, of the guidance of the fortunes of the broad, toiling masses in all the continents; and our loyal effort, without any clog of selfish interest, to lead them forward out of the miseries into which they have been plunged back to the broad highroad of freedom and justice. This is the highest honour and the most glorious opportunity which could ever have come to any branch of the human race.

London, August 24, 1941

The meeting was therefore symbolic. That is its prime importance. It symbolizes, in a form and manner which everyone can understand in every land and in every clime, the deep underlying unities which stir, and at decisive moments rule, the English-speaking peoples throughout the world. Would it be presumptuous for me to say that it symbolizes something even more majestic – namely, the marshalling of the good forces of the world against the evil forces which are now so formidable and triumphant, and which have cast their cruel spell over the whole of Europe and a large part of Asia?

London, August 24, 1941

Atomic Bomb

It would nevertheless be wrong and imprudent to entrust the secret knowledge or experience of the atomic bomb, which the United States, Great Britain and Canada now share, to the world organization, while it is still in its infancy. It would be criminal madness to cast it adrift in this still agitated and non-united world. No one in any country has slept less well in their beds because this knowledge, and the method and the raw materials to apply it, are at present largely retained in American hands. I do not believe we should all have slept so soundly had the position been reversed and if some Communist or Neo-Fascist State monopolized for the time being these dread agencies. The fear of them alone might easily have been used to enforce totalitarian systems upon the free democratic world, with consequences appalling to human imagination.

Fulton, Missouri, March 5, 1946

The decision to use the atomic bomb was taken by President Truman and myself at Potsdam, and we approved the military plans to unchain the dread, pent-up forces.

Commons, August 16, 1945

'It would be criminal madness to cast the secret knowledge of the atomic bomb adrift in this still agitated and non-united world'

41

'In these present days we dwell strangely and precariously under the shield of the atomic bomb'

In these present days we dwell strangely and precariously under the shield and protection of the atomic bomb. The atomic bomb is still only in the hands of a State and nation which we know will never use it except in the cause of right and freedom. But it may well be that in a few years this awful agency of destruction will be widespread and the catastrophe following from its use by several warring nations will not only bring to an end all that we call civilization, but may possibly disintegrate the globe itself.

Zürich University, September 19, 1946

On July 17th there came to us at Potsdam the eagerly-awaited news of the trial of the atomic bomb in the Mexican desert. Success beyond all dreams crowded this sombre, magnificent venture of our American allies. The detailed reports of the Mexican desert experiment, which were brought to us a few days later by air, could leave no doubt, in the minds of the very few who were informed, that we were in the presence of a new factor in human affairs, and possessed of powers which were irresistible.

Commons, August 16, 1945

Atomic Power

This revelation of the secrets of nature, long mercifully withheld from man, should arouse the most solemn reflections in the mind and conscience of every human being capable of comprehension. We must indeed pray that these awful agencies will be made to conduce to peace among the nations, and that instead of wreaking measureless havoc upon the entire globe, may become a perennial fountain of world prosperity.

London, August 6, 1945

Atomic Weapons

The dark ages may return – the Stone Age may return on the gleaming wings of science; and what might now shower immeasurable material blessings upon mankind may even bring about its total destruction. Beware I say! Time may be short.

Fulton, Missouri, March 5, 1946

Atrocities

Field-Marshal Goering – who is one of the few Germans who has been having a pretty good time for the last few years – says that we have been spared so far because Nazi Germany is so humane. They cannot bear to do anything to hurt anybody. All they ask for is the right to live and to be let alone to conquer and kill the weak. Their humanity forbids them to apply severities to the strong. It may be true: but when we remember the bestial atrocities they have committed in Poland, we do not feel we wish to ask for any favours to be shown us. We shall do our duty as long as we have life and strength.

Commons, November 8, 1939

Attlee, Clement

Mr Attlee combines a limited outlook with strong qualities of resistance.

Royal Albert Hall, London, April 27, 1951

Attrition

It is in the dragging-out of the war at enormous expense, until the democracies are tired or bored or split, that the main hopes of Germany and Japan must now reside. We must destroy this hope, as we have destroyed so many others, and for that purpose we must beware of every topic, however attractive, and every tendency, however natural, which turns our minds and energies from this supreme objective of the general victory of the United Nations. By singleness of purpose, by steadfastness of conduct, by tenacity and endurance such as we have so far displayed – by these, and only by these, can we discharge our duty to the future of the world and to the destiny of man.

The Congress, Washington, May 19, 1943

Auchinleck, General

Although the battle is not yet finished, I have no hesitation in saying that, for good or ill, it is General Auchinleck's battle. Watching these affairs, as it is my duty to do, from day to day, and often from hour to hour, and seeing the seamy side of the reports as they come in, I have felt my confidence in General Auchinleck grow continually, and although everything is hazardous in war, I believe we have found in him, as we have also found in General Wavell, a military figure of the first order.

Commons, December 11, 1941

Austerity

This is no time for ease and comfort. It is the time to dare and endure.

Manchester, January 27, 1940

Austria, Conquest of

The public mind has been concentrated upon the moral and sentimental aspects of the Nazi conquests of Austria – a small country brutally struck down, its Government scattered to the winds, the oppression of the Nazi party doctrine imposed upon a Catholic population, and upon the working classes of Austria and of Vienna, the hard ill-usage of persecution which indeed will ensue – which is probably in progress at the moment – of those who, this time last week, were exercising their undoubted political rights, discharging their duties faithfully to their own country.

Commons, March 14, 1938

The gravity of the event of the 11th of March [the occupation] cannot be exaggerated. Europe is confronted with a programme of aggression, nicely calculated and timed, unfolding stage by stage, and there is only one choice open, not only to us, but to other countries who are unfortunately concerned – either to submit, like Austria, or else to take effective measures while time remains to ward off the danger and, if it cannot be warded off, to cope with it.

Commons, March 14, 1938

Autarchy

If the French woke up tomorrow morning and found that all the rest of the world had sunk under the sea, and that they were alone, they could make a pretty good living for themselves from their fertile soil. But if Britain woke up tomorrow morning and found nothing but salt water on the rest of the globe, about one-third of our people would disappear.

Town Hall, Leeds, February 4, 1950

Authority

I entirely agree that the civil authority has supreme authority over the military men.

Commons, October 31, 1950

Authorship

Writing a book was an adventure. To begin with it was a toy, and amusement; then it became a mistress, and then a master, and then a tyrant.

London, November 2, 1949

Autocracy

There is a deep fund of common sense in the English race and they have all sorts of ways, as has been shown in the past, of resisting and limiting the imposition of State autocracy.

Usher Hall, Edinburgh, February 14, 1950

Avalanche, The German

More than a million German soldiers, including all their active divisions and armoured divisions, are drawn-up ready to attack, at a few hours' notice, all along the frontiers of Luxembourg, of Belgium and of Holland.

45

At any moment these neutral countries may be subjected to an avalanche of steel and fire; and the decision rests in the hands of a haunted, morbid being, who, to their eternal shame, the German peoples in their bewilderment have worshipped as a god.

London, March 30, 1940

Averages

There is exhilaration in the study of insurance questions because there is a sense of elaborating new and increased powers which have been devoted to the service of mankind. It is not only a question of order in the face of confusion. It is not only a question of collective strength of the nation to render effective the thrift and the exertions of the individual, but we bring in the magic of averages to the aid of the million.

Commons, May 25, 1911

NOW THIS IS NOT THE END.

It is not even the beginning of the end.

But it is, perhaps, the end of the beginning.

Mansion House, London, November 10, 1942

Baden-Powell, Lord

I first met B-P many years before the birth of the Scout Movement. He was a man of character, vision and enthusiasm, and he passed these qualities on to the movement which has played, and is playing, an important part in moulding the character of our race. Sturdiness, neighbourliness, practical competence, love of country, and above all, in these times, indomitable resolve, daring and enterprise in the face of the enemy, these are the hallmarks of a scout. … "Be Prepared" to stand up faithfully for right and truth however the winds may blow.

London, July 16, 1942

Balance of Power

I say quite frankly, though I may shock the House, that I would rather see another ten or twenty years of one-sided armed peace than see a war between equally well-matched powers or combinations of power – and that may be the choice.

Commons, November 23, 1932

Never before has the choice of blessings or curses been so plainly, vividly, even brutally, offered to mankind. The choice is open. The dreadful balance trembles. It may be that our island and all the Commonwealths it has gathered around it may, if we are worthy, play an important, perhaps even a decisive, part in turning the scales of human fortune from bad to good, from fear to confidence, from miseries and crimes immeasurable to blessings and gains abounding.

Free Trade Hall, Manchester, May 9, 1938

Baldwin, Lord

In those days Mr Baldwin was wiser than he is now; he used frequently to take my advice.

Commons, May 22, 1935

It has been my fortune to have ups and downs in my political relations with him, the downs on the whole predominating perhaps, but at any rate we have always preserved agreeable personal relations, which, so far as I am concerned, are greatly valued. I am sure he would not wish in his conduct of public affairs that there should be any shrinking from putting the real issues of criticism which arise, and I shall certainly proceed in that sense.

Commons, November 12, 1936

Balfour, A J

Office at any price was his motto, at the sacrifice of any friend or colleague, at the sacrifice of any principle, by the adoption of any manoeuvre, however miserable or contemptible.

Commons, April 5, 1905

The Hon Gentleman looked upon the hours spent in the House as a spell upon the Parliamentary treadmill, and as part of the purchase price of office and power.

Commons, August 14, 1903

Baltic, Command of the

The German navy in the next few years will not be able to form a line of battle for a general engagement. One would expect that cruisers and submarines would be sent out to attack commerce, but I think you may take it as absolutely certain that the prime object of the German navy will be to preserve command of the Baltic, which is of supreme consequence to Germany, not only because of the supplies she can obtain from the Scandinavian countries, and the influence she can exert over them, but because the loss of naval command in the Baltic would lay the whole of the Baltic shores of Germany open to attack or possible invasions from other Baltic powers, of which the largest and most important is, of course, the Soviet Union.

Commons, March 16, 1939

Barbarism

Wickedness, enormous, panoplied, embattled, seemingly triumphant, casts its shadow over Europe and Asia. Laws, customs and traditions are broken up. Justice is cast from her seat. The rights of the weak are trampled down. The grand freedoms of which the President of the United States has spoken so movingly are spurned and chained. The whole stature of man, his genius, his initiative and his nobility, is ground down under systems of mechanical barbarism and of organized and scheduled terror.

London, June 16, 1941

Barbs

I am not at all worried about anything that may be said about me. Nobody would attempt to take part in controversial politics and not expect to be attacked.

Commons, December 6, 1945

Bargaining, Collective

We support the principle of collective bargaining between recognized and responsible trade unions and employers, and we include in collective bargaining the right to strike. They [the trade unions] have a great part to play in the life of the country and we think they should keep clear of Party politics.

Conservative Trades Union Congress, London, October 13, 1949

Barracking

I must say I do not think any public man charged with a high mission from this country ever seemed to be barracked from his homeland in his absence – unintentionally, I can well believe – to the extent that befell me while on this visit to the United States; and only my unshakable confidence in the ties which bind me to the mass of the British people upheld me through those days of trial.

Commons, July 2, 1942

Basic English

Some months ago I persuaded the British Cabinet to set up a committee of Ministers to study and report upon Basic English. Here you have a plan. There are others, but here you have a very carefully wrought plan for an international language capable of a very wide transaction of practical business and interchange of ideas. The whole of it is comprised in about 650 nouns and 200 verbs or other parts of speech – no more indeed than can be written on one side of a single sheet of paper.

Harvard University, September 6, 1943

Basic English is not intended for use among English-speaking people, but to enable a much larger body of people who do not have the good fortune to know the English language to participate more easily in our society.

Commons, November 4, 1943

Battle

I have often thought that it is sometimes unwise of generals to try to foresee with meticulous exactness just what will happen after a battle has been fought. A battle hangs like a curtain across the future. Once that curtain is raised or rent we can all see how the scenery is arranged, what actors are left upon the scene, and how they appear to be related to one another.

Commons, October 31, 1944

Battle of Britain

The three great days of August 15th, September 15th and September 27th have proved to all the world that here at home over our own island we have the mastery of the air. That is a tremendous fact. It marks the laying down of the office [of Chief of the Air Staff] which he has held with so much distinction for the last three years by Sir Cyril Newall, and it enables us to record our admiration to him for the services he has rendered. It also marks the assumption of new and immense responsibilities by Sir Charles Portal, an officer who, I have heard from every source and every side, commands the enthusiastic support and confidence of the Royal Air Force.

Commons, October 8, 1940

Battleships

We always believed before the war that battleships could never be laid down without our knowledge. The Germans were entitled to build 10,000-ton ships according to the Treaty, but they, by a concealment which the Admiralty were utterly unable to penetrate, converted these into 26,000-ton ships. Let us be careful when we see all these extremely awkward incidents occurring.

Commons, July 22, 1935

The offensive power of modern battleships is out of all proportion to their defensive power. Never was the disproportion so marked. If you want to make a true picture in your mind of a battle between great modern ironclad ships you must not think of it as if it were two men in armour striking at each other with heavy swords. It is more like a battle between two egg-shells striking each other with hammers.

Commons, March 17, 1914

Before the Battle

In that supreme emergency we shall not hesitate to take every step, even the most drastic, to call forth from our people the last ounce and the last inch of effort of which they are capable. The interests of property, the hours of labour, are nothing compared with the struggle for life and honour, for right and freedom, to which we have vowed ourselves.

London, May 19, 1940

Beginning, The End of the

The fight between the British and the Germans was intense and fierce in the extreme. It was a deadly grapple. The Germans have been outmatched and outfought with the very kind of weapons with which they have beaten down so many small peoples, and also large unprepared peoples. They have been beaten by the very technical apparatus on which they counted

'We shall not hesitate to take every step to call forth from our people the last ounce of effort'

to gain them the domination of the world. Especially is this true of the air and of the tanks and of the artillery, which has come back into its own on the battlefield. The Germans have received back again that measure of fire and steel which they have so often meted out to others.

Now this is not the end. It is not even the beginning of the end. But it is, perhaps, the end of the beginning.

Mansion House, London, November 10, 1942

Belligerents

There is nothing improper in belligerents meeting to discuss their affairs even while actual battles are going on. All history abounds in precedents.

Commons, February 25, 1954

Beresford, Lord Charles, MP

He is one of those orators of whom it was well said, "Before they get up, they do not know what they are going to say; when they are speaking, they do not know what they are saying; and when they sit down, they do not know what they have said."

Commons, December 20, 1912

Bevan, Aneurin

I should think it was hardly possible to state the opposite of the truth with more precision. I back up those who seek to establish democracy and civilization. The Hon Member must learn to take as well as to give. There is no one more free with interruptions, taunts, and jibes than he is. I saw him – I heard him, not saw him – almost assailing some of the venerable figures on the bench immediately below him. He need not get so angry because the House laughs at him: he ought to be pleased when they only laugh at him.

Commons, December 8, 1944

Bevin, Ernest

He takes his place among the great Foreign Secretaries of our country, and in his steadfast resistance to Communist aggression, in his strengthening of our ties with the United States and in his share of building up the Atlantic Pact, he has rendered services to Britain and to the cause of peace which will long be remembered.

London, March 17, 1951

Big Three

The future of the whole world, and certainly the future of Europe, perhaps for several generations, depends upon the cordial, trustful and comprehending association of the British Empire, the United States and Soviet Russia, and no pains must be spared and no patience grudged which are necessary to bring that supreme hope to fruition.

Commons, September 28, 1944

No meeting during this war would carry with it so much significance for the future of the world as a meeting between the heads of the three Governments, for, without the close, cordial and lasting association between Soviet Russia and the other great Allies, we might find ourselves at the end of the war only to have entered upon a period of deepening confusion.

Commons, September 21, 1943

Black Market

If you destroy a free market you create a black market. If you have 10,000 regulations you destroy all respect for the law.

Commons, February 3, 1949

Blackmail

Never in our history have we been in a position where we could be liable to be blackmailed, or forced to surrender our possessions, or take some action which the wisdom of the country or its conscience would not allow.

Commons, November 28, 1934

Blessings, Counting

We have to look back along the path we have trodden these last three years of toil and strife, to value properly all that we have escaped and all that we have achieved. No mood of boastfulness, of vain glory, of over-confidence must cloud our minds; but I think we have a right which history will endorse to feel that we had the honour to play a part in saving the freedom and the future of the world.

London, November 29, 1942

Blood, River of

A river of blood has flowed and is flowing between the German race and the peoples of nearly all Europe. It is not the hot blood of battle, where good blows are given and returned. It is the cold blood of the execution yard and the scaffold, which leaves a stain indelible for generations and for centuries.

Mansion House, London, November 10, 1941

Blur

The English never draw a line without blurring it.

Commons, November 16, 1948

'Bolshevism is a great evil, but it has arisen out of great social evils'

Bolsheviks

The Bolsheviks robbed Russia at one stroke of two most precious things, peace and victory – the victory that was within her grasp and the peace which was her dearest desire. Both were swept away from her. The victory was turned into defeat. As for the peace, her life ever since has been one long struggle of agonizing war.

Commons, November 5, 1919

I think the day will come when it will be recognized without doubt, not only on one side of the House but throughout the civilized world, that the strangling of Bolshevism at its birth would have been an untold blessing to the human race.

Commons, January 26, 1949

Bolshevism is a great evil, but it has arisen out of great social evils.

Commons, May 29, 1919

My hatred of Bolshevism and Bolsheviks is not founded on their silly system of economics or their absurd doctrine of an impossible equality. It arises from the bloody and devastating terrorism which they practise in every land into which they have broken, and by which alone their criminal régime can be maintained.

Commons, July 8, 1920

Bombing

The Hon Gentleman opposite made our flesh creep the other night by suggesting the dropping of bombs from airships on the House of Commons. If that event should happen, I am confident that the Members of this House would gladly embrace the opportunity of sharing the perils which the soldiers and the sailors have to meet.

Commons, March 26, 1913

If all of a sudden two powers with equal forces went to war, and one threw its bombs upon cities so as to kill as many women and children as possible, and the other threw its bombs on the aerodromes and air bases and factories and arsenals and dockyards and railway focal points of the other side, can any one doubt that next morning the one who had committed the greatest crime would not be the one who had reaped the greatest advantage?

Commons, March 14, 1933

The House will, I think, be favourably surprised to learn that the total number of flying bombs launched from the enemy's stations have killed almost exactly one person per bomb. That is a very remarkable fact, and it has kept pace roughly week by week. Actually the latest figures are 2,754 flying bombs launched and 2,752 fatal casualties sustained. They are the figures up to six o'clock this morning. Well, I am bound to say I was surprised when, some time ago, I perceived this wonderful figure. This number of dead will be somewhat increased by people who die of their injuries in hospital. Besides these there has been a substantially larger number of injured, and many minor injuries have been caused by splinters of glass.

Commons, July 6, 1944

Books

Books in all their variety are often the means by which civilization may be carried triumphantly forward.

Ministry of Information Film, 1941

Certainly I have been fully qualified so far as the writing of books about wars is concerned; in fact, already in 1900, which is a long time ago, I could boast to have written as many books as Moses, and I have not stopped writing them since, except when momentarily interrupted by war, in all the intervening period.

London, July 4, 1950

Boomerangs

Such is life with its astonishing twists and turns. You never can tell what is going to happen next, nor can you tell what will be the consequences of any action you may take. The principle of the boomerang, a weapon which we owe to the genius of the Australian aboriginals, is, it would seem, increasingly operative in human affairs.

Westminster, May 7, 1946

Both

Some people say: "Put your trust in the League of Nations." Others say: "Put your trust in British rearmament." I say we want both. I put my trust in both.

Commons, October 24, 1935

Brakes

If a train is running on the wrong lines downhill at sixty miles an hour it is no good trying to stop it by building a brick wall across the track. That would only mean that the wall was shattered, that the train was wrecked and the passengers mangled. First you have to put on the brakes.

London, December 22, 1951

Bread Rationing

The German U-boats in their worst endeavour never made bread rationing necessary in war. It took a Socialist Government and Socialist planners to fasten it on us in time of peace when the seas are open and the world harvests good. At no time in the two world wars have our people had so little bread, meat, butter, cheese and fruit to eat.

Conservative Party Conference, Blackpool, October 5, 1946

Breathing Space

I believe that we have a considerable breathing space in which to revive again those lights of goodwill and reconciliation in Europe which shone, so brightly but so briefly, on the morrow of Locarno. We shall never do that merely by haggling about cannons, tanks, aeroplanes and submarines, or measuring swords with one another, among nations already eyeing each other with so much vigilance.

Commons, November 23, 1932

Bribery

It was very much better to bribe a person than kill him, and very much better to be bribed than to be killed.

Commons, April 30, 1953

Bricklayer

I have always been a firm supporter of British trade unionism. I believe it to be the only foundation upon which the relations of employers and employed can be harmoniously adjusted. I have always advised Conservatives and Liberals to join the trade unions. I tried to join the Bricklayers' Trade Union and it is a complicated legal point whether I have in fact succeeded in doing so.

Woodford Green, July 10, 1948

Britain Alone

And now it has come to us to stand alone in the breach, and face the worst that the tyrant's might and enmity can do. Bearing ourselves humbly before God, but conscious that we serve an unfolding purpose, we are ready to defend our native land against the invasion by which it is threatened. We are fighting by ourselves alone; but we are not fighting for ourselves alone.

Commons, July 14, 1940

Britain and America

The experience of a long life and the promptings of my blood have wrought in me the conviction that there is nothing more important for the future of the world than the fraternal association of our two peoples in righteous work both in war and peace.

Broadcast from the Capitol, Washington, DC, May 19, 1943

Britain

In order that our naval defence shall be fully effective, there must be sufficient military force in this country to make it necessary for an invader to come in such large numbers that he will offer a target to the Navy, and certainly would be intercepted if he embarked.

Commons, March 17, 1914

When we aspire to lead all Europe back from the verge of the abyss on to the uplands of law and peace, we must ourselves set the highest example. We must keep nothing back. How can we bear to continue to lead our comfortable, easy life here at home, unwilling even to pronounce the word "compulsion", unwilling even to take the necessary measure by which the armies that we have promised can alone be recruited and equipped? How can we continue – let me say it with particular frankness and sincerity – with less than the full force of the nation incorporated in the governing instrument? These very methods, which the Government owe it to the nation to take, are not only indispensable to the duties that we have accepted but, by their very adoption, they may rescue our people and the people of many lands from the dark, bitter waters which are rising fast on every side.

Commons, April 13, 1939

> 'Today we may say aloud, "We are still masters of our fate. We still are captains of our soul"'

Thus far then have we travelled along the terrible road we chose at the call of duty. The mood of Britain is wisely and rightly averse from every form of shallow or premature exultation. This is no time for boasts or glowing prophecies, but there is this – a year ago our position looked forlorn and well nigh desperate to all eyes but our own. Today we may say aloud before an awestruck world, "We are still masters of our fate. We still are captains of our soul."

Commons, September 9, 1941

The outside world which a little while ago took only a moderate view of our prospects, now believes that Britain will survive. But between immediate survival and lasting victory there is a long road to tread. In treading it, we shall show the world the perseverance and steadfastness of the British race and the glorious resilience and flexibility of our ancient institutions.

Mansion House, London, November 9, 1940

Britain and Poland

It would be affectation to pretend that the attitude of the British, and, I believe, the United States Governments towards Poland is identical with that of the Soviet Union. Every allowance must be made for the different conditions of history and geography which govern the relationship of the western democracies on the one hand and the Soviet Government on the other with the Polish nation. Marshal Stalin has repeatedly declared himself in favour of a strong, friendly Poland, sovereign and independent. In this our great Eastern Ally is in the fullest accord with His Majesty's Government, and also, judging from American public statements, with the United States. We in this island and throughout our Empire, who drew the sword against mighty Germany on account of her aggression against Poland, have sentiments and duties towards Poland which deeply stir the British race. Everything in our power has been and will be done to achieve, both in the letter and in the spirit, the declared purposes towards Poland of the three great allies.

Commons, September 28, 1944

Britain at War

In our wars the episodes are largely adverse, but the final results have hitherto been satisfactory. Away we dash over the currents that may swirl around us, but the tide bears us forward on its broad, resistless flood. In the last war the way was uphill almost to the end. We met with continual disappointments, and with disasters far more bloody than anything we have experienced so far in this one. But in the end all the oppositions fell together, and all our foes submitted themselves to our will.

Mansion House, London, November 10, 1942

It must always be assumed, of course, that Great Britain will stand by her obligations. Probably she will be better than her legal word.

Commons, March 23, 1933

Britain's Part in Europe

Our country has a very important part to play in Europe, but it is not so large a part as we have been attempting to play, and I advocate for us in future a more modest role than many of our peace-preservers and peace-lovers have sought to impose upon us.

Commons, April 13, 1933

Britannia, Rule

The tasks which the navy has performed in peacetime are hardly less magnificent than those they have achieved in war. From Trafalgar onwards, for more than 100 years Britannia ruled the waves. There was a great measure of peace, the freedom of the seas was maintained, the slave trade was extirpated, the Monroe Doctrine of the United States found its sanction in British naval power – and that has been pretty well recognized on the other side of the Atlantic – and in those happy days the cost was about £10 million a year.

Commons, March 8, 1948

British, The

They [the British] are the only people who like to be told how bad things are – who like to be told the worst.

Commons, June 10, 1941

I go about the country whenever I can escape for a few hours or for a day from my duty at headquarters, and I see the damage done by the enemy attacks; but I also see side by side with the devastation and amid the ruins quiet, confident, bright and smiling eyes, beaming with a consciousness of being associated with a cause far higher and wider than any human or

'Among the various forces that hold the British Empire together is "enlightened self-interest"'

personal issue. I see the spirit of an unconquerable people. I see a spirit bred in freedom, nursed in a tradition which has come down to us through the centuries, and which will surely at this moment, this turning-point in the history of the world, enable us to bear our part in such a way that none of our race who come after us will have any reason to cast reproach upon their sires.

Bristol University, April 12, 1941

British Empire

Governments who have seized upon power by violence and by usurpation have often resorted to terrorism in their desperate efforts to keep what they have stolen; but the august and venerable structure of the British Empire, where lawful authority descends from hand to hand and generation after generation, does not need such aid. Such ideas are absolutely foreign to the British way of doing things.

Commons, July 8, 1920

Among the various forces that hold the British Empire together is – and I certainly do not object to the expression which my Hon Friend and Member for Seaham used – "enlightened self-interest". That has a valuable and important part to play, but I am sure he would not make the mistake of placing it in front of those deeper and more mysterious influences which cause human beings to do the most incalculable, improvident, and, from the narrow point of view, profitless things. It is our union in freedom and for the sake of our way of living which is the great fact, reinforced by tradition and sentiment, and it does not depend upon anything that could ever be written down in any account kept in some large volume.

Commons, April 21, 1944

If the British Empire is fated to pass from life into history, we must hope it will not be by the slow process of dispersion and decay, but in some supreme exertion for freedom, for right and for truth.

Canada Club, London, April 20, 1939

It is a sober fact that the British Empire produces within its limits every commodity which luxury can imagine or industry require.

Commons, March 8, 1905

British Influence

It is known, alike by peoples and rulers that, upon the whole – and it is upon the whole that we must judge these things – British influence is a kindly and healthy influence and makes for the general happiness and welfare of mankind.

Commons, May 17, 1901

British at War

When the British people make up their minds to go to war they expect to receive terrible injuries. That is why we tried to remain at peace as long as possible.

Commons, September 5, 1940

Brotherhood among Men

I rejoice in the prospect, now becoming sure and certain, that the Nazi ideology, enforced in a hideous manner upon a vast population, will presently be beaten to the ground. These facts and manifestations, which I see taking place continually as the world war crashes onwards to its close, make me increasingly confident that when it is won, when the hateful aggressive Nazi and Fascist systems have been laid low, and when every precaution has been taken against their ever rising again, there may be a new brotherhood among men which will not be based upon crude antagonisms of ideology but upon broad, simple, homely ideals of peace, justice and freedom. Therefore, I am glad that the war is becoming less an ideological war between rival systems and more and more the means by which high ideals and solid benefits may be achieved by the broad masses of the people in many lands and ultimately in all.

Commons, August 2, 1944

Bulldogs

The nose of the bulldog has been slanted backwards so that he can breathe without letting go.

Description of naval strategy in 1914

Bureaucracy Rejected

Of all races in the world our people would be the last to consent to be governed by a bureaucracy. Freedom is their life-blood.

London, March 21, 1943

Bureaucrat

A State official or employee has only to keep his office hours punctually and do his best and if anything goes wrong he can send in the bill to the Chancellor of the Exchequer. He is truly what is called "disinterested" in the sense that he gains no advantage from wisdom and suffers no penalty for error.

Liverpool, October 2, 1951

Butchery

The Russian armies and all the peoples of the Russian Republic have rallied to the defence of their hearths and homes. For the first time Nazi blood has flowed in a fearful torrent. Certainly a million-and-a-half, perhaps two millions, of Nazi cannon-fodder have bit the dust of the endless plains of Russia. The tremendous battle rages along nearly two thousand miles of front. The Russians fight with magnificent devotion; not only that, our generals who have visited the Russian front line report with admiration the efficiency of their military organization and the excellence of their equipment. The aggressor is surprised, startled, staggered. For the first time in his experience mass murder has become unprofitable. He retaliates by the most frightful cruelties. As his armies advance, whole districts are being exterminated. Scores of thousands – literally scores of thousands – of executions in cold blood are being perpetrated by the German police-troops upon the Russian patriots who defend their native soil. Since the Mongol invasions of Europe in the sixteenth century, there has never been methodical, merciless butchery on such a scale, or approaching such a scale. And this is but the beginning. Famine and pestilence have yet to follow in the bloody ruts of Hitler's tanks. We are in the presence of a crime without a name.

London, August 24, 1941.

THE INHERENT VICE OF CAPITALISM IS THE UNEQUAL SHARING OF BLESSINGS.

The inherent virtue of Socialism is the equal sharing of miseries.

Commons, October 22, 1945

Cacophony

I must not say how much better we are than at the twenty-third month of the last war, nor how our output compares with the peak of the last war, because it is contended conditions have changed. This is rather easy money for the critics. A handful of Members can fill a couple of days' debate with disparaging charges against our war effort, and every ardent or disaffected section of the Press can take it up, and the whole can cry a dismal cacophonous chorus of stinking fish all round the world.

Commons, July 29, 1941

Calculations

The human story does not always unfold like a mathematical calculation on the principle that two and two make four. Sometimes in life they make five or minus three; and sometimes the blackboard topples down in the middle of the sum and leaves the class in disorder and the pedagogue with a black eye.

London, May 7, 1946

Cameramen

It is the misfortune of a good many Members to encounter in our daily walks an increasing number of persons armed with cameras to take pictures for the illustrated Press which is so rapidly developing.

Commons, May 25, 1911

Canada

Canada is the linchpin of the English-speaking world. Canada, with those relations of friendly affectionate intimacy with the United States on the one hand and with her unswerving fidelity to the British Commonwealth and the Motherland on the other, is the link which, spanning the oceans, brings the continents into their true relation and will prevent in future generations any growth of division between the proud and the happy nations of Europe and the great countries which have come into existence in the New World.

Mansion House, London, September 4, 1941

There are no limits to the majestic future which lies before the mighty expanse of Canada with its virile, aspiring, cultured and generous-hearted people. Canada is the vital link in the English-speaking world and joins across the Atlantic Ocean the vast American democracy of the United States with our famous old island and the fifty millions who keep the flag flying here.

Guildhall, London, November 19, 1951

Cant

I care as little as any man in this House for the cant of Empire which plays so large a part in the jargon of modern political discussion, but I should like to see the great English-speaking nations work together in majesty, in freedom, and in peace.

February 15, 1911

Capitalism and Socialism

The inherent vice of capitalism is the unequal sharing of blessings. The inherent virtue of Socialism is the equal sharing of miseries.

Commons, October 22, 1945

Casualties

We have inflicted losses on the enemy which are about double those we have suffered ourselves. It is remarkable considering we were the challengers, and unusual compared with the experiences of the last war.

Commons, August 2, 1944

Excluding Dominion and allied squadrons working with the Royal Air Force, the British islanders have lost 38,300 pilots and air crews killed and 10,400 missing, and over 10,000 aircraft since the beginning of the war – and they have made nearly 900,000 sorties into the North European theatre.

Commons, February 22, 1944

Now, we know exactly what our casualties have been. On that particular Thursday night 180 persons were killed in London as a result of 251 tons of bombs. That is to say, it took one ton of bombs to kill three-quarters of a person.

Commons, October 8, 1940

The total of personnel, officers and men, of the Royal Navy lost since the war started is just over 30 per cent of its pre-war strength, the figures being 41,000 killed out of 133,000, which was its total strength on the outbreak of war.

Commons, February 22, 1944

We have had hardly any losses at sea in our heavily escorted troop convoys. Out of about 3,000,000 soldiers who have been moved under the protection of the British Navy about the world, to and fro across the seas and oceans, about 1,348 have been killed or drowned, including missing. It is about 2,200 to one against your being drowned if you travel in British troop convoys in this present war.

Commons, February 11, 1943

Causation, Chain of

In order to have the correct perspective and proportion of events, it is necessary to survey the whole chain of causation, the massive links of which have been forged by the diligence and burnished with the devotion and skill of our combined forces and their commanders until they shine in the sunshine of today, and will long shine in the history of war.

Commons, September 21, 1943

Cause, The

We are all of us defending something which is, I won't say dearer, but greater than a country, namely a cause. That cause is the cause of freedom and of justice; that cause is the cause of the weak against the strong; it is the cause of law against violence, of mercy and tolerance against brutality and iron-bound tyranny. That is the cause we are fighting for. That is the cause which is moving slowly, painfully but surely, inevitably and inexorably to victory; and when the victory is gained you will find that you are – I will not say in a new world, but a better world; you are in a world

'If we are together nothing is impossible. If we are divided all will fail'

which can be made more fair, more happy, if only all the peoples will join together to do their part, and if all classes and all parties stand together to reap the fruits of victory as they are standing together to bear, and to face, and to cast back the terrors and menaces of war.

Town Hall, Bradford, December 5, 1942

If we are together nothing is impossible. If we are divided all will fail. I therefore preach continually the doctrine of the fraternal association of our two peoples, not for any purpose of gaining material advantages for either of them, not for territorial aggrandizement or the vain pomp of earthly domination, but for the sake of service to mankind and for the honour that comes to those who faithfully serve great causes.

Harvard University, September 6, 1943

In ordinary day-to-day affairs of life, men and women expect rewards for successful exertion, and this is often right and reasonable. But those who serve causes as majestic and high as ours need no reward; nor are our aims limited by the span of human life. If success come to us soon, we shall be happy. If our purpose is delayed, if we are confronted by obstacles and inertia, we may still be of good cheer, because in a cause, the righteousness of which will be proclaimed by the march of future events and the judgment of happier ages, we shall have done our duty, we shall have done our best.

The Royal Albert Hall, London, May 14, 1947

Century, The New

The advantages of the nineteenth century, the literary age, have been largely put away by this terrible twentieth century with all its confusion and exhaustion of mankind.

University of London, November 18, 1948

Chamber, Size of Parliamentary

The second characteristic of a Chamber formed on the lines of the House of Commons is that it should not be big enough to contain all its Members at once without over-crowding, and that there should be no question of every Member having a separate seat reserved for him. The reason for this has long been a puzzle to uninstructed outsiders, and has frequently excited the curiosity and even the criticism of new Members. Yet it is not so difficult to understand if you look at it from a practical point of view. If the House is big enough to contain all its Members, nine-tenths of its debates will be conducted in the depressing atmosphere of an almost empty or half-empty Chamber. The essence of good House of Commons speaking is the conversational style, the facility for quick, informal interruptions and interchanges. Harangues from a rostrum would be a bad substitute for the conversational style in which so much of our business is done. But the conversational style requires a fairly small space, and there should be a sense of the importance of much that is said, and a sense that great matters are being decided, there and then, by the House.

Commons, October 28, 1943

Chamberlain, Neville

He was, like his father and his brother Austen before him, a famous Member of the House of Commons, and we here assembled this morning, Members of all parties, without a single exception, feel that we do ourselves and our country honour in saluting the memory of one whom Disraeli would have called an "English worthy".

Commons, November 12, 1940

It fell to Neville Chamberlain in one of the supreme crises of the world to be contradicted by events, to be disappointed in his hopes, and to be deceived and cheated by a wicked man. But what were these wishes in which he was frustrated? What was that faith that was abused? They were surely among the most noble and benevolent instincts of the human heart – the love of peace, the toil for peace, the strife for peace, the pursuit of peace, even at great peril, and certainly to the utter disdain of popularity or clamour. Whatever else history may or may not say about these terrible tremendous years, we can be sure that

Neville Chamberlain acted with perfect sincerity according to his lights and strove to the utmost of his capacity and authority, which were powerful, to save the world from the awful, devastating struggle in which we are now engaged. This alone will stand him in good stead as far as what is called the verdict of history is concerned.

Commons, November 12, 1940

Champions of Right

Ought we not to produce in defence of Right, champions as bold, missionaries as eager, and, if need be, swords as sharp as are at the disposal of the leaders of totalitarian states?

Free Trade Hall, Manchester, May 9, 1938

Change

Changes in personnel are caused from time to time by the march of events and by the duty of continual improvement. Changes in machinery are enjoined by experience, and, naturally, while we live we ought to learn. Change is agreeable to the human mind, and gives satisfaction, sometimes short-lived, to ardent and anxious public opinion.

Commons, July 29, 1941

Change of Mind

It is always bad for a government to change its mind, yet it ought to do so from time to time, out of respect to the House of Commons and out of the influence made upon its collective mind by the debates. But what is still worse is to change your mind and then have to change it again. That is a double disadvantage, and we must certainly avoid that.

Commons, October 6, 1944

'Whatever else history may say about these years, we can be sure that Neville Chamberlain acted with perfect sincerity'

'So long as I am acting from duty and conviction, I am indifferent to taunts and jeers'

Change, Resistance to

The oldest habit in the world for resisting change is to complain that unless the remedy to the disease can be universally applied it should not be applied at all. But you must begin somewhere.

Commons, May 25, 1911

Character, British

A few critical or scathing speeches, a stream of articles in the newspapers, showing how badly the war is managed and how incompetent are those who bear the responsibility – these obtain the fullest publicity; but the marvellous services of seamanship and devotion, and the organization behind them, which prove at every stage and step the soundness of our national life; the inconquerable, the inexhaustible adaptiveness and ingenuity of the British mind, the iron, unyielding, unwearying tenacity of the British character, by which we live, by which alone we can be saved, and by which we shall certainly be saved – and save the world – these, though fully realized by our foes abroad, are sometimes overlooked by our friends at home.

Commons, June 25, 1941

Chiang Kai-Shek, Mme

Madame Chiang Kai-Shek is also a most remarkable and fascinating personality. Her perfect command of English, and complete comprehension of the world struggle as a whole, enable her to be the best of all interpreters in matters in which she herself plays a notable part.

Commons, February 22, 1944

China

For five long years the Japanese military factions, seeking to emulate the style of Hitler and Mussolini, taking all their posturing as if it were a new

European revelation, have been invading and harrying the five hundred million inhabitants of China. Japanese armies have been wandering about that vast land in futile excursions, carrying with them carnage, ruin and corruption, and calling it the "Chinese Incident".

London, August 24, 1941

The Japanese military performances in China had not seemed remarkable. The Chinese had always been a weak nation, divided, and traditionally unwarlike. We knew that they were very ill-armed and ill-supplied, especially with every weapon that matters in modern war. And yet for four and a half years the Japanese, using as many as a million men at a time, had failed to quell or conquer them.

Commons April 23, 1942

Choice of Evils

I will not pretend that, if I had to choose between Communism and Nazism, I would choose Communism. I hope not to be called upon to survive in the world under a government of either of those dispensations.

Commons, April 14, 1937

Church and State

In the present age the State cannot control the Church in spiritual matters; it can only divorce it.

Commons, June 14, 1928

Churchill

So long as I am acting from duty and conviction, I am indifferent to taunts and jeers. I think they will probably do me more good than harm.

Commons, December 6, 1945

I am not a business man. I am only a politician. I can only apply my common sense, sharpened by political experience, to this topic.

Commons, March 27, 1919

I am certainly not one of those who need to be prodded. In fact, if anything, I am a prod.

Commons, November 11, 1942

Churchill and America

I feel greatly honoured that you should have invited me to enter the United States Senate Chamber and address the representatives of both branches of Congress. The fact that my American forebears have for so many generations played their part in the life of the United States, and that here I am, an Englishman, welcomed in your midst, makes this experience one of the most moving and thrilling in my life, which is already long and has not been entirely uneventful. I wish indeed that my mother, whose memory I cherish across the vale of years, could have been here to see. By the way, I cannot help reflecting that if my father had been American and my mother British, instead of the other way round, I might have got here on my own. In that case, this would not have been the first time you would have heard my voice. In that case I should not have needed any invitation, but if I had, it is hardly likely it would have been unanimous. So perhaps things are better as they are. I may confess, however, that I do not feel quite like a fish out of water in a legislative assembly where English is spoken.

The Congress, Washington, DC, December 26, 1941

'It is not a question of opposing Nazism or Communism, but of opposing tyranny'

Churchill and Scotland

I have myself some ties with Scotland which are to me of great significance – ties precious and lasting. First of all, I decided to be born on St Andrew's day – and it was to Scotland I went to find my wife, who is deeply grieved not to be here today through temporary indisposition. I commanded a Scottish battalion of the famous 21st Regiment for five months in the line in France in the last war. I sat for 15 years as the representative of "Bonnie Dundee", and I might be sitting for it still if the matter had rested entirely with me.

Usher Hall, Edinburgh, October 12, 1942

Churchill and Toryism

The second question I have asked myself is much more personal. Am I by temperament and conviction able sincerely to identify myself with the main historical conceptions of Toryism, and can I do justice to them and give expression to them spontaneously in speech and action? My life, such as it has been, has been lived for forty years in the public eye, and very varying opinions are entertained about it – and about particular phases in it. I shall attempt no justification, but this I will venture most humbly to submit and also to declare, because it springs most deeply from the convictions of my heart, that at all times according to my lights and throughout the changing scenes through which we are all hurried, I have always faithfully served two public causes which I think stand supreme – the maintenance of the enduring greatness of Britain and her Empire and the historical continuity of our island life.

Caxton Hall, London, October 9, 1940

Churchill's Case

It is no part of my case that I am always right.

Commons, May 21, 1952

Churchill's Message

In these last years of life there is a message of which I conceive myself to be a bearer. It is a very simple message which can be well understood by the people of both our countries. It is that we should stand together. We should stand together in malice to none, in greed for nothing, but in defence of those causes which we hold dear not only for our own benefit, but because we believe they mean the honour and the happiness of long generations of men.

The General Assembly of Virginia, Richmond, March 8, 1946

Civil War in Spain

It is not a question of opposing Nazism or Communism, but of opposing tyranny in whatever form it presents itself; and, as I do not find in either of these two Spanish factions which are at war any satisfactory guarantee that the ideals which I care about would be preserved, I am not able to throw myself in this headlong fashion into the risk of having to fire cannon immediately on the one side or the other of this trouble. I have found it easier to maintain this feeling of detachment from both sides because, before we gave any help to either side we ought to know what the victory of that side would mean to those who are beaten.

Commons, April 14, 1937

Civilization

There are few words which are used more loosely than the word "civilization". What does it mean? It means a society based upon the opinion of civilians. It means that violence, the rule of warriors and despotic chiefs, the conditions of camps and warfare, or riot and tyranny, give place to parliaments where laws are made, and independent courts of justice in which over long periods those laws are maintained. That is civilization – and in its soil grow continually freedom, comfort and culture.

University of Bristol, July 2, 1938

Civilization will not last, freedom will not survive, peace will not be kept, unless a very large majority of mankind unite together to defend them and show themselves possessed of a constabulary power before which barbaric and atavistic forces will stand in awe.

University of Bristol, July 2, 1938

Clarion Call

Come then: let us to the task, to the battle, to the toil – each to our part, each to our station. Fill the armies, rule the air, pour out the munitions, strangle the U-boats, sweep the mines, plough the land, build the ships, guard the streets, succour the wounded, uplift the downcast and honour the brave. Let us go forward together in all parts of the Empire, in all parts of the island. There is not a week, nor a day, nor an hour to lose.

Free Trade Hall, Manchester, January 27, 1940

Class Hatred

There have always been men of power and position, who have sacrificed and exerted themselves in the popular cause; and that is why there is so little class hatred here, in spite of all the squalor and misery which we see around us.

Kinnaird Hall, Dundee, May 14, 1908

'The British people have always been superior to the British climate. They have shown themselves capable of rising above it'

Classics

I should like to say that I have changed my mind about the classics. I had very strong views about them when at Harrow; I have changed my mind about them since. Knowledge of the ancient world of the Greek and Roman literature was a great unifying force in Europe, which is now, I fear, rapidly becoming extinct and I should like to say that university education ought not to be too practical.

University of London, November 18, 1948

Climate, British

The British people have always been superior to the British climate. They have shown themselves capable of rising above it, and certainly they have derived from it many of those strong enduring principles and ways of life which make their existence in our island home different from any other community in the world.

Woodford Green, July 10, 1948

Climax of War

It is a reasonable assumption that, unless we make some grave mistakes in strategy, the year 1944 will see the climax of the European war. Unless some happy event occurs on which we have no right to count, and the hand of Providence is stretched forth in some crowning mercy, 1944 will see the greatest sacrifice of life by British and American armies, and battles far larger and more costly than Waterloo or Gettysburg will be fought. Sorrow will come to many homes in the United Kingdom and throughout the great Republic. British and American manhood – true brothers in arms – will attack and grapple with the deadly foe.

Mansion House, London, November 9, 1943

Testing, trying, adverse, painful times lie ahead of us. We must all strive to do our duty to the utmost of our strength. As the war rises remorselessly to its climax, the House of Commons, which is the foundation of the British life struggle – this House of Commons which has especial responsibilities – will have the opportunity once again of proving to the world that the firmness of spirit, sense of proportion, steadfastness of purpose, which have gained it renown in former days, will now once again carry great peoples and a greater cause to a victorious deliverance.

Commons, April 23, 1942

Coal

The foundation of this island's commerce was cheap and abundant coal. Upon this the brains, inventiveness, good business management and enterprise of our people enabled our population to double itself in a century. Now here, living, breathing, toiling, suffering, what is to happen if the foundation fails?

Belle Vue, Manchester, December 6, 1947

Coins, Nickel

And now the British housewife, as she stands in the queues to buy her bread ration, will fumble in her pocket in vain for a silver sixpence. Under the Socialist Government nickel will have to be good enough for her. In future we shall be able to say: "Every cloud has a nickel lining."

Blackpool, October 5, 1946

Cold War

What we are faced with is not a violent jerk but a prolonged pull.

Commons, March 5, 1953

Combustion, Internal

When internal combustion becomes a realized fact – of course, it has lagged on the road in the last two years, but when it becomes a realized fact – all the advantages which have been described with regard to oil will

'I like commanders on land and sea and in the air to feel they have behind them a strong Government'

be very greatly increased, and every ton of oil will do three or four times as much work as is now possible.

Commons, March 17, 1914

Commanders

I shall always urge that the tendency in the future should be to prolong the courses of instruction at the colleges rather than to abridge them, and to equip our young officers with that special technical professional knowledge which soldiers have the right to expect from those who can give them orders, if necessary, to go to their deaths. It is quite clear that class or wealth or favour will not be allowed in the modern world to afford dividing lines. Professional attainment, based upon prolonged study, and collective study at colleges, rank by rank, and age by age – those are the title deeds of the commanders of the future armies, and the secret of future victories.

The Pentagon, Washington, March 9, 1946

I like commanders on land and sea and in the air to feel they have behind them a strong Government. They will not run risks unless they feel that they need not look over their shoulders or worry about what is happening at home, unless they feel they can concentrate their gaze upon the enemy.

Commons, July 2, 1942

Common Bond

However we may differ in political opinion, however divergent our Party interests, however diverse our callings and stations, we have this in common. We mean to defend our island from tyranny and aggression, and so far as we can, we mean to hold out a helping hand to others who may be in an even more immediate danger than at this moment we are ourselves.

Manchester, May 9, 1938

Common Man

Little did we guess that what has been called "The Century of the Common Man" would witness as its outstanding feature more common men killing each other with greater facilities than any other five centuries put together in the history of the world.

Boston, Massachusetts, March 31, 1949

Commons, House of

In this war the House of Commons has proved itself to be the rock upon which an Administration, without losing the confidence of the House, has been able to confront the most terrible emergencies. The House has shown itself able to face the possibility of national destruction with classical composure. It can change governments in long, adverse, disappointing struggles through many dark, grey months and even years until the sun comes out again. I do not know how else this country can be governed than by the House of Commons playing its part in all its broad freedom in British public life.

Commons, October 28, 1943

On the night of May 10, 1941, with one of the last bombs of the last serious raid, our House of Commons was destroyed by the violence of the enemy, and we have now to consider whether we should build it up again, and how, and when. We shape our buildings, and afterwards our buildings shape us. Having dwelt and served for more than forty years in the late Chamber, and having derived very great pleasure and advantage, therefrom, I, naturally, should like to see it restored in all essentials to its old form, convenience and dignity.

Commons, October 28, 1943

Communism

Everyone can see how Communism rots the soul of a nation; how it makes it abject and hungry in peace, and proves it base and abominable in war.

London, January 20, 1940

I tell you – it's no use arguing with a Communist. It's no good trying to convert a Communist or persuade him. You can only deal with them on the following basis ... you can only do it by having superior force on your side on the matter in question – and they must also be convinced that you will use – you will not hesitate to use – those forces, if necessary, in the most ruthless manner. You have not only to convince the Soviet Government that you have a superior force – that they are confronted by superior force – but that you are not restrained by any moral consideration if the case arose from using that force with complete material ruthlessness. And that is the greatest chance of peace, the surest road to peace.

New York, March 25, 1949

Company

We are no longer alone. We are in the midst of a great company. Three-quarters of the human race are now moving with us. The whole future of mankind may depend upon our action and upon our conduct. So far we have not failed. We shall not fail now.

London, February 15, 1942

Complacency, Anti-

All the disadvantages are not on one side, and certainly they are not all on our side. I think that conforms to the standards of anti-complacency opinion in this country.

Commons, February 11, 1943

Comradeship

The other day I crossed the Atlantic again to see President Roosevelt. This time we met not only as friends, but as comrades, standing side by side and shoulder to shoulder, in a battle for dear life and dearer honour, in the common cause, and against a common foe. When I survey and compute the power of the United States and its vast resources and feel that they are now in with us, with the British Commonwealth of Nations all together, however long it lasts, till death or victory, I cannot believe there is any other fact in the whole world which can compare with that. That is what I have dreamed of, aimed at and worked for, and now it has come to pass.

London, February 15, 1942

Concentration of Force

I could not see how better you can prevent war than by confronting an aggressor with the prospect of such a vast concentration of force, moral and material, that even the most reckless, even the most infuriated leader, would not attempt to challenge those great forces.

Commons, July 13, 1934

Concessions

I do not think that we need break our hearts in deploring the treatment that Germany is receiving now. Germany is not satisfied; but no concession which has been made has produced any very marked appearance of gratitude. Once it has been conceded it has seemed less valuable than when it was demanded.

Commons, April 13, 1933

Confidence

I have, myself, full confidence that if all do their duty, if nothing is neglected and if the best arrangements are made, as they are being made, we shall prove ourselves once again able to defend our island home, to ride out the storm of war, and to outlive the menace of tyranny, if necessary for years, if necessary alone. At any rate, that is what we are going to try to do.

Commons, June 4, 1940

Confidence in Government

I shall be asked, "Have you no confidence in His Majesty's Government?" Sir, I say "Yes" and "No". I have great confidence that these Hon and Right Hon Friends of mine will administer faithfully and well the Constitution of this country, that they will guard its finances in a thrifty manner, that they will hunt out corruption wherever it may be found, that they will preserve the peace and order of our streets and the impartiality of our courts and keep a general hold upon Conservative principles. [Laughter.] In all these matters I have a sincere and abiding confidence in them. But if you ask me whether I have confidence in their execution of defence programmes, or even in their statements as to the degree to which those defence programmes have at any moment advanced – then I must beg the House not to press me too far. [Renewed laughter.]

Commons, November 17, 1938

I ask the House for a Vote of Confidence. I hope that those, if such there be, who sincerely in their hearts believe that we are not doing our best and that they could do much better, I hope that they will carry their opinion to its logical and ultimate conclusion in the Lobby. Here I must point out, only for the benefit of foreign countries, that they would run no risk in doing so. They are answerable only to their consciences and to their constituents. It is a free Parliament in a free country. We have succeeded in maintaining, under difficulties which are unprecedented, and in dangers which, in some cases, might well be mortal, the whole process and reality of Parliamentary institutions. I am proud of this. It is one of the things for which we are fighting.

Commons, May 7, 1941

It is because things have gone badly and worse is to come that I demand a Vote of Confidence.

Commons, January 27, 1942

Conquest of the Air

The conquest of the air and the perfection of the art of flying fulfilled the dream which for thousands of years had glittered in human imagination. Certainly it was a marvellous and romantic event. Whether the bestowal of this gift upon an immature civilization composed of competing nations, whose nationalization grew with every advance of democracy, and who were as yet devoid of international organization, whether this gift was a blessing or a curse has yet to be proved.

Massachusetts Institute of Technology, Boston, March 31, 1949

Conscience

Conscience and muddle cannot be reconciled; conscience apart from truth is mere stupidity, regrettable, but by no means respectable.

Commons, July 15, 1948

A nation without a conscience is a nation without a soul. A nation without a soul is a nation that cannot live.

London, September 16, 1951

Conscription

I have regarded compulsion not as the gathering together of men as if they were heaps of shingle, but the fitting of them into their places like the pieces in the pattern of a mosaic. The great principle of equality of sacrifice requires in practice to be applied in accordance with the maxim, "A place for every man and every man in his place".

Commons, May 23, 1916

There are many countries where a national army on a compulsory basis is the main foundation of the State, and is regarded as one of the most important safeguards of democratic freedom. It is not so here. On the contrary, the civil character of our Government institutions is one of the most deeply cherished convictions of our island life, a conviction which our island position alone has enabled us to enjoy.

Commons, February 23, 1920

Consistency

In this world of human error and constant variations, usually of an unexpected character, the Liberal Party can range themselves in Party doctrine, few but impeccable. They have no need to recur for safety or vindication to that well-known maxim, or dictum, that "Consistency is the last resort of feeble and narrow minds."

Commons, March 31, 1947

It is better to be both right and consistent. But if you have to choose – you must choose to be right.

Scarborough, October 11, 1952

Constantinople

All this year I have offered the same counsel to the Government – undertake no operation in the west which is more costly to us in life than to the enemy; in the east, take Constantinople; take it by ship, if you can; take it by soldiers if you must; take it whichever plan, military or naval, commends itself to your military experts, but take it, and take it soon, and take it while time remains.

Commons, November 15, 1915

Constitution, American

We must be very careful nowadays – I perhaps all the more, because of my American forebears – in what we say about the American Constitution. I will, therefore, content myself with the observation that no Constitution was written in better English.

Coronation Luncheon, Westminster Hall, London, May 27, 1953

Constitution, The British

The British Constitution is mainly British common sense.

Kinnaird Hall, Dundee, May 14, 1908

Construction

If in erecting some great building it is found that a girder in the lowest story is defective, the building becomes a cause of peril and danger to the public, but it is not possible immediately to withdraw it. To wrench it away would be to involve the certainty of ruin; but to whom? The jerry-builder might have decamped. The contractor might have made a fortune from the job and retired. It is upon the humble occupants that the miseries of the downfall would descend.

Commons, February 22, 1906

Consultation

Well one can always consult a man and ask him: "Would you like your head cut off tomorrow?" and after he has said: "I would rather not," cut it off. "Consultation" is a vague and elastic term.

Commons, May 7, 1947

Consuming the Substance

How are we keeping going from day to day? Let me tell you. We are living on the last remaining assets and overseas investments accumulated under the capitalistic system – that is what we are living on: we are living on them in the hope that we may bridge the gap before the new American grant-in-aid under the Marshall plan comes in. Our last reserves will then be nearly gone, and even with the American help there will be a heavy deficit to be met each year on all our overseas purchases.

London, February 14, 1948

Contest of Wills

The Germans in this war have gained many victories. They have easily overrun great countries and beaten down strong powers with little resistance offered to them. It is not only a question of the time that is gained by fighting strongly, even if at a disadvantage, for important points. There is also this vitally important principle of stubborn resistance to the will of the enemy.

Commons, June 10, 1941

Contributions

The great Napoleon for many years insisted on maintaining the whole fabric of his Empire on contributions levied by force on foreign States, but I am not of opinion that the ultimate historical conclusion of that great experiment could be said to be profitable for Napoleon or the country over which he presided.

Commons, June 2, 1908

Controls

Control for control's sake is senseless. Controls under the pretext of war or its aftermath which are in fact designed to favour the accomplishment of quasi-totalitarian systems, however innocently designed, whatever guise they assume, whatever liveries they wear, whatever slogans they mouth, are a fraud which should be mercilessly exposed to the British public.

Central Hall, Westminster, March 15, 1945

Convictions

I have two convictions in my heart. One is that, somehow or other, we shall survive, though for a time at a lower level then hitherto. The late Lord Fisher used to say: "Britain never succumbs." The second is that things are going to get worse before they are better.

Commons, March 12, 1947

Co-ordination

It would seem, on the face of it, rather odd to invite the co-ordinator after the co-ordination is, according to the Government White Paper, already perfect and complete; to appoint the man who is to concert the plan after it has already been made and embodied in the detailed Estimates for the current year. The usual process, if I may model myself on the somewhat simple types of exposition in which my Right Hon and learned Friend [Sir John Simon] excels, is to put the horse before the cart, the idea being, I presume, although I do not wish to take anything for granted, that as the horse moves forward he, as it were, drags the cart behind him. That, of course, would be the usual and normal procedure, but no doubt there may be very good reasons for having adopted the contrary one in this case.

Commons, March 10, 1936

Correctives

I am inclined to think that in a free community every evil carries with it its own corrective, and so I believe that sensationalism of all kinds is playing itself out, and, overdoing, is itself undone.

Free Trade Hall, Manchester, May 23, 1909

The old Radical campaign against exploitation, monopolies, unfair rake-offs and the like, in which I took a part in my young days, was a healthy and necessary corrective to the system of free enterprise. But this grotesque idea of managing vast enterprises by centralized direction from London can only lead to bankruptcy and ruin.

Perth, May 28, 1948

Correspondents

There never has been in this war a battle in which so much liberty has been given to war correspondents. They have been allowed to roam all over the battlefield, taking their chance of getting killed, and sending home their very full messages whenever they can reach a telegraph office. This is what the Press have always asked for, and it is what they got. These war correspondents, moving about amid the troops and sharing their perils, have also shared their hopes and have been inspired by their buoyant spirit. They have sympathized with the fighting men whose deeds

'By all means follow your lines of hope and your paths of peace, but do not close your eyes to the fact we are entering a corridor of deepening and darkening danger'

they have been recording, and they have, no doubt, been extremely anxious not to write anything which would spread discouragement or add to their burdens.

Commons, July 2, 1942

Corridor of Danger

It would be folly for us to act as if we were swimming in a halcyon sea, as if nothing but balmy breezes and calm weather were to be expected and everything were working in the most agreeable fashion. By all means follow your lines of hope and your paths of peace, but do not close your eyes to the fact that we are entering a corridor of deepening and darkening danger, and that we shall have to move along it for many months and possibly for years to come.

Commons, May 31, 1935

Country First

Before they [the Socialists] nationalized our industries they should have nationalized themselves. They should have set country before Party, and shown that they were Britons first, and Socialists only second.

Commons, March 12, 1947

Courage

However tempting it might be to some, when much trouble lies ahead, to step aside adroitly and put someone else up to take the blows, I do not intend to take that cowardly course, but, on the contrary, to stand to my post and persevere in accordance with my duty as I see it.

Commons, February 25, 1942

'It is no use espousing a cause without having a plan by which that cause may be made to win'

Courts of Law

We are reminded how in a state of savagery every man is armed and is a law unto himself, but that civilization means that courts are established, that men lay aside arms and carry their causes to the tribunal. This presupposes a tribunal to which men, when they are in doubt or anxiety, may freely have recourse. It presupposes a tribunal which is not incapable of giving a verdict.

Commons, May 2, 1935

Covenant of the League of Nations

It is no use espousing a cause without having also a method and a plan by which that cause may be made to win. I would not affront you with generalities. There must be the vision. There must be a plan, and there must be action following upon it. We express our immediate plan and policy in a single sentence: "Arm, and stand by the Covenant". In this alone lies the assurance of safety, the defence of freedom, and the hope of peace.

Free Trade Hall, Manchester, May 9, 1938

I think we ought to place our trust in those moral forces which are enshrined in the Covenant of the League of Nations. Do not let us mock at them, for they are surely on our side. Do not mock at them, for this may well be a time when the highest idealism is not divorced from strategic prudence. Do not mock at them, for these may be years, strange as it may seem, when Right may walk hand in hand with Might.

Commons, March 4, 1937

Craft

Craft is common both to skill and deceit.

Commons, November 11, 1947

Crete

I think it would be most unfair and wrong, and very silly, in the midst of a defence which has so far been crowned with remarkable success, to select the loss of the Crete salient as an excuse and pretext for branding with failure or belittling with taunt the great campaign for the defence of the Middle East, which has so far prospered beyond all expectations, and is now entering upon an even more intense and critical phase.

Commons, June 10, 1941

Crime

Hitler has told us that it was a crime in such circumstances on our part to go to the aid of the Greeks. I do not wish to enter into argument with experts. This is not a kind of crime of which he is a good judge.

Commons, May 7, 1941

Cripps, Sir Stafford

Sir Stafford Cripps is an able and upright man, tortured and obsessed by his Socialist tenets.

Ayr, May 16, 1947

Stafford Cripps was a man of force and fire. His intellectual and moral passions were so strong that they not only inspired but not seldom dominated his actions. They were strengthened and also governed by the working of a powerful, lucid intelligence and by a deep and lively Christian faith. He strode through life with a remarkable indifference to material satisfaction or worldly advantages.

Commons, April 23, 1952

Criticism

We do not resent the well-meant criticism of any man who wishes to win the war. We do not shrink from any fair criticism, and that is the most dangerous of all. On the contrary, we take it earnestly to heart and seek to profit by it. Criticism in the body politic is like pain in the human body. It is not pleasant, but where would the body be without it? No health or sensibility would be possible without continued correctives and warnings of pain.

Commons, January 27, 1940

'It is the golden circle of the Crown which alone embraces the loyalties of so many States and races'

I am not one, and I should be the last, unduly to resent unfair criticism, or even fair criticism, which is so much more searching. I have been a critic myself – I cannot at all see how I should have stood the test of being a mere spectator in the drama which is now passing. But there is a kind of criticism which is a little irritating. It is like a bystander who, when he sees a team of horses dragging a heavy waggon painfully up a hill, cuts a switch from the fence, and there are many switches, and belabours them lustily. He may well be animated by a benevolent purpose, and who shall say the horses may not benefit from his efforts, and the waggon get quicker to the top of the hill.

Commons, May 7, 1941

I have derived continued benefit from criticism at all periods of my life, and I do not remember any time when I was ever short of it.

November 27, 1914

Critics

We are certainly aided by a great volume of criticism and advice from which it will always be our endeavour to profit in the highest degree. Naturally when one is burdened by the very hard labour of the task and its cares, sorrows and responsibilities, there may sometimes steal across the mind a feeling of impatience at the airy and jaunty detachment of some of those critics who feel so confident of their knowledge and feel so sure of their ability to put things right. If I should be forced – as I hope I shall not be – to yield to such a temptation, I hope you will remember how difficult it is to combine the attitude of proper meekness and humility towards assailants at home with those combative and pugnacious qualities, with the spirit of offensive and counter-attack, which we feel were never more needful than now against the common enemy.

Caxton Hall, London, March 26, 1942

Crossing the Floor

I am a convinced supporter of the Party system in preference to the group system. I have seen many earnest and ardent Parliaments destroyed by the group system. The Party system is much favoured by the oblong form of Chamber. It is easy for an individual to move through those insensible gradations from Left to Right, but the act of crossing the floor is one which requires serious consideration. I am well informed on this matter, for I have accomplished that difficult process, not only once but twice.

Commons, October 28, 1943

Crossman, R H S (MP)

The Hon Member is never lucky in the coincidence of his facts with the truth.

Commons, July 14, 1954

Crown

It is the golden circle of the Crown which alone embraces the loyalties of so many States and races all over the world. It is the symbol which gathers together and expresses those deep emotions and stirrings of the human heart which make men travel far to fight and die together, and cheerfully abandon material possessions and enjoyments for the sake of abstract ideas.

Commons, May 15, 1945

In the British Empire we not only look out across the seas towards each other, but backwards to our own history, to Magna Charta, to Habeas Corpus, to the Petition of Right, to Trial by Jury, to the English Common Law and to Parliamentary democracy. These are the milestones and monuments that mark the path along which the British race has marched to leadership and freedom. And over all this, uniting each Dominion with the other and uniting us all with our majestic past, is the golden circle of the Crown. What is within the circle? Not only the glory of an ancient unconquered people, but the hope, the sure hope, of a broadening life for hundreds of millions of men.

Canada Club, London, April 20, 1939

The prerogatives of the Crown have become the privileges of the people.
Harrow, December 1, 1944

It is natural for Parliament to talk and for the Crown to shine. The oldest here will confirm me that we are never likely to run short of Members and of Ministers who can talk. And the youngest here are sure that they will never see the Crown sparkle more gloriously than in these joyous days.
Coronation Luncheon, Westminster Hall, London, May 27, 1953

Cup of Success

Can we produce that complete unity and that impulse in time to achieve decisive military victory with the least possible prolongation of the world's misery, or must we fall into jabber, babel and discord while victory is still unattained? It seems to me to be the supreme question alike of the hour and the age. This is no new problem in the history of mankind. Very often have great combinations almost attained success and then, at the last moment, cast it away. Very often have the triumphs and sacrifices of armies come to naught at the conference table. Very often the eagles have been squalled down by the parrots. Very often, in particular, the people of this island, indomitable in adversity, have tasted the hard-won cup of success only to cast it away.

Commons, January 18, 1945

Curzon Line, The

We speak of the Curzon Line. A line is not a frontier. A frontier has to be surveyed and traced on the ground and not merely put in on a map with a pencil and ruler.

Commons, February 27, 1945

I have been censured for wrongly championing the Russian claims to the Curzon Line. So far as the Curzon Line is concerned, I hold strongly that this was a rightful Russian frontier, and that a free Poland should receive compensation at the expense of Germany both in the Baltic and in the west, going even to the line of the Oder and the Eastern Neisse. If I and my colleagues erred in these decisions, we must be judged in relation to the circumstances of the awful conflict in which we were engaged.

Commons, June 5, 1946

Czechoslovakia

To English ears, the name Czechoslovakia sounds outlandish. No doubt they are only a small democratic State, no doubt they have an army only two or three times as large as ours, no doubt they have a munitions supply only three times as great as that of Italy, but still they are a virile people; they have their treaty rights, they have a line of fortresses, and they have a strongly manifested will to live freely.

Commons, March 14, 1938

Many people at the time of the September crisis thought they were only giving away the interests of Czechoslovakia, but with every month that passes you will see that they were also giving away the interests of Britain, and the interests of peace and justice.

Waltham Abbey, March 14, 1939

Let us look for a moment at what Nazi Germany inflicts upon the peoples she has subjugated to her rule. The German invaders pursue with every method of cultural, social and economic oppression their intention of destroying the Czech nation. Students are shot by scores and tormented in concentration camps by thousands. All the Czech Universities have been closed – amongst them the Charles University of Prague which, founded in 1348, was the first University in Central Europe; the clinics, the laboratories, the libraries of the Czech Universities have been pillaged or destroyed. The works of their national writers have been removed from the public libraries. More than two thousand periodicals and newspapers have been suppressed. Prominent writers, artists and professors have been herded into the concentration camps. The public administration and judicature have been reduced to chaos. The Czech lands have been plundered, and every scrap of food and useful portable article carried off into Germany by organized brigandage or common theft. The property of the Churches is maladministered and engrossed by German commissars. A hundred thousand Czech workmen have been led off into slavery to be toiled to death in Germany. Eight millions of Czechs – a nation famous and recognizable as a distinct community for many centuries past in Europe – writhe in agony under the German and Nazi tyranny.

Free Trade Hall, Manchester, January 27, 1940

NO ONE PRETENDS THAT DEMOCRACY IS PERFECT OR ALL-WISE.

Democracy is the worst form of government except all those other forms that have been tried.

Commons, November 11, 1947

Dalton, Dr Hugh

Dr Dalton, the practitioner who never cured anyone.

London, February 14, 1948

Danger

> When danger is far off we may think of our weakness, when it is near we must not forget our strength.
>
> *Commons, June 28, 1939*

If I support the Government today, it is not because I have changed my views. It is because the Government have in principle and even in detail adopted the policy I have urged. I only hope they have not adopted it too late to prevent war. When danger is at a distance, when there is plenty of time to make the necessary preparations, when you can bend twigs instead of having to break massive boughs – it is right, indeed it is a duty, to sound the alarm. But when danger comes very near, when it is plain that not much more can be done in the time that may be available, it is no service to dwell upon the shortcomings or neglects of those who have been responsible. The time to be frightened is when evils can be remedied; when they cannot be fully remedied they must be faced with courage.

Commons, June 28, 1939

Dangers in the air are sudden and might have become catastrophic, but the dangers to our seaborne traffic mature much more slowly.

Commons, November 5, 1940

It is no use examining national defence in the abstract and talking in vague and general terms about hypothetical dangers and combinations which cannot be expressed.

Commons, July 30, 1934

Dangerous Corner

We did not make this war, we did not seek it. We did all we could to avoid it. We did too much to avoid it. We went so far at times in trying to avoid it as to be almost destroyed by it when it broke upon us. But the dangerous corner has been turned, and with every month and every year that passes we shall confront the evil-doers with weapons as plentiful, as sharp, and as destructive as those with which they have sought to establish their hateful domination.

Ottawa, December 30, 1941

Danzig

What is Danzig? Danzig is not only a city. It has become a symbol. An act of violence against the Polish Republic, whether it arises from without or from within, will raise an issue of world importance. The Foreign Secretary has told us that force will be met by force, and no one voice in Britain has been raised to contradict him. An attack upon Poland at the present time would be a decisive and irrevocable event. It is of the highest importance that the Nazi Party in Germany should not mislead themselves upon the temper of the British and French democracies.

City Carlton Club, London, June 28, 1939

Datum Line

I have tried to find a datum line, and I take as the datum line the three months after Dunkirk. Then, it will be admitted, our people worked to the utmost limit of their moral, mental and physical strength. Men fell exhausted at their lathes, and workmen and working women did not take their clothes off for a week at a time. Meals, rest and relaxation all faded from their minds, and they just carried on to the last ounce of their strength.

Commons, July 29, 1941

Dawn of 1943

The dawn of 1943 will soon loom red before us, and we must brace ourselves to cope with the trials and problems of what must be a stern and terrible year. We do so with the assurance of ever-growing strength, and we do so as a nation with a strong will, a bold heart and a good conscience.

London, November 29, 1942

Deadlock

It is always an error in diplomacy to press a matter when it is quite clear that no further progress is to be made. It is also a great error if you ever give the impression abroad that you are using language which is more concerned with your domestic politics than with the actual fortunes and merits of the various great countries upon the Continent to whom you offer advice.

Commons, March 14, 1934

Death

We have to organize our lives and the life of our cities on the basis of dwelling under fire and of having always this additional – not very serious – chance of death added to the ordinary precarious character of human existence.

Commons, October 8, 1940

Death Duties

There is no real gain to British democracy when some family leaves a home of its ancestors and hands it over to a transatlantic millionaire or wartime profiteer.

Commons, April 15, 1930

Death Penalty

If I was assured that abolishing the death penalty would bring all murders to an end, I would certainly be in favour of that course.

Commons, July 15, 1948

Death of Soldiers

Soldiers must die, but by their death they nourish the nation which gave them birth.

London, July 14, 1943

Decision

War is a hard and brutal job, and there is no place in it for misgivings or reserves. Nobody ever launched an attack without having misgivings beforehand. You ought to have misgivings before; but when the moment of action is come, the hour of misgivings is passed. It is often not possible to go backward from a course which has been adopted in war. A man must answer "Aye" or "No" to the great questions which are put; and by that decision he must be bound.

Commons, November 15, 1915

Deeds

It seems to me, therefore, that words cannot form a foundation for our action unless they are accompanied by deeds; and the likelihood of deeds being done in Germany at the present time which will remove the present danger, seems to me remote when you consider what a dire effect it would have upon the immediate economic, industrial and labour situation within that country.

Commons, May 22, 1935

Defeat

It is only where great strategic issues of policy come that it is fitting for us here to endeavour to form a final opinion. Defeat is bitter. There is no use in trying to explain defeat. People do not like defeat and they do not like the explanations, however elaborate or plausible, which are given of them. For defeat there is only one answer. The only answer to defeat is victory.

Commons, June 10, 1941

The penalties of defeat are frightful. After the blinding flash of catastrophe, the stunning blow, the gaping wounds, there comes an onset of the diseases of defeat. The central principle of a nation's life is broken, and all healthy, normal control vanishes, there are few societies that can withstand the conditions of subjugation. Indomitable patriots take different paths; quislings and collaborationists of all kinds abound; guerilla leaders, each with their personal followers, quarrel and fight.

Commons, February 22, 1944

103

Defence

> Pending some new discovery, the only
> direct measure of defence upon a great
> scale is the certainty of being able to inflict
> simultaneously upon the enemy as great
> damage as he can inflict upon ourselves.
>
> *Commons, November 28, 1934*

We should have a greater chance of applying the gifts of science broadly to the whole texture of our defensive arrangements if there were a reception of all these new inventions and discoveries from a common elevated point of view, removed from the prejudice of any one particular uniformed profession.

Commons, March 21, 1934

I submit to you that these matters of national defence and foreign policy ought to be considered upon a plane above Party, and apart from natural antagonisms which separate a Government and an Opposition. They affect the life of the nation. They influence the fortunes of the world.

Corn Exchange, Cambridge, May 19, 1939

Defiance

All the world, even our best friends, thought that our end had come. Accordingly, we prepared ourselves to conquer or perish. We were united in that solemn, majestic hour; we were all equally resolved at least to go down fighting. We cast calculations to the winds; no wavering voice was heard; we hurled defiance at our foes; we faced our duty; and, by the mercy of God, we were preserved.

It fell to me in those days to express the sentiments and resolves of the British nation in that supreme crisis of its life. That was to me an honour far beyond any dreams or ambitions I had ever nursed, and it is one that cannot be taken away.

London, May 10, 1942

Deficiencies in Armaments

We are now in the third year of openly avowed rearmament. Why is it, if all is going well, there are so many deficiencies? Why, for instance, are the Guards drilling with flags instead of machine-guns? Why is it that our small Territorial Army is in a rudimentary condition? Is that all according to schedule? Why should it be, when you consider how small are our forces? Why should it be impossible to equip the Territorial Army simultaneously with the Regular Army?

Commons, May 25, 1938

Degrees

I am surprised that in my later life I should have become so experienced in taking degrees, when as a schoolboy I was so bad at passing examinations. In fact one might almost say that no one ever passed so few examinations and received so many degrees. From this a superficial thinker might argue that the way to get the most degrees is to fail in the most examinations. This would, however, Ladies and Gentlemen, be a conclusion unedifying in the academic atmosphere in which I now preen myself, and I therefore hasten to draw another moral with which I am sure we shall be in accord: namely, that no boy or girl should ever be disheartened by lack of success in their youth but should diligently and faithfully continue to persevere and make up for lost time.

University of Miami, February 26, 1946

Deluge

I should advise the Right Hon Gentleman [Mr Arnold Foster, Secretary of State for War] not to worry too much about details, because, after all, there would be an election some day, and when it came the waters of the boundless ocean would come in and all the castles on the sands would be washed away.

Commons, February 23, 1905

'All the world thought our end had come. Accordingly, we prepared ourselves to conquer or perish'

Democracy

With all their virtues, democracies are changeable. After a hot fit, comes the cold. Are we to see again, as we saw the last time, the utmost severities inflicted upon the vanquished, to be followed by a period in which we let them arm anew, and in which we then seek to appease their wrath?

Commons, June 5, 1946

Democracy does not express itself in clever manoeuvres by which a handful of men survive from day to day, or another handful of men try to overthrow them.

London, March 17, 1951

Under our representative institutions it is occasionally necessary to defer to the opinions of other people.

Commons, July 16, 1909

Democracy is not a caucus, obtaining a fixed term of office by promises, and then doing what it likes with the people. We hold that there ought to be a constant relationship between the rulers and the people. Government of the people, by the people, for the people, still remains the sovereign definition of democracy.

Commons, November 11, 1947

We welcome any country where the people own the Government, and not the Government the people.

The Hague, May 7, 1948

The foundation of all democracy is that the people have the right to vote. To deprive them of that right is to make a mockery of all the high-sounding phrases which are so often used. At the bottom of all the tributes paid to democracy is the little man, walking into the little booth, with a little pencil, making a little cross on a little bit of paper – no amount of rhetoric or voluminous discussion can

'Government of the people, by the people, for the people, still remains the sovereign definition of democracy'

possibly diminish the overwhelming importance of that point.

Commons, October 31, 1944

Peaceful Parliamentary countries, which aim at freedom for the individual and abundance for the mass, start with a heavy handicap against a dictatorship whose sole theme has been war, the preparation for war, and the grinding up of everything and everybody into its military machine.

Commons, November 8, 1939

If democracy and Parliamentary institutions are to triumph in this war, it is absolutely necessary that Governments resting upon them shall be able to act and dare, that the servants of the Crown shall not be harassed by nagging and snarling, that enemy propaganda shall not be fed needlessly out of our own hands and our reputation disparaged and undermined throughout the world.

Commons, July 2, 1942

Many forms of government have been tried, and will be tried, in this world of sin and woe ... No one pretends that democracy is perfect or all-wise. Indeed it has been said that democracy is the worst form of government except all those other forms that have been tried from time to time.

Commons, November 11, 1947

107

Demon of the Air

Hitler made a contract with the demon of the air, but the contract ran out before the job was done, and the demon has taken on an engagement with the rival firm. How truly it has been said that nations and people very often fall by the very means which they have used, and built their hopes upon, for their rising-up.

Commons, July 2, 1942

Depopulation

A continuance of Socialist experiments in theory, and of their ineptitude and incompetence in practice, will bring upon us not only worse privations and restrictions than those we now bear, but economic ruin; and not only economic ruin but the depopulation of the British Isles on a scale which no one has ever imagined or predicted.

The Royal Albert Hall, London, April 21, 1948

Desert Army

This noble Desert Army, which has never doubted its power to beat the enemy, and whose pride had suffered cruelly from retreats and disasters which they could not understand, regained in a week its ardour and self-confidence. Historians may explain Tobruk. The Eighth Army has done better; it has avenged it.

Commons, November 11, 1942

This desert warfare has to be seen to be believed. Large armies, with their innumerable transport and tiny habitations, are dispersed and scattered as if from a pepper-pot over the vast indeterminate slopes and plains of the desert, broken here and there only by a sandy crease or tuck in the ground or an outcrop of rock.

Commons, September 8, 1942

'We stand here still the champions. If we fail, all fails, and if we fall, all will fall together'

Desperation

We have to reckon with a gambler's desperation. We have to reckon with a criminal who by a mere gesture has decreed the death of three or four million Russian and German soldiers. We stand here still the champions. If we fail, all fails, and if we fall, all will fall together.

Commons, July 29, 1941

Destiny

It is not our power to anticipate our destiny.

Commons, November 23, 1932

These are not the days when you can order the British nation or the British Empire about as if it were a pawn on the chessboard of Europe. You cannot do it.

Of course, if the United States were willing to come into the European scene as a prime factor, if they were willing to guarantee to those countries who take their advice that they would not suffer for it, then an incomparably wider and happier prospect would open to the whole world. If they were willing not only to sign, but to ratify, treaties of that kind, it would be an enormous advantage.

It is quite safe for the British Empire to go as far in any guarantee in Europe as the United States is willing to go, and hardly any difficulty in the world could not be solved by the faithful co-operation of the English-speaking peoples. But that is not going to happen tomorrow.

Commons, November 23, 1932

> It is a mistake to look too far ahead. Only one link in the chain of destiny can be handled at a time.
>
> *Commons, February 18, 1945*

It is not in the power of one nation, however formidably armed, still less is it in the power of a small group of men, violent, ruthless men, who have always to cast their eyes back over their shoulders, to cramp and fetter the forward march of human destiny.

London, October 16, 1938

Destroyers

There will be no delay in bringing the American destroyers into active service; in fact, British crews are already meeting them at the various ports where they are being delivered. You might call it the long arm of coincidence. I really do not think that there is any more to be said about the whole business at the present time. This is not the appropriate occasion for rhetoric. Perhaps I may, however, very respectfully, offer this counsel to the House: When you have got a thing where you want it, it is a good thing to leave it where it is.

Commons, September 5, 1940

The destroyer has two functions. Its first function is to destroy the enemy's torpedo craft by gunfire in its own waters. Its second function is the attack by the torpedo on the heavy ships of the enemy.

Commons, March 17, 1914

Determination

We shall not flag or fail. We shall go on to the end. We shall fight in France, we shall fight on the seas and oceans, we shall fight with growing confidence and growing strength in the air. We shall defend our island, whatever the cost may be. We shall fight on the beaches, we shall fight on the landing-grounds, we shall fight in the fields and in the streets, we shall fight in the hills. We shall never surrender, and even if, which I do not for a moment believe, this island or a large part of it were subjugated and starving, then our Empire beyond the seas, armed and guarded by the British Fleet, would carry on the struggle, until, in God's good time, the New World, with all its power and might, steps forth to the rescue and liberation of the Old.

Commons, June 4, 1940

I am confident that we shall succeed in defeating and largely destroying this most tremendous onslaught by which we are now threatened, and anyhow, whatever happens, we will all go down fighting to the end.

Commons, September 17, 1940

Deterrents

It is my belief that by accumulating deterrents of all kinds against aggression we shall, in fact, ward off the fearful catastrophe, the fears of which darken the life and mar the progress of all the peoples of the globe.

Congress, Washington, DC, January 17, 1952

Major war of the future will differ, therefore, from anything we have known in the past in this one significant respect, that each side, at the outset, will suffer what it dreads the most, the loss of everything that it has ever known of. The deterrents will grow continually in value. In the past, an aggressor has been tempted by the hope of snatching an early advantage. In future, he may be deterred by the knowledge that the other side has the certain power to inflict swift, inescapable, and crushing retaliation.

Commons, March 1, 1955

'We shall fight on the beaches, we shall fight on the landing-grounds, we shall fight in the fields and in the streets, we shall fight in the hills. We shall never surrender'

A country like ours, possessed of immense territory and wealth, whose defence has been neglected, cannot avoid war by dilating upon its horrors, or even by a continuous display of pacific qualities, or by ignoring the fate of the victims of aggression elsewhere. War will be avoided, in present circumstances, only by the accumulation of deterrents against the aggressor.

Commons, March 24, 1938.

Devolution

I am convinced that no Party in the future would refuse to consider the delegation of administrative and legislative functions to provincial and national boards. I believe in the extension of local government on a scale hitherto quite unknown, in the creation of national boards in the four parts of the Kingdom, and the handing over to them of large slices and blocks of business which could not properly be dealt with at Westminster.

Commons, February 20, 1905

In the conduct of vast, nation-wide administration there must be division of functions, and there must be proper responsibility assigned to the departmental chiefs. They must have the power and authority to do their work, and be able to take a proper pride in it when it is done, and be held accountable for it if it is not done.

Commons, July 29, 1941

Dictators

If we do not stand up to the dictators now, we shall only prepare the day when we shall have to stand up to them under far more adverse conditions. Two years ago it was safe, three years ago it was easy, and four years ago a mere dispatch might have rectified the position. But where shall we be a year hence?

Commons, March 24, 1938

Like the Communists, the Nazis tolerate no opinion but their own. Like the Communists, they feed on hatred. Like the Communists, they must seek, from time to time, and always at shorter intervals, a new target, a new prize, a new victim. The dictator in all his pride, is held in the grip of his Party machine. He can go forward; he cannot go back. He must blood his hounds and show them sport, or else, like Actaeon of old, be devoured by them. All-strong without, he is all-weak within.

London, October 16, 1938

As a freeborn Englishman, what I hate is the sense of being at anybody's mercy or in anybody's power, be it Hitler or Attlee. We are approaching very near to dictatorship in this country, dictatorship that is to say – I will be quite candid with the House – without either its criminality or its efficiency.

Commons, November 11, 1947

Dictatorships

It is in this fear of criticism that the Nazi and Bolshevik dictatorships run their greatest risk. They silence all criticism by the concentration camp, the rubber truncheon, or the firing party. Thus the men at the top must very often only be fed with the facts which are palatable to them. Scandals, corruption and shortcomings are not exposed, because there are no independent voices. Instead of being exposed, they continue to fester behind the pompous frontage of the State. The men at the top may be very fierce and powerful, but their ears are deaf, their fingers are numb; they cannot feel their feet as they move forward in the fog and darkness of the immeasurable and the unknown.

Free Trade Hall, Manchester, January 27, 1940

Diplomatic Relations

The reason for having diplomatic relations is not to confer a compliment, but to secure a convenience.

Commons, November 17, 1949

Disarmament

It may be very virtuous and high-minded to press disarmament upon nations situated as these nations are, but if not done in the right way and

113

in due season, and in moderation, with regard for other people's points of view as well as our own sentiments, it may bring war nearer rather than peace, and may lead us to be suspected and hated instead of being honoured and thanked as we should wish to be.

Commons, April 13, 1933

Once upon a time all the animals in the zoos decided that they would disarm, and they arranged to have a conference to arrange the matter. So the Rhinoceros said when he opened the proceedings that the use of teeth was barbarous and horrible and ought to be strictly prohibited by general consent. Horns, which were mainly defensive weapons, would, of course, have to be allowed.

The Buffalo, the Stag, the Porcupine, and even the little Hedgehog all said they would vote with the Rhino, but the Lion and the Tiger took a different view. They defended teeth and even claws, which they described as honourable weapons of immortal antiquity.

The Panther, the Leopard, the Puma, and the whole tribe of small cats all supported the Lion and the Tiger. Then the Bear spoke. He proposed that both teeth and horns should be banned and never used again for fighting by any animal. It would be quite enough if animals were allowed to give each other a good hug when they quarrelled.

No one could object to that. It was so fraternal, and that would be a great step towards peace. However, all the other animals were very offended with the Bear, and the Turkey fell into a perfect panic.

The discussion got so hot and angry, and all those animals began thinking so much about horns and teeth and hugging when they argued about the peaceful intentions that had brought them together that they began to look at one another in a very nasty way.

Luckily the keepers were able to calm them down and persuade them to go back quietly to their cages, and they began to feel quite friendly with one another again.

Aldersbrook Road, West Essex, October 25, 1928

False ideas have been spread about the country that disarmament means peace.

Commons, March 14, 1934

'False ideas have been spread about the country that disarmament means peace'

Disaster

Our thankfulness at the escape of our army and so many men, whose loved ones have passed an agonizing week, must not blind us to the fact that what has happened in France and Belgium is a colossal military disaster. The French army has been weakened, the Belgian army has been lost, a large part of those fortified lines upon which so much faith had been reposed is gone, many valuable mining districts and factories have passed into the enemy's possession, the whole of the Channel ports are in his hands, with all the tragic consequences that follow from that, and we must expect another blow to be struck almost immediately at us or at France.

Commons, June 4, 1940

Discipline

The bond of discipline is subtle and sensitive. It may be as tense as steel or as brittle as glass. The main element of discipline in the British Service is a sense of justice and a sense of willing association among great bodies of men with the general policy of their country.

Commons, March 3, 1919

Discretion

I make it a rule, as far as I possibly can, to say nothing in this House upon matters which I am not sure are already known to the General Staffs of foreign countries.

Commons, November 12, 1936

It would be better to do what has been promised, that is, have a discussion without the enemy listening. I know a good deal about all this business. I have very good advisers who check, I can assure Hon Members, what I say, so that I do not inadvertently let out something detrimental; but Hon Members have not the same opportunity. A perfectly well-meaning speech might be resented by the troops when it got around and make them say:

"Well, they have said this in the House of Commons." We must be careful, and therefore I should not recommend a public debate.

Commons, July 6, 1944

Dishcloth

When you have to hold a hot coffee pot, it is better not to break the handle off until you are sure that you will get another equally convenient and serviceable, or, at any rate, until there is a dishcloth handy.

Commons, February 22, 1944

Dismissal

It is an unwholesome way of conducting public affairs in time of peace that ministers or viceroys should be dismissed or should resign, and should not feel it necessary to their self-respect to explain to the nation the reasons for their departure.

Commons, March 6, 1947

Dispersal

People must be taught not to despise the small shelter. Dispersal is the sovereign remedy against heavy casualties.

Commons, October 8, 1940

Dispersal of Production

There is no doubt that this method of the widely distributed manufacture of components ought to be as much a part of the life of an industrial country in this present unhappy modern age as the practice of archery on the village green was in medieval England. It is the simplest and most primary method by which the freedom of a country can be assured, and it is the very heart of modern national defence.

Commons, March 10, 1936

Dispersion of Forces

It is not the enemy in front that I fear, but the division which too often makes itself manifest in progressive ranks – it is that division, that dispersion of forces, that internecine struggle in the moments of great emergency, in the moments when the issue hangs in the balance – it is that which, I fear, may weaken our efforts and may perhaps deprive us of success otherwise within our grasp.

Kinnaird Hall, Dundee, May 14, 1908

Divergences

When you have half a dozen theatres of war in various parts of the globe, there are bound to be divergences of view when the problem is studied from different angles. There were many divergences of view before we came together, and it was for that reason that I had been pressing for so many months for the meeting of as many of the great Allies as possible. These divergences are of emphasis and priority rather than of principle. They can only be removed by the prolonged association of consenting and instructed minds. Human judgment is fallible. We may have taken decisions which will prove to be less good than we hoped, but at any rate anything is better than not having a plan. You must be able to answer every question in these matters of war, and have a good, clear, plain answer to the question: what is your plan, what is your policy? But it does not follow that we always give the answer. It would be foolish.

Commons, February 11, 1943

Division of Mankind

The world was divided into peoples that owned the governments and governments that owned the peoples.

Massachusetts Institute of Technology, Boston, March 31, 1949

Division of the World

We live in a period, happily unique in human history, when the whole world is divided intellectually and to a large extent geographically between the creeds of Communist discipline and individual freedom, and when at the same time, this mental and psychological division is accompanied by the possession by both sides of the obliterating weapons of the nuclear age.

Commons, March 1, 1955

Dog Doesn't Eat Dog

I was not invited to the conference that took place last week in Downing Street between the Prime Minister and the leader of the Liberal Party, but "my Hon Friend the Member for Treorchy" gave me a very shrewd account of the interview between the two Party leaders. After the usual compliments, the Prime Minister said: "We have never been colleagues, we have never been friends – at least, not what you would call holiday friends – but we have both been Prime Minister, and dog doesn't eat dog. Just look at this monstrous Bill the trade unions and our wild fellows have foisted on me. Do me a service, and I will never forget it. Take it upstairs and cut its dirty throat."

Commons, January 28, 1931

Doing the Necessary

It is no use saying: "We are doing our best." You have got to succeed in doing what is necessary.

Commons, March 7, 1916

Doing Without

We have had to dispense with the indispensable.

Commons, July 11, 1922

Dominions

We have fully informed and consulted all the self-governing Dominions, these great communities far beyond the oceans who have been built up on our laws and on our civilization, and who are absolutely free to choose their course, but are absolutely devoted to the ancient Motherhood, and who feel themselves inspired by the same emotions which lead me to stake our all upon duty and honour.

Commons, June 18, 1940

'It is no use saying: "We are doing our best." You have got to succeed in doing what is necessary'

Doom of Britain

I went through, as a minister, some of the worst periods of the U-boat attack in the last year. I have studied the conditions long and carefully, and have thought often about them in the intervening years. Nothing that happened then, nothing that we imagined in the interval, however alarming it seemed at the time, was comparable to the dangers and difficulties which now beset us. I repeat that every high authority I know of, if asked in cold blood a year ago how we should get through, would have found it impossible to give a favourable answer. I have no doubt that the able experts who advise Hitler told him that our doom was certain.

Commons, June 25, 1941

Doom of Mankind

When Mr Sterling Cole, the Chairman of the United States Congressional Committee, gave out a year ago – February 17, 1954 – the first comprehensive review of the hydrogen bomb, the entire foundation of human affairs was revolutionized, and mankind placed in a situation both measureless and laden with doom.

Commons, March 1, 1955

Doom, Ring of

I have always expected that this war would become worse in severity as the guilty Nazis feel the ring of doom remorselessly closing in upon them.

Usher Hall, Edinburgh, October 12, 1942

Downing Street, 11

There seemed to be something about the air of 11 Downing Street peculiarly exhilarating, something which not only gave to the occupant of that building clear views on financial questions, but which very often imparted to him the courage of a martyr and the most unalterable convictions. It was all the more remarkable that the atmosphere should have the effect when they reflected upon the obscurity which prevailed at the residence of the Prime Minister next door, and the very dangerous and poisonous fumes which, until a recent date, issued from the Colonial Office across the road.

Commons, May 16, 1904

Dread Nought

We have the means, and we have the opportunity, of marshalling the whole vast strength of the British Empire, and of the Mother Country, and directing these steadfastly and unswervingly to the fulfilment of our purpose, and the vindication of our cause, and for each and for all, as for the Royal Navy, the watchword should be, "Carry on, and dread nought."

Commons, December 6, 1939

Dreaded Day, The

I dread the day when the means of threatening the heart of the British Empire should pass into the hands of the present rulers of Germany. I think we should be in a position which would be odious to every man who values freedom of action and independence, and also in a position of the utmost peril for our crowded, peaceful population, engaged in their daily toil. I dread that day, but it is not, perhaps, far distant.

Commons, March 8, 1934

Drift

We seem to be moving, drifting, steadily, against our will, against the will of every race and every people and every class, towards some hideous catastrophe. Everybody wishes to stop it, but they do not know how.

Commons, April 14, 1937

Drones

We cannot afford to have idle people. Idlers at the top make idlers at the bottom. No one must stand aside in his working prime to pursue a life of selfish pleasure. There are wasters in all classes. Happily they are only a small minority in every class. But anyhow we cannot have a band of drones in our midst, whether they come from the ancient aristocracy or the modern plutocracy or the ordinary type of pub crawler.

London, March 21, 1943

Drugs

The recent advances in medicine are most remarkable and inspiring. Human inventiveness has been fanned by the fierce wings of war. New drugs of a remarkable healing potency are becoming commonplaces of science, and even the latest textbooks on many diseases require to have very considerable annotations and additions made to them. I personally have never failed to pay my tribute of respect and gratitude to M and B; although I am not competent to give you an exact description of how it works, it certainly has in my case always been attended by highly beneficial results. Then there is penicillin, which has broken upon the world just at a moment when human beings are being gashed and torn and poisoned by wounds on the field of war in enormous numbers, and when so many other diseases, hitherto insoluble, cry for treatment.

Royal College of Physicians, London, March 2, 1944

Dunkirk

We must be very careful not to assign to this deliverance the attributes of victory. Wars are not won by evacuations. But there was a victory inside this deliverance which should be noted. It was gained by the Air Force.

Commons, June 4, 1940

This struggle was protracted and fierce. Suddenly the scene has cleared, the crash and thunder has for the moment – but only for the moment – died away. A miracle of deliverance, achieved by valour, by perseverance, by perfect discipline, by faultless service, by resource, by skill, by unconquerable fidelity, is manifest to us all. The enemy was hurled back by the retreating British and French troops. He was so roughly handled that he did not hurry their departure seriously. The Royal Air Force engaged the main strength of the German air force, and inflicted upon them losses of at least four to one; and the navy, using merely 1,000 ships of all kinds, carried over 335,000 men, French and British, out of the jaws of death and shame, to their native land and to the tasks which lie immediately ahead.

Commons, June 4, 1940

In the fighting over Dunkirk, which was a sort of no-man's-land, we undoubtedly beat the German air force, and gained the mastery of the local air, inflicting here a loss of three to four to one day after day. Anyone who looks at the photographs which were published a week or so ago of the re-embarkation, showing the masses of troops assembled on the beach and forming an ideal target for hours at a time, must realize that this re-embarkation would not have been possible unless the enemy had resigned all hope of recovering air superiority at that time and at that place.

Commons, June 18, 1940

Duty

The destiny of mankind is not decided by material computation. When great causes are on the move in the world, stirring all men's souls, drawing them from their firesides, casting aside comfort, wealth, and the pursuit of happiness in response to impulses at once awe-striking and irresistible, we learn that we are spirits, not animals, and that something is going on in space and time, and beyond space and time, which, whether we like it or not, spells duty.

London, June 16, 1941

Victory or defeat are things which happen, but duty is a thing which is compulsory and has to go on irrespective, and carries with it its own rewards whatever the upshot of the struggle may be.

Ritz-Carlton Hotel, New York, March 25, 1949

It is not given to the cleverest and the most calculating of mortals to know with certainty what is their interest. Yet it is given to quite a lot of simple folk to know every day what is their duty.

London, August 31, 1943

It is always a comfort in times of crisis to feel that you are treading the path of duty according to the lights that are granted you.

Guildhall, London, November 9, 1951

WHAT IS EUROPE NOW?

It is a rubble-heap, a charnel-house, a breeding-ground of pestilence and hate.

Ancient nationalistic feuds and modern ideological factions distract and infuriate the unhappy, hungry populations. False guides point to unsparing retribution as the pathway to prosperity.

The Royal Albert Hall, London, May 14, 1947

Earth in Control of Air

I wish to draw the attention of the House and of the public to a question connected with air defence. The point is limited, and largely technical and scientific in its character. Nevertheless it is important. It is concerned with the methods which can be invented, adopted or discovered to enable the earth to control the air, to enable defence from the ground to exercise control – domination – upon aeroplanes high above its surface.

Commons, June 7, 1935

Economic Structure of Britain

The attempt to socialize Great Britain is fraught with mortal danger. There has never been a community in the world like ours. Here in this small island we maintain forty-six millions of people, who played a greater part per head in winning the world war than any other people, and who, before the war, had developed a standard of living and social services above that of any country in Europe and in many respects above that of the United States. These forty-six millions differ from every other community that has ever existed in the world by the fact that they are perched upon the completely artificial foundation of not providing even one half of their food, and being dependent for the purchase of the bulk of their food and raw materials on persuading foreign customers to accept the wares and the services they offer. Vast, intricate, delicate, innumerable, are the methods of acquiring external wealth which the British nation has developed in recent generations, and the population has grown step by step upon the livelihood produced.

Friends House, London, November 28, 1945

Economy of Nature

In looking at the views of these two Hon Members [the brothers Sir Edgar Vincent and Col. Sir C E H Vincent], I have always marvelled at the economy of nature which had contrived to grow from a single stock the nettle and the dock.

Commons, July 24, 1905

Eden, Anthony

He is the one fresh figure of the first magnitude arising out of a generation which was ravaged by the war.

Commons, February 1938

124

Here is the moment when the House should pay its tribute to the work of my Right Hon Friend the Foreign Secretary. I cannot describe to the House the aid and comfort he has been to me in all our difficulties. His hard life when quite young in the infantry in the last war, his constant self-preparation for the tasks which have fallen to him, his unequalled experience as a minister at the Foreign Office, his knowledge of foreign affairs and their past history, his experience of conferences of all kinds, his breadth of view, his powers of exposition, his moral courage, have gained for him a position second to none among the Foreign Secretaries of the Grand Alliance. It is not only my own personal debt, but even more that of the House to him, which I now acknowledge.

Commons, February 27, 1945

Education

Human beings are endowed with infinitely varying qualities and dispositions, and each one is different from the others. We cannot make them all the same. It would be a pretty dull world if we did. It is in our power, however, to secure equal opportunities for all. The facilities for advanced education must be evened out and multiplied. No one who can take advantage of a higher education should be denied this chance. You cannot conduct a modern community except with an adequate supply of persons upon whose education, whether humane, technical, or scientific, much time and money have been spent.

London, March 21, 1943

Owing to the pressure of life and everyone having to earn their living, a university education of the great majority of those who enjoy that high privilege is usually acquired before twenty. These are great years for young people. The world of thought and history and the treasures of learning are laid open to them. They have the chance of broadening their minds, elevating their view and arming their moral convictions by all the resources that free and wealthy communities can bestow.

University of Miami, February 26, 1946

Egypt

It was always said that Egypt could never be successfully invaded across the Western Desert, and certainly that historical fact has now been established upon modern and far stronger foundations.

Commons, February 11, 1943

Eighth Army

The Desert Army is the product of three years of trial and error and the continued perfecting of transport, communications, supplies and signals, and the rapid moving forward of airfields and the like.

Commons, February 11, 1943

Eisenhower, General

General Eisenhower assumed the command of the Expeditionary Force gathered in Britain. No man has ever laboured more skilfully or intensely for the unification and goodwill of the great forces under his command than General Eisenhower. He has a genius for bringing all the allies together, and is proud to consider himself an allied as well as a United States commander.

Commons, August 2, 1944

Election

A friend of mine, an officer, was in Zagreb when the results of the late General Election came in. An old lady said to him, "Poor Mr Churchill! I suppose now he will be shot." My friend was able to reassure her. He said the sentence might be mitigated to one of the various forms of hard labour which are always open to His Majesty's subjects.

Commons, August 16, 1945

I never remember a General Election which was not followed by a disagreeable, sterile, bickering over election pledges.

Commons, March 6, 1919

Electioneering

It would indeed be disastrous if we were led into a fierce division here at home about foreign policy. An election fought on ordinary domestic issues is a process with which we are all familiar; but an election turning on the dread issues of defence and foreign policy might leave us a deeply divided nation, with an evenly balanced, incoherent Parliament, and this at the very moment when the danger on the Continent had reached its height.

Free Trade Hall, Manchester, May 9, 1938

Eleventh Hour

Now is the time at last to rouse the nation. Perhaps it is the last time it can be roused with a chance of preventing war, or with a chance of coming through to victory should our efforts to prevent war fail. We should lay aside every hindrance and endeavour by uniting the whole force and spirit of our people to raise again a great British nation standing up before all the world; for such a nation, rising in its ancient vigour, can even at this hour save civilization.

Commons, March 24, 1938

Emigration

Under Socialism, with all its malice and class jealousy, with all its hobbling and crippling of diligence, initiative and enterprise, it will not be possible for more than two-thirds of our present population to live in this island. That is why there is all this talk of emigration.

Royal Wanstead School, September 27, 1947

Empire

Some foreigners mock at the British Empire because there are no parchment bonds or hard steel shackles which compel its united action. But there are other forces, far more subtle and far more compulsive, to which the whole fabric spontaneously responds.

These deep tides are flowing now. They sweep away in their flow differences of class and Party. They override the vast ocean spaces which separate the Dominions of the King. The electric telegraph is an old story;

the wireless broadcast is a new one; but we rely on a process far more widespread and equally instantaneous. There are certain things which could happen, which it would not be necessary for us to argue about. No Constitutional issues would arise. Everyone, in the loneliest ranch, or in the most self-centred legislature, would see duty staring him in the face, and all hearts would have the same conviction. And not only the same conviction, but the same resolve to action.

Commons, April 20, 1939

All sorts of greedy appetites have been excited and many itching fingers are stretching and scratching at the vast pillage of a derelict Empire.

Royal Albert Hall, London, March 18, 1931

> # The British Empire existed on the principles of a family and not on those of a syndicate.
>
> *Imperial Conference, Downing Street, May 7, 1907*

Let us then seek to impress year after year upon the British Empire an inclusive and not an exclusive character. We who sit on this side of the House, who look forward to larger brotherhoods and more exact standards of social justice, value and cherish the British Empire because it represents, more than any other similar organization has ever represented, the peaceful co-operation of all sorts of men in all sorts of countries, and because we think it is, in that respect at least, a model of what we hope the whole world will some day become.

Commons, July 15, 1907

Already Mr Gandhi moves about surrounded by a circle of wealthy men, who see at their finger-tips the acquisition of an Empire on cheaper terms than were ever yet offered in the world. Sir, the Roman senator, Didius Julianus, was dining in a restaurant when they told him that the Praetorian Guard put the Empire up to auction and were selling it in the ditch in their camp; he ran out, and, according to Gibbon, bought it for £200 sterling per soldier. That was fairly cheap; but the terms upon which the Empire is being offered to this group surrounding Mr Gandhi are cheaper still.

Commons, March 12, 1931

I remember coming out of the Cabinet meeting on an August afternoon in 1914, when war was certain and the fleet was already mobilized, with this feeling: "How are we to explain it all to Canada, Australia, South Africa and New Zealand; nay, how are we to explain it all to our own people in the short time left?" But, when we came out from the fierce controversy of the Cabinet room into the open air, the whole of the peoples of the British Empire, of every race and every clime, had already sprung to arms. Our old enemies, recent enemies, Generals Botha and Smuts, were already saddling their horses to rally their commandos to the attack on Germany, and Irishmen, whose names I always bear in my memory with regard, John Redmond and his brother, and others of the old Irish Parliamentary Party, which fought us for so many years in this House, pleading the cause of Ireland, with great eloquence and Parliamentary renown; there they were, making these speeches of absolute support and unity with this country until everybody said everywhere: "The brightest spot in the world is Ireland." It may be that a grand opportunity was lost then. We must keep our eyes open. I always keep mine open on the Irish question.

Commons, April 21, 1944

Emulation

A natural and healthy emulation between the two Chambers may be conducive to their ultimate efficiency and improvement.

Commons, July 15, 1948

Encirclement of Germany

What then, is this talk about encirclement? It is all nonsense. There is nothing that we ask for ourselves under collective security that we will not willingly concede, nay earnestly proffer, to Germany. Let her join the club, and make her great contribution and share its amenities and immunities.

Commons, November 5, 1936

Endurance

We are passing through a bad time now, and it will probably be worse before it is better, but that it will be better, if we only endure and persevere, I have no doubt whatever.

Commons, November 15, 1915

Enemy's Two Hopes

The enemy has two hopes. The first is that by lengthening the struggle he may wear down our resolution; the second, and more important, hope is that division will arise between the three great powers by whom he is assailed, and whose continued union spells his doom. His hope is that there will be some rift in this Alliance; that the Russians may go this way, the British and Americans that; that quarrels may arise about the Balkans or the Baltic, about Poland or Hungary, which he hopes will impair the union of our councils and, consequently, the symmetry and momentum of our converging advance. There is the enemy's great hope. It is to deprive that hope of all foundation and reality that our efforts must necessarily be bent.

Commons, October 27, 1944

England

There are a few things I will venture to mention about England. They are spoken in no invidious sense. Here it would hardly occur to anyone that the banks would close their doors against their depositors. Here no one questions the fairness of the courts of law and justice. Here no one thinks of persecuting a man on account of his religion or his race. Here everyone, except the criminals, looks on the policeman as a friend and servant of the public. Here we provide for poverty and misfortune with more compassion, in spite of all our burdens, than any other country. Here we can assert the rights of the citizen against the State, or criticize the Government of the day, without failing in our duty to the Crown or in our loyalty to the King. This ancient, mighty London in which we are gathered is still the financial centre of the world. From the Admiralty building, half a mile away, orders can be sent to a fleet which, though much smaller than it used to be, or than it ought to be, is still unsurpassed on the seas. More than 80 per cent of the British casualties of the Great War were English. More than 80 per cent of the taxation is paid by the English taxpayers. We are entitled to mention these facts, and to draw authority and courage from them.

Royal Society of St George, London, April 24, 1933

Stripped of her Empire in the Orient, deprived of the sovereignty of the seas, loaded with debt and taxation, her commerce and carrying trade shut out by foreign tariffs and quotas, England would sink to the level of a fifth-rate power, and nothing would remain of all her glories except a population much larger than this island can support.

Royal Society of St George, London, April 24, 1933

On this one night in the whole year we are allowed to use a forgotten, almost a forbidden word. We are allowed to mention the name of our own country, to speak of ourselves as "Englishmen," and we may even raise the slogan "St George for Merrie England."

Royal Society of St George, London, April 24, 1933

English, The

We are at once more experienced and more truly united than any people in the world.

Royal Society of St George, London, April 24, 1933

English-Speaking Nations

I should like to set the great English-speaking nations to work together in majesty, in freedom and in peace. The road is open.

Commons, February 15, 1911

Enough

Enough is as good as a feast.

Commons, April 25, 1918

Entanglement

It must be remembered that Great Britain will have more power and will run far less risk in pressing for the redress of grievances than in pressing for disarmament. We can only promote disarmament by giving further guarantees of aid. We can press for the redress of grievances by merely threatening, if our counsels are not attended to, to withdraw ourselves at the proper time from our present close entanglement in European affairs. The first road of pressing for disarmament and offering more aid only leads us deeper and deeper into the European situation. The second either removes the cause of danger or leads us out of the danger zone.

Commons, November 23, 1932

Entente

For forty years or more I have believed in the greatness and virtue of France, often in dark and baffling days I have not wavered, and since the Anglo-French Agreement of 1904 I have always served and worked actively with the French in the defence of good causes.

London, August 31, 1943

Enterprise

We certainly could never earn our living by world trade or even exist in this island without full recognition of all forms of exceptional individual contribution, whether by genius, contrivance, skill, industry or thrift.

Woodford Green, October 9, 1951

This is no country of vast spaces and simple forms of mass production. We have important and substantial basic industries. We have an agriculture which out of self-preservation we are expanding to the utmost. But it is by many thousands of small individual enterprises and activities that the margin by which alone we can maintain ourselves has been procured.

Friends House, London, November 28, 1945

Entrenchment

There is no surer method of economizing and saving money than in the reduction of the number of officials.

Commons, April 24, 1928

Envisage

Envisage – an unpleasant and overworked word.

Commons, March 5, 1953

Epitaph
"Not in vain" may be the pride of those who have survived and the epitaph of those who fell.

Commons, September 28, 1944

Epoch
We live in a terrible epoch of the human story, but we believe there is a broad and sure justice running through its theme.

County Hall, London, July 14, 1941

Equality
A man may be poor; he may have nothing at all except his labour to sell; he may be a manual worker for a weekly wage, but in a free Commonwealth he must enjoy as good a right of citizenship as any lord, or prelate, or capitalist in the country.

Commons, May 30, 1911

The only safe rule for doing justice electorally between man and man was to assume – a large assumption in some cases – that all men are equal and that all discriminations between them are unhealthy and undemocratic.

Commons, July 31, 1906

The foundation of our political system is the equality of rights and the equal importance and value of the political rights enjoyed by persons in every class.

Commons, May 30, 1911

During this war great changes have taken place in the minds of men, and there is no change which is more marked in our country than the continual and rapid effacement of class differences.

Harrow School, Harrow, December 1, 1944

Equilibrium
One set of evils is balanced against another set of evils, and we are invited to admire a perfect equilibrium.

Commons, April 18, 1947

Espionage

The House may be sure that the Soviet Government know perfectly well what we have got in the navy and in the forces in Europe, and that they have got a lot of good friends moving freely about in this country, who will not hesitate to tell them about any little points on which they may be short.

Commons, March 31, 1947

Ethics

The light of Christian ethics remains the most precious guide. Their revival and application is a practical need, whether spiritual or secular in nature, whether to those who find comfort and solace in revealed religion or those who have to face the mystery of human destiny alone. And on this foundation alone will come the grace of life and that reconciliation of the right of the individual with the needs of society from which the happiness, the safety, and the glory, of mankind may spring.

University of London, November 18, 1948

Europe

One can imagine that under a world institution embodying or representing the United Nations, and some day all nations should bring into being a Council of Europe and a Council of Asia. As, according to the forecast I am outlining, the war against Japan will still be raging, it is upon the creation of the Council of Europe and the settlement of Europe that the first practical task will be centred. Now this is a stupendous business. In Europe lie most of the causes which have led to these two world wars. In Europe dwell the historic parent-races from whom our western civilization has been so largely derived. I believe myself to be what is called a good European, and deem it a noble task to take part in reviving the fertile genius and in restoring the true greatness of Europe.

London, March 21, 1943

In our task of reviving the glories and happiness of Europe, and her prosperity, it can certainly be said that we start at the bottom of her fortunes. Here is the fairest, most temperate, most fertile area of the globe. The influence and the power of Europe and of Christendom have for centuries shaped and dominated the course of history. The sons and daughters of Europe have gone forth and carried their message to every part of the world. Religion, law, learning, art, science, industry, throughout the world all bear, in so many lands, under every sky and in every clime, the stamp of European origin, or the trace of European influence.

The Royal Albert Hall, London, May 14, 1947

If Europe were once united in the sharing of its common inheritance, there would be no limit to the happiness, to the prosperity and glory, which its three or four hundred million people would enjoy. Yet it is from Europe that have sprung the series of frightful nationalistic quarrels, originated by the Teutonic nations, which we have seen, even in this twentieth century and in our own lifetime, wreck the peace and mar the prospects of all mankind.

Zürich University, September 19, 1946

What is Europe now? It is a rubble-heap, a charnel-house, a breeding-ground of pestilence and hate. Ancient nationalistic feuds and modern ideological factions distract and infuriate the unhappy, hungry populations. Evil teachers urge the paying-off of old scores with mathematical precision, and false guides point to unsparing retribution as the pathway to prosperity.

The Royal Albert Hall, London, May 14, 1947

There can be no hope for the world unless the peoples of Europe unite together to preserve their freedom, their culture and their civilization, founded upon Christian ethics.

The Royal Albert Hall, London, April 21, 1948

Evil

Time passes quickly. Everything is in constant change. When the first beginnings of evil which may subsequently challenge peace and freedom and even the life of the State make their appearance on the horizon, it is right then to sound the alarm and to try, even by frantic exertions, to arouse somnolent authority to novel dangers; but once we are in the danger zone, once everybody can see that we are marching through that long, dark valley of which I spoke to the House two years ago, then a mood of coolness and calmness is enjoined.

Commons, March 4, 1937

> **Evils**
>
> ## Evils can be created much quicker than they can be cured.
>
> *Liverpool, October 2, 1951*

Excise

Spirits hold their own somewhat better under bleak conditions, but they must be expected in normal weather to resume their continuous descent.

Commons, April 24, 1928

Exertions

Because we feel easier in ourselves and see our way more clearly through our difficulties and dangers than we did some months ago, because foreign countries, friends and foes, recognize the giant, enduring, resilient strength of Britain and the British Empire, do not let us dull for one moment the sense of the awful hazards in which we stand. Do not let us lose the conviction that it is only by supreme and superb exertions, unwearying and indomitable, that we shall save our souls alive. No one can predict, no one can even imagine, how this terrible war against German and Nazi aggression will run its course or how far it will spread or how long it will last. Long, dark months of trials and tribulations lie before us. Not only great dangers, but many more misfortunes, many shortcomings, many mistakes, many disappointments, will surely be our lot. Death and sorrow will be the companions of our journey; hardship our garment; constancy and valour our only shield. We must be united, we must be undaunted, we must be inflexible. Our qualities and deeds must burn and glow through the gloom of Europe until they become the veritable beacon of its salvation.

Commons, October 8, 1940

Exhaustion

We have sacrificed everything in this war. We shall emerge from it, for the time being, more stricken and impoverished than any other victorious country. The United Kingdom and the British Commonwealth are the only unbroken force which declared war on Germany of its own free will. We declared war not for any ambition or material advantage, but for the sake of our obligation to do our best for Poland against German aggression, in which aggression, there or elsewhere, it must also in fairness be stated, our own self-preservation was involved.

Commons, January 18, 1945

Expediency

There was a difference in a policy when it was put forward on the faith and honour of a public man and when it was put forward avowedly as a matter of convenient political tactics.

Commons, March 29, 1904

Expenditure

Expenditure always is popular; the only unpopular part about it is the raising of the money to pay the expenditure.

Commons, May 13, 1901

Experience

The electors, based on universal suffrage, may do what they like. And afterwards they have to like what they do. There is a saying in England, "Experience bought is better than taught." We have bought the experience. I do not complain at all of the workings of our constitutional democratic system. If the majority of the people of Britain, on the morrow of our survival and victory, felt as they did, it was right that they should have their way.

Blackpool, October 5, 1946

Experience in Parliament

Five or ten years' experience as a Member of this House [of Commons] is as fine an all-round education in public affairs as any man can obtain.

Commons, May 23, 1940

Expert Evidence

I am very well accustomed to weigh expert evidence, and most of the important decisions which have been taken in the last three or four years at the Admiralty have been taken by me on a divergence of expert evidence.

Commons, November 15, 1915

Experts

Expert knowledge, however indispensable, is no substitute for a generous and comprehending outlook upon the human story with all its sadness and with all its unquenchable hope.

University of Miami, February 26, 1946

Experts and Government

It was a principle of our Constitution not to employ experts, whether business men or military men, in the highest affairs of State.

Commons, March 23, 1902

I LIKE THE MARTIAL AND COMMANDING AIR WITH WHICH THE RIGHT HON GENTLEMAN TREATS FACTS.

He stands no nonsense from them.

Commons, February 19, 1909

Faction

I suppose we are all in this House admirers of the Party system of government, but I do not think that we should any of us carry our admiration of that system so far as to say that the nation is unfit to enjoy the privilege of managing its own affairs unless it can find some one to quarrel with and plenty of things to quarrel about.

Commons, December 17, 1906

Facts

> I like the martial and commanding air with which the right Hon Gentleman treats facts. He stands no nonsense from them.
>
> *Commons, February 19, 1909*

You must look at facts because they look at you.

Commons, May 7, 1925

We must be on our guard equally against pessimism and against optimism. There are, no doubt, temptations to optimism. It is the fact that the mighty Russian State, so foully and treacherously assaulted, has struck back with magnificent strength and courage, and is inflicting prodigious and well-deserved slaughter for the first time upon the Nazi armies. It is the fact that the United States, the greatest single power in the world, is giving us aid on a gigantic scale and advancing in rising wrath and conviction to the very verge of war. It is the fact that the German air superiority has been broken, and that the air attacks on this country have for the time being almost ceased. It is a fact that the Battle of the Atlantic, although far from won, has, partly through American intervention, moved impressively in our favour. It is the fact that the Nile Valley is now far safer than it was twelve months ago or three months ago. It is the fact that the enemy has lost all pretence of theme or doctrine, and is sunk ever deeper in moral and intellectual degradation and bankruptcy, and that almost all his conquests have proved burdens and sources of weakness.

Commons, July 29, 1941

A balloon goes up quite easily for a certain distance, but after a certain distance it refuses to go up any farther, because the air is too rarefied to float it and sustain it. And, therefore, I would say, let us examine the concrete facts.

St Andrew's Hall, Glasgow, October 11, 1906

Failure

They [the Baldwin-Chamberlain Governments] neither prevented Germany from rearming, nor did they rearm ourselves in time. They quarrelled with Italy without saving Ethiopia. They exploited and discredited the vast institution of the League of Nations. They neglected to make alliances and combinations which might have repaired previous errors; and thus they left us in the hour of trial without adequate national defence or effective international security.

Commons, October 5, 1938

Fair Play

Britain, like any other country, is always changing but, like nature, never draws a line without smudging it. We have not the sharp logic of Continental countries. We seek to benefit private enterprise with the knowledge and guiding power of modern Governments, without sacrificing the initiative and drive of individual effort under free, competitive conditions. Our policy is based on the two main principles of fair play and adequate opportunity. We seek to establish a minimum standard of life and labour, below which no one who is prepared to meet the obligations of good citizenship should be allowed to fall. Above that minimum standard, we wish to give the fullest possible play for competitive individual enterprise and every chance for the native genius of our island race, springing perennially from every class, to win its full and fair reward.

Ayr, May 16, 1947

Fair Traders

They watch the river flowing to the sea, and they wonder how long it will be before the land is parched and drained of all its water. They do not observe the fertilizing showers by which in the marvellous economy of nature the water is restored to the land.

Commons, July 29, 1903

Faith

Faith is given to us, to help and comfort us when we stand in awe before the unfurling scroll of human destiny. And I proclaim my faith that some of us will live to see a fourteenth of July when a liberated France will once again stand forward as the champion of the freedom and the rights of man. When the day dawns, as dawn it will, the soul of France will turn with comprehension and with kindness to those Frenchmen and Frenchwomen, wherever they may be, who in the darkest hour did not despair of the Republic.

Commons, July 14, 1940

I ask you to witness, Mr Speaker, that I have never promised anything or offered anything but blood, tears, toil and sweat, to which I will now add our fair share of mistakes, shortcomings and disappointments, and also that this may go on for a very long time, at the end of which I firmly believe – though it is not a promise or a guarantee, only a profession of faith – that there will be complete, absolute, and final victory.

Commons, May 7, 1941

Faith-Healing

There was nothing more remarkable than this doctrine of faith-healing. The principle was very simple; you said a thing was so and it was so, or you said it was not so, and it was not so.

Commons, April 3, 1905

Family, The

Where does the family start? It starts with a young man falling in love with a girl. No superior alternative has yet been found!

Commons, November 6, 1950

Faroe Islands

We are also at this moment occupying the Faroe Islands, which belong to

Denmark and which are a strategic point of high importance, and whose people showed every disposition to receive us with warm regard. We shall shield the Faroe Islands from all the severities of war and establish ourselves there conveniently by sea and air until the moment comes when they will be handed back to the Crown and people of Denmark, liberated from the foul thraldom in which they have been plunged by the German aggression.

Commons, April 11, 1940

Fear

It is much better to be frightened beforehand than when the danger actually comes to pass. Or it is much better to be frightened now than to be killed hereafter.

Commons, November 28, 1934

Fifth Year of War

It is only in the proper framework that we can take any decision for the time that lies before us. The task is long, and the toil is heavy. The fifth year of the war in which everyone has given the utmost in him weighs harsh and heavy on our minds and on our shoulders. Do not let us add to our difficulties by any lack of clarity of thinking or any restive wavering in resolve. Upon the whole, with all our faults and the infirmities of which we are rightly conscious, this island is a model to the world in its unity and its perservance towards the goal. However intense may be the strain of the fifth year upon us, it will be far worse for our enemies; and we have to continue to show them what they are now beginning reluctantly to realize, that our flexible system of free democratic government is capable alike of pursuing the most complex designs of modern war and of bearing invincibly all the varied strains which come upon our soldiers on the battlefield and upon all of us whose duty lies behind the fighting fronts.

Commons, October 13, 1943

Fifty Millions

Never forget that fifty millions have come into being in Great Britain under the impact and inspiration of former generations; and now if our native genius is cribbed, cabined and confined these fifty millions will be left physically stranded and gasping, like whales which swum upon the high tide into a bay from which the waters have receded.

Woodford Green, July 21, 1951

Fighter Pilots

There never has been, I suppose, in all the world, in all the history of war, such an opportunity for youth. The Knights of the Round Table, the Crusaders, all fall back into the past: not only distant but prosaic; these young men, going forth every morn to guard their native land and all that we stand for, holding in their hands these instruments of colossal and shattering power.

Commons, June 4, 1940

The gratitude of every home in our island, in our Empire, and indeed throughout the world, except in the abodes of the guilty, goes out to the British airmen who, undaunted by odds, unwearied in their constant challenge and mortal danger, are turning the tide of the world war by their prowess and by their devotion. Never in the field of human conflict was so much owed by so many to so few. All hearts go out to the fighter pilots, whose brilliant actions we see with our own eyes day after day.

Commons, August 20, 1940

Fighting French, The

The Germans by their oppression, will soon procure for us the unity of Metropolitan France. That unity can now only take an anti-German form. In such a movement the spirit of the Fighting French must be continually in the ascendant. Their reward will come home on the tide. We must try to bring about as speedily as possible a working arrangement and ultimately a consolidation between all Frenchmen outside the German power. The character and constitution of Admiral Darlan's Government must be continuously modified by the introduction of fresh and, from our point of view, clean elements. We have the right, and I believe we have the power, to effect these necessary transformations so long as Great Britain and the United States act harmoniously together. But meanwhile, above all, let us get on with the war.

Commons, December 10, 1942

'We have only to endure and to persevere, to conquer'

Final Victory

As in the last war, so in this, we are moving through many reverses and defeats to complete and final victory. We have only to endure and to persevere, to conquer. Now we are no longer unarmed; we are well armed. Now we are not alone; we have mighty allies, bound irrevocably by solemn faith and common interests to stand with us in the ranks of the United Nations. There can only be one end. When it will come, or how it will come, I cannot tell. But, when we survey the overwhelming resources which are at our disposal, once they are fully marshalled and developed – as they can be, as they will be – we may stride forward into the unknown with growing confidence.

London, May 10, 1942

Finance

There can be no true efficiency of Government without a sound and careful system of finance.

Commons, April 25, 1918

Finest Hour

Let us therefore brace ourselves to our duties, and so bear ourselves that, if the British Empire and its Commonwealth last for a thousand years, men will still say, "This was their finest hour."

Commons, June 18, 1940

Finland

Only Finland – superb, nay sublime – in the jaws of peril – Finland shows what free men can do. The service rendered by Finland to mankind is magnificent. They have exposed, for all the world to see, the military incapacity of the Red Army and of the Red Air Force. Many illusions about Soviet Russia have been dispelled in these few fierce weeks of fighting in the Arctic Circle.

London, January 20, 1940

Finucane

If ever I feel a bitter feeling rising in me, in my heart, about the Irish, the hands of heroes like Finucane seem to stretch out to soothe it away.

Commons, October 28, 1948

Fire, Living under

We have to make a job of this business of living and working under fire, and I have not the slightest doubt that, when we have settled down to it, we shall establish conditions which will be a credit to our island society and to the whole British family, and will enable us to maintain the production of those weapons in good time upon which our whole safety and future depend.

Commons, October 8, 1940

Fire Power

It is remarkable and indeed odd that the more efficient fire-arms have become, the fewer people are killed by them. The explanation of this apparent paradox is simply that human beings are much more ingenious in getting out of the way of missiles which are fired at them than they are at improving the direction and guidance of these individual missiles. In fact, the semi-automatic and automatic rifles have already, in a certain sense, gained their triumph by largely putting an end to the very mass attacks they were originally devised to destroy.

Commons, February 1, 1954

Flag of Freedom

Upon Britain fell the proud but awful responsibility of keeping the Flag of Freedom flying in the Old World till the forces of the New World could arrive. But now the tornado has passed away. The thunder of the cannons has ceased, the terror from the skies is over, the oppressors are cast out and broken, and we find ourselves breathless but still alive, exhausted but free. The future stands before us to make or mar.

Brussels, November 16, 1945

Flame, Cleansing

The fact that the British Empire stands invincible, and that Nazidom is still being resisted, will kindle again the spark of hope in the breasts of hundreds of millions of down-trodden or despairing men and women throughout Europe, and far beyond its bounds, and from these sparks there will presently come cleansing and devouring flame.

Commons, August 20, 1940

Flattery

The Rector has mentioned the trials and tribulations through which we have passed, and he has referred to my contribution to our efforts during

'Upon Britain fell the proud but awful responsibility of keeping the Flag of Freedom flying in the Old World till the forces of the New World could arrive'

that time in a manner which no man should hear until he is dead. I shall long remember the eloquent words which he has used, and I hope that I shall do nothing in the span of life which still remains to me to cause him to alter his opinion.

University of Oslo, May 12, 1948

Fleet

There was one advantage we possessed over other countries in Europe, which enabled us to have a navy far greater and better than they could have, no matter how great were the sacrifices they made, and that was, while all these powers had to depend upon a great army and to consider enormous land preparations for the defence of their frontiers, we, in this island, were able to concentrate the whole of our energies and strength upon the fleet.

Commons, May 14, 1903

The command of a battle fleet is far more intimate and personal than any function discharged by generals on land.

Commons, March 7, 1916

The First Sea Lord moves the fleet. No one else moves it.

Commons, March 5, 1917

Flexibility

The best method of acquiring flexibility is to have three or four plans for all the probable contingencies, all worked out with the utmost detail. Then it is much easier to switch from one to the other as and when the cat jumps.

Commons, September 21, 1943

Flocculence

Everyone knows how ardently he [the Prime Minister] desires to work for peace, and everyone knows that there are no limits to his courage in such a calling. He said last month, to a deputation from the Churches which waited upon him: "I hope you will go on pressing and pressing and pressing. Do help us to do the broad, just, fundamental, eternal thing." We all admire such sentiments. Dressed in noble, if somewhat flocculent eloquence, they obtain the allegiance of all.

Commons, November 23, 1932

Foch, Marshal

At a moment of great disaster, when it seemed that the French and British armies might well be severed from one another by the German advance, the illustrious Marshal took command of the stricken field, and after a critical and even agonizing month, restored the fortunes of the war. General Weygand, who was head of his military family – as the French put it – said: "If Marshal Foch were here now, he would not waste time deploring what has been lost. He would say: 'Do not yield another yard.'"

Corn Exchange, Cambridge, May 19, 1939

Foe, The

The British and Americans do not war with races or governments as such. Tyranny, external or internal, is our foe whatever trappings and disguises it wears, whatever language it speaks or perverts.

Dorchester Hotel, London, July 4, 1953

Folk, The Little

My hope is that the generous instincts of unity will not depart from us … [so that we] become the prey of the little folk who exist in every country and who frolic alongside the Juggernaut car of war to see what fun or notoriety they can extract from the proceedings.

Commons, February 22, 1944

Folly

It would be a great reform in politics if wisdom could be made to spread as easily and as rapidly as folly.

Commons, August 16, 1947

Food in War

Many of the most valuable foods are essential to the manufacture of vital war material. Fats are used to make explosives. Potatoes make the alcohol for motor spirit. The plastic materials now so largely used in the construction of aircraft are made of milk. If the Germans use these commodities to help them to bomb our women and children, rather than to feed the populations who produce them, we may be sure that imported foods would go the same way, directly or indirectly, or be employed to relieve the enemy of the responsibilities he has so wantonly assumed.

Commons, August 20, 1940

Force

The dominant forces in human history have come from the perception of great truths and the faithful pursuance of great causes.

Commons, March 28, 1950

No more force should be used than is necessary to secure compliance with the law.

Commons, July 8, 1920

Foreign Affairs

My knowledge, such as it is, is not mainly derived from books and documents about foreign affairs, but from living through them for a long time.

Commons, May 11, 1953

Foreign Policy

There must be a moral basis for British foreign policy. People in this country, after all we have gone through, do not mean to be drawn into another terrible war in the name of old-world alliances or diplomatic combinations. If deep causes of division are to be removed from our midst, if all our energies are to be concentrated upon the essential task of increasing our strength and security, it can only be because of lofty and unselfish ideals which command the allegiance of all classes here at home, which rouse their echoes in the breasts even of the dictator-ridden peoples themselves, and stir the pulses of the English-speaking race in every quarter of the globe.

Free Trade Hall, Manchester, May 9, 1938.

When we think of the great power and influence which this country exercises we cannot look back with much pleasure on our foreign policy in the past five years. They certainly have been disastrous years.

Commons, March 26, 1936

Forewarning

I hold to the conviction I expressed some months ago, that if in April, May or June, Great Britain, France and Russia had jointly declared that they would act together upon Nazi Germany if Herr Hitler committed an act of unprovoked aggression against this small state [Czechoslovakia], and if they had told Poland, Yugoslavia and Rumania what they meant to do in good time, and invited them to join the combination of peace-defending powers, I hold that the German dictator would have been confronted with such a formidable array that he would have been deterred from his purpose.

London, October 16, 1938

Forfeit

You will not have any means of abridging this war, or, indeed, of emerging from it safely, unless risks are run. Risks do imply that when forfeit is exacted, as it may be when a great ship is sunk or some bold attack repulsed with heavy slaughter, the House must stand by the Government and the military commanders.

Commons, December 19, 1940

Fortifications

Germany is now fortifying the Rhine zone, or is about to fortify it. No doubt it will take some time.

We are told that in the first instance only field entrenchments will be erected, but those who know to what perfection the Germans can carry field entrenchments like the Hindenburg Line, with all the masses of concrete and the underground chambers included – those who remember that will realize that field entrenchments differ only in degree from permanent fortifications, and work steadily up from the first cutting of the sods to their final and perfect form.

Commons, April 6, 1936

Fortune

I am afraid I cannot give any explanation of the freaks of fortune in the world.

Commons, April 20, 1910

Fox Hunting

Mr Jorrocks has described fox hunting as providing all the glory of war with only 35 per cent of its danger.

Commons, August 7, 1911

France

Even an isolationist would, I think, go so far as to say: "If we have to mix ourselves up with the Continent, let us, at any rate, get the maximum of safety from our commitments."

Commons, March 24, 1938

For more than thirty years I have defended the cause of friendship, of comradeship, and of alliance between France and Great Britain. I have never deviated from that policy throughout the whole of my life. For so many years past have these two nations shared the glories of western Europe that they have become indispensable to each other. It is a fundamental principle of British policy that the alliance with France should be unshakable, constant and effective.

Paris, November 11, 1944

As long as France is strong and Germany is but inadequately armed there is no chance of France being attacked with success, and therefore no obligation will arise under Locarno for us to go to the aid of France. I am sure, on the other hand, that France, which is the most pacific nation in Europe at the present time, as she is, fortunately, the most efficiently armed, would never attempt any violation of the Treaty or commit an overt act against Germany without the sanction of the Treaty, without reference to the Treaty, and, least of all, in opposition to the country with which she is in such amicable relations – Great Britain.

Commons, March 23, 1933

I am not reciting these facts for the purpose of recrimination. That I judge to be utterly futile and even harmful. We cannot afford it. I recite them in order to explain why it was we did not have, as we could have had, between twelve and fourteen British divisions fighting in the line in this great battle instead of only three. Now I put all this aside. I put it on the shelf, from which the historians, when they have time, will select their documents to tell their stories. We have to think of the future and not of the past.

Commons, June 18, 1940

The news from France is very bad and I grieve for the gallant French people who have fallen into this terrible misfortune. Nothing will alter our feelings towards them or our faith that the genius of France will rise again. What has happened in France makes no difference to our actions and purpose. We have become the sole champions now in arms to defend the world cause. We shall do our best to be worthy of this honour. We shall defend our island home, and with the British Empire we shall fight on unconquerable until the curse of Hitler is lifted from the brows of mankind. We are sure that in the end all will come right.

London, June 17, 1940

When you have a friend and comrade at whose side you have faced tremendous struggles, and your friend is smitten down by a stunning blow, it may be necessary to make sure that the weapon that has fallen from his hands shall not be added to the resources of your common enemy. But you need not bear malice because of your friend's cries of delirium and gestures of agony. You must not add to his pain; you must

'We shall fight on unconquerable until the curse of Hitler is lifted from the brows of mankind. In the end all will come right' work for his recovery. The association of interest between Britain and France remains. The cause remains. Duty inescapable remains.

Commons, July 14, 1940

Many of these countries have been poisoned by intrigue before they were struck down by violence. They have been rotted from within before they were smitten from without. How else can you explain what has happened to France? – to the French army, to the French people, to the leaders of the French people?

Commons, July 14, 1940

Many ask themselves the question: Is France finished? Is that long and famous history, adorned by so many manifestations of genius and valour, bearing with it so much that is precious to culture and civilization, and above all to the liberties of mankind – is all that now to sink for ever into the ocean of the past, or will France rise again and resume her rightful place in the structure of what may one day be again the family of Europe? I declare to you here, on this considerable occasion, even now when misguided or suborned Frenchmen are firing upon their rescuers, I declare to you my faith that France will rise again. While there are men like General de Gaulle and all those who follow him – and they are legion throughout France – and men like General Giraud, that gallant warrior whom no prison can hold, while there are men like those to stand forward in the name and in the cause of France, my confidence in the future of France is sure.

Mansion House, London, November 10, 1942

I wish to make it quite clear that I regard the restoration of France as one of the great powers of Europe as a sacred duty from which Great Britain will never recede. This arises not only from the sentiments which we hold towards France, so long our comrade in victory and misfortune, but also from the fact that it is one of the most enduring interests of Great Britain in Europe that there should be a strong France and a strong French army.

Commons, September 21, 1943

We all know that the French are pacific. They are quite as pacific as we are. They want to be left alone, as we do, and, I would add, as the people of Soviet Russia also wish to be left alone. But the French seem much nearer to the danger than we are. There is no strip of salt water to guard their land and their liberties. We must remember that they are the only other great European country that has not reverted to despotism or dictatorship in one form or another.

Commons, October 24, 1935

By all kinds of sly and savage means he [Hitler] is plotting and working to quench for ever the fountain of characteristic French culture and of French inspiration to the world. ... Never will I believe that the soul of France is dead.

London, December 1, 1940

France and Germany

I am now going to say something that will astonish you. The first step in the re-creation of the European family must be a partnership between France and Germany. In this way only can France recover the moral and cultural leadership of Europe. There can be no revival of Europe without a spiritually great France and a spiritually great Germany.

Zürich, September 19, 1946

Franchise

It has often been remarked by bewildered foreign observers that every extension of the franchise in Great Britain has left the Conservative Party in a stronger position. But the reason, or one of the main reasons, which they do not see for this undoubted fact is the steady and ceaseless improvement in the education of the people and in the conditions of their life, and in their growing conscious power to govern their country effectively.

Central Hall, Westminster, March 15, 1945

Fraternal Association

The drawing together in fraternal association of the British and American peoples, and of all the peoples of the English-speaking world may well be regarded as the best of the good things that have happened to us and to the world in this century of tragedy and storm.

Dorchester Hotel, London, July 4, 1950

'This is not the end of the tale. The stars proclaim the deliverance of mankind. Not so easily shall the lights of freedom die'

Free Enterprise

Where you find that State enterprise is likely to be ineffective, then utilize private enterprises, and do not grudge them their profits.

St Andrew's Hall, Glasgow, October 11, 1906

At the head of our mainmast we, like the United States, fly the flag of free enterprise. We are determined that the native genius and spirit of adventure, of risk-taking in peace as in war, shall bear our fortunes forward, finding profitable work and profitable trade for our people, and also we are determined that good and thrifty house-keeping, both national and private, shall sustain our economy.

Central Hall, Westminster, March 15, 1945

The old Radical campaign against exploitation, monopolies, unfair rake-offs and the like, in which I took a part in my young days, was a healthy and necessary corrective to the system of free enterprise.

Perth, May 28, 1948

Free Speech

Free speech carries with it the evil of all foolish, unpleasant and venomous things that are said; but on the whole we would rather lump them than do away with it.

Commons, July 15, 1952

Freedom

The cause of freedom has in it a recuperative power and virtue which can draw from misfortune new hope and new strength.

London, October 16, 1938.

And now the old lion with her lion cubs at her side stands alone against hunters who are armed with deadly weapons and impelled by desperate and destructive rage. Is the tragedy to repeat itself once more? Ah no! This is not the end of the tale. The stars in their courses proclaim the deliverance of mankind. Not so easily shall the onward progress of the people be barred. Not so easily shall the lights of freedom die.

London, June 16, 1941

It is not only the supreme question of self-preservation that is involved in the realization of these dangers, but also the human and the world cause of the preservation of free Governments and of western civilization against the ever advancing forces of authority and despotism.

Commons, May 31, 1935

We have our mistakes, our weaknesses and failings, but in the fight which this island race has made, had it not been the toughest of the tough, if the spirit of freedom which burns in the British breast had not been a pure, dazzling, inextinguishable flame, we might not yet have been near the end of this war.

Bristol University, Bristol, April 21, 1945

'The question arises, "What is freedom?" There are one or two quite simple, practical tests by which it can be known'

It has been said that the price of freedom is eternal vigilance. The question arises, "What is freedom?" There are one or two quite simple, practical tests by which it can be known in the modern world in peace conditions – namely:

Is there the right to free expression of opinion and of opposition and criticism of the Government of the day?

Have the people the right to turn out a Government of which they disapprove, and are constitutional means provided by which they can make their will apparent?

Are their courts of justice free from violence by the Executive and from threats of mob violence, and free of all association with political Parties?

Will these courts administer open and well-established laws which are associated in the human mind with the broad principles of decency and justice?

Will there be fair play for poor as well as for rich, for private persons as well as Government officials?

Will the rights of the individual, subject to his duties to the State, be maintained and asserted and exalted?

Is the ordinary peasant or workman, who is earning a living by daily toil and striving to bring up a family, free from the fear that some grim police organization under the control of a single Party, like the Gestapo, started by the Nazi and Fascist Parties, will tap him on the shoulder and pack him off without fair or open trial to bondage or ill-treatment?

London, August 28, 1944

French Ships

During the last fortnight the British navy, in addition to blockading what is left of the German fleet and chasing the Italian fleet, has had imposed upon it the sad duty of putting effectually out of action for the duration of the war the capital ships of the French navy. These, under the Armistice terms, signed in the railway coach at Compiègne, would have been placed within the power of Germany. The transference of these ships to Hitler would have endangered the security of both Great Britain and the United States. We, therefore, had no choice but to act as we did, and to act forthwith. Our painful task is now complete. Although the unfinished battleship the Jean Bart still rests in a Moroccan harbour and there are a number of French warships at Toulon and in various French ports all over the world, these are not in a condition or of a character to derange our preponderance of naval power. As long, therefore, as they make no attempt to return to ports controlled by Germany or Italy, we shall not molest them in any way. That melancholy phase in our relations with France has, so far as we are concerned, come to an end.

Commons, July 14, 1940

French Navy

Under the long care of Admiral Darlan and M Campinchi, the Minister of Marine, a magnificent fighting and seafaring force has been developed. Not only have we been assisted in every way agreed upon before the war, but besides a whole set of burdens have been lifted off our shoulders by the loyal and ever-increasingly vigorous co-operation of the French fleet. It seems to me a wonderful thing that when France is making so great an effort upon land she should at the same time offer to the allied cause so powerful a reinforcement by sea.

Commons, November 8, 1939

Frenchmen

The Almighty in His infinite wisdom did not see fit to create Frenchmen in the image of Englishmen.

Commons, December 10, 1942

Frenzy

The human race is going through tormenting convulsions, and there is a profound longing for some breathing space, for some pause in the frenzy.

London, October 8, 1951

Friendships

Here in this country, the forerunner of all the democratic and Parliamentary conceptions of modern times, we in this country, who are very old at the game of Party politics hard fought out, have learned how to carry through and debate great fiercely-contested political issues without the severance of personal and private friendships.

Commons, November 9, 1944

Fuel

We used to be a source of fuel; we are increasingly becoming a sink. These supplies of foreign liquid fuel are no doubt vital to our industry, but our ever-increasing dependence upon them ought to arouse serious and timely reflection. The scientific utilization, by liquefaction, pulverization, and other processes, of our vast and magnificent deposits of coal, constitutes a national object of prime importance.

Commons, April 24, 1928

Future

Let us see how the course of events develops, and let us not endeavour to pry too closely or speculate too audaciously upon those mysteries of the future which are veiled from our eyes, and which, if they were not veiled from our eyes by the wisdom of Providence, would confront us with a state of existence here below very much less interesting and exciting than that in which we find ourselves.

Cairo, February 3, 1943

YOU MUST NEVER UNDERRATE THE POWER OF THE GERMAN MACHINE.

It is the most terrible machine that has been created.

Westminster Central Hall, London, October 31, 1942

Gab, Gift of the

It is a very old saying that one man can make more assertions in the course of half an hour than another can offer in a week.

Commons, April 13, 1927

Gallipoli

I will not have it said that this was a civilian plan, foisted by a political amateur upon reluctant officers and experts.

Commons, November 15, 1915

I am concerned to make it clear to the House, and not only to the House but to the navy, that this enterprise was profoundly, maturely, and elaborately considered, that there was a great volume of expert opinion behind it, that it was framed entirely by expert and technical minds, and that in no circumstances could it have been regarded as having been undertaken with carelessness or levity.

Commons, November 15, 1915

Gallup Poll

Nothing is more dangerous in wartime than to live in the temperamental atmosphere of a Gallup Poll, always feeling one's pulse and taking one's temperature.

Commons, September 30, 1941

Gandhi

I am against this surrender to Gandhi. I am against these conversations and agreements between Lord Irwin and Mr Gandhi. Gandhi stands for the permanent exclusion of British trade from India. Gandhi stands for the substitution of Brahmin domination for British rule in India. You will never be able to come to terms with Gandhi.

The Royal Albert Hall, London, March 18, 1931

Ganging Up

Here let me deal with two expressions of prejudice which are now used in an endeavour to prevent friendly peoples' coming together to mutual advantage without hostility to anyone else in the world. The first is the word "bloc". To be on good, easy, sympathetic terms with your neighbours is to form a bloc. To form a bloc is a crime, according to every Communist in every land, unless it be a Communist bloc. So much for the word "bloc". It happens also that we are closely associated with the United States. We think very much alike on great world problems on the morrow of our victory – because the British and Americans did have something to do with the victory. The Foreign Secretary often finds himself at these conferences in agreement with Mr Byrnes, just as my Right Hon Friend the Member for Warwick and Leamington [Mr Eden] was often in agreement with Mr Hull, and just as I was often in agreement with President Roosevelt, and, after him, with President Truman. Now all this process, without which I can assure Hon Members we should not be sitting here this afternoon, is to be condemned and ruled out by the expression "ganging up". If two countries who are great friends agree on something which is right, they are "ganging up", so they must not do it. We should brush aside these terms of prejudice, which are used only to darken counsel, and which replace, in certain minds, the ordinary processes of thought and human feeling.

Commons, June 5, 1946

'There shall be no halting, or half-measures, there shall be no compromise, or parley'

Gangsterdom

There shall be no halting, or half-measures, there shall be no compromise, or parley. These gangs of bandits have sought to darken the light of the world; have sought to stand between the common people of all the lands and their march forward into their inheritance. They shall themselves be cast into the pit of death and shame, and only when the earth has been cleansed and purged of their crimes and their villainy shall we turn from the task which they have forced upon us, a task which we were reluctant to undertake, but which we shall now most faithfully and punctiliously discharge.

Ottawa, December 30, 1941

Gasoline

The African excursions of the two dictators have cost their countries in killed and captured 950,000 soldiers, in addition to nearly 2,400,000 tons of shipping destroyed, both of these figures being exclusive of large numbers of ships and aircraft damaged. There have also been lost to the enemy 6,200 guns, 2,550 tanks and 70,000 trucks, which is the American name for lorries, and which, I understand, has been adopted by the combined staffs in North-West Africa in exchange for the use of the word petrol in place of gasoline.

The US Congress, Washington, DC, May 19, 1943

Gaulle, General de

That General de Gaulle was right in believing that the majority of Frenchmen in Dakar was favourable to the Free French movement, I have no doubt; indeed, I think his judgment has been found extremely surefooted, and our opinion of him has been enhanced by everything we have seen of his conduct in circumstances of peculiar and perplexing difficulty. His Majesty's Government have no intention whatever of abandoning the cause of General de Gaulle until it is merged, as merged it will be, in the larger cause of France.

Commons, October 8, 1940

In these last four years I have had many differences with General de Gaulle, but I have never forgotten, and can never forget, that he stood forth as the first eminent Frenchman to face the common foe in what seemed to be the hour of ruin of his country, and possibly of ours; and it is only fair and becoming that he should stand first and foremost in the days when France shall again be raised, and raise herself, to her rightful place among the great powers of Europe and of the world.

Commons, August 2, 1944

General Strike

We now know with accuracy the injury which has been done, at any rate to our finances. We meet this afternoon under the shadow of last year. It is not the time to bewail the past; it is the time to pay the bill. It is not for me to apportion the blame; my task is only to apportion the burden. I cannot present myself before the Committee in the guise of an impartial judge; I am only the public executioner.

Commons, April 11, 1927

Generalities

We are often told that "The House of Commons thinks this" or "feels that". Newspapers write: "The general feeling was of grave uneasiness", "There was much disquiet in the Lobby", etc. All this is telegraphed all over the world and produces evil effects. No one has a right to say what is the opinion of the House of Commons. We suffer now from not having divisions. We have debates, to which a very small minority of Members are able to contribute because of the time available. They express their anxiety and grievances and make our affairs out as bad as they possibly can, and these views bulk unduly in the reports which reach the public or are heard abroad. These Members do not represent the opinion of the House of Commons or of the nation, nor do their statements give a true picture of the prodigious war efforts of the British people. Parliament should be an arena in which grievances and complaints became vocal. The Press also should be a prompt and vigilant alarm bell, ringing when things are not going right. But it is a heavy burden added to the others we have to bear if, without a vote being cast, the idea should be spread at home and abroad that it is the opinion of the House of Commons that our affairs are being conducted in an incompetent and futile manner and that the whole gigantic drive of British industry is just one great muddle and flop.

Commons, July 29, 1941

Geography and Bombing

The next point is a matter of geography. The frontiers of Germany are very much nearer to London than the sea-coasts of this island are to Berlin, and whereas practically the whole of the German bombing air force can reach London with an effective load, very few, if any, of our aeroplanes can reach Berlin with any appreciable load of bombs.

That must be considered as one of the factors in judging between the two countries.

Commons, March 19, 1935

George VI, King

I have seen the King, gay, buoyant, and confident when the stones and rubble of Buckingham Palace lay newly scattered in heaps upon its lawns.

Edinburgh, October 12, 1942

George, David Lloyd

He launched the Liberal and Radical forces of this country effectively into the broad stream of social betterment and social security along which all modern Parties now steer.

Commons, March 28, 1955

His warm heart was stirred by the many perils which beset the cottage homes, the health of the bread-winner, the fate of his widow, the nourishment and upbringing of his children, the meagre and haphazard provision of medical treatment and sanatoria, and the lack of any organized accessible medical service from which the mass of the wage earners and the poor in those days suffered so severely. All this excited his wrath. Pity and compassion lent their powerful wings. He knew the terror with which old age threatened the toiler – that after a life of exertion he could be no more than a burden at the fireside and in the family of a struggling son.

Commons, March 28, 1955

I was his lieutenant in those bygone days, and shared in a minor way in the work. I have lived to see long strides taken, and being taken, and going to be taken, on this path of insurance by which the vultures of utter ruin are driven from the dwellings of the nation. The stamps we lick, the roads we travel, the system of progressive taxation, the principal remedies that have so far been used against unemployment – all these to a very great extent were part not only of the mission but of the actual achievement of Lloyd George; and I am sure that as time passes, his name will not only live but shine on account of the great, laborious, constructive work he did for the social and domestic life of our country.

Commons, March 28, 1945

When the calm, complacent, self-satisfied tranquillities of the Victorian era had exploded into the world convulsions and wars of the terrible twentieth century, Lloyd George had another part to play on which his fame will stand with equal or even greater firmness. Although unacquainted with the military arts, although by public repute a pugnacious pacifist, when the life of our country was in peril he rallied to the war effort and cast aside all other thoughts and aims.

Commons, March 28, 1945

German Air Armaments

Here, again, mystery shrouds all German preparations. At various points facts emerge which enable a general view to be taken. Enormous sums of money are being spent on German aviation and upon other armaments. I wish we could get at the figures which are being spent upon armaments. I believe that they would stagger us with the terrible tale they would tell of the immense panoply which that nation of nearly 70,000,000 of people is assuming, or has already assumed.

Commons, May 19, 1935

German Air Superiority

If Germany continues this expansion and if we continue to carry out our scheme, then some time in 1936 Germany will be definitely and substantially stronger in the air than Great Britain.

Commons, July 30, 1934

German Arms Production

The arms production has the first claim on the entire industry of Germany. The materials required for the production of armaments are the first charge on the German exchange. The whole of their industry is woven into an immediate readiness for war. You have a state of preparedness in German industry which was not attained by our industry until after the late War had gone on probably for two years.

Commons, May 31, 1935

German General Staff

The German General Staff system, which we failed to liquidate after the last war, represents an order comprising many thousands of highly trained officers and a school of doctrine of long, unbroken continuity. It possesses great skill, both in the handling of troops in action and in their rapid movement from place to place. The recent fighting in Italy should leave no doubt on these points.

Commons, February 22, 1944

German Politics

Politics in Germany are not what they are over here. There you do not leave Office to go into Opposition. You do not leave the Front Bench to sit below in the Gangway. You may well leave your high office at a quarter of an hour's notice to drive to the police station, and you may be conducted thereafter, very rapidly, to an even harder ordeal.

Commons, July 13, 1934

German Rearmament

Now the demand is that Germany should be allowed to rearm. Do not delude yourselves. Do not let His Majesty's Government believe – I am sure they do not believe – that all that Germany is asking for is equal status. I believe the refined term now is equal qualitative status, or, as an alternative, equal quantitative status by indefinitely deferred stages. That is not what Germany is seeking. All these bands of sturdy Teutonic youths, marching through the streets and roads of Germany, with the light of desire in their eyes to suffer for their Fatherland, when they have the weapons, believe me they will then ask for the return of lost territories and lost colonies, and when that demand is made it cannot fail to shake and possibly shatter to their foundations every one of the countries I have mentioned, and some other countries I have not mentioned.

Commons, November 23, 1932

German War Machine

You must never underrate the power of the German machine. It is the most terrible machine that has been created. After the last war they kept the brains of the German army together. They kept their Great Staff together. Although their weapons were taken away, this tremendous association of people who think nothing but war, studying war, ruthless scientific war, was held together, thousands of them, and they were able to train and build up an army which, as you saw, in a few weeks shattered to pieces the once famous army of France, and which has marched into country after country and laid it low, and laid low every form of opposition, and only now in the vast spaces of Russia is confronted with this immense and valiant race which has stood against them.

Westminster Central Hall, London, October 31, 1942

Germans, The

They combine in the most deadly manner the qualities of the warrior and the slave. They do not value freedom themselves, and the spectacle of it in others is hateful to them. Whenever they become strong they seek their prey, and they will follow with an iron discipline anyone who will lead them to it.

Commons, September 21, 1943

Those who fight the Germans fight a stubborn and resourceful foe, a foe in every way worthy of the doom prepared for him.

Commons, December 11, 1941

I bear no grudge; I have no prejudice against the German people. I have many German friends, and I have a lively admiration for their splendid qualities of intellect and valour and for their achievements in science and art. The re-entry into the European circle of a Germany at peace within itself, with a heart devoid of hate, would be the most precious benefit for which we could strive, and a supreme advantage which alone would liberate Europe from its peril and its fear, and I believe that the British and French democracies would go a long way in extending the hand of friendship to realize such a hope.

Commons, October 24, 1935

Germany, Bombing of

Even if the Nazi legions stood triumphant on the Black Sea, or indeed upon the Caspian, even if Hitler was at the gates of India, it would profit him nothing if at the same time the entire economic and scientific apparatus of German war power lay shattered and pulverized at home.

Commons, August 20, 1940

Germany, Cause of Anxiety

There is even a theory that the Germans are rearming only out of national self-respect and that they do not mean to hurt anyone at all. Whatever you believe, whatever you think, I venture to submit that we cannot have any anxieties comparable to the anxiety caused by German rearmament.

Commons, October 24, 1935

Germany, Defeat of

While the German lines extend far beyond their frontiers, while their flag flies over conquered capitals and subjugated provinces, while all the appearances of military successes attend their arms, Germany may be defeated more fatally in the second or third year of the war than if the allied armies had entered Berlin in the first.

Commons, November 15, 1915

The character of Hitler's Nazi Party was such as to destroy almost all independent elements in the German people. The struggle was fought to the bitter end. The mass of the people were forced to drain the cup of defeat to the dregs. A headless Germany has fallen into the hands of the conquerors.

Commons, August 16, 1945

I must say that in talking about all these various campaigns that are going on at once all over the world, I have left the obvious, essential fact till this point, namely, that it is the Russian armies who have done the main work in tearing the guts out of the German army. In the air and on the oceans we could maintain our place, but there was no force in the world which could have been called into being, except after several more years, that would have been able to maul and break the German army unless it had been subjected to the terrible slaughter and manhandling that has befallen it through the strength of the Russian Soviet armies.

Commons, August 2, 1944

Defeat to Germany at sea means nothing but loss of the ships sunk or damaged in battle. Behind the German "Dread-noughts" stand four and a half million soldiers and a narrow sea-front bristling with fortresses and batteries. Nothing we could do, after a naval victory, could effect the safety or freedom of a single German hamlet.

Commons, March 17, 1914

Germany in Europe
My hope is that free, liberal civilization and democratic Parliamentary processes will win the soul of Germany for Europe, and that the great

underlying harmonies of the European family will predominate over the feuds that have hitherto rent our famous parent Continent and brought upon it miseries and humiliations beyond the power of statistics to measure or language to describe.

Commons, October 28, 1948

Germany, Hostility to

Certainly we see the Germans hated as no race has ever been hated in human history, or with such good reason. We see them sprawled over a dozen once free and happy countries, with their talons making festering wounds, the scars of which will never be effaced. Nazi tyranny and Prussian militarism, those two loathsome dominations, may well foresee and dread their approaching doom.

London, August 31, 1943

Germany, Negotiations with

When we are asked whether we will grasp the proffered hand of German friendship, I think we should answer: "Yes," but at the same time one wants to know what happens after that. Often when these conversations begin they go nicely for a certain time, and then it appears that what the Germans want is that peace and goodwill should be translated forthwith into tangible and solid immediate benefits to themselves. Very often it is suggested that we should promise to do something, or, what is perhaps even more difficult, stand by and see something or other done that may not be desirable. When the conversations reach that point, they become halting and embarrassed.

Commons, December 21, 1937

Germany, Punishment of

The allies are resolved that Germany shall be totally disarmed, that Nazism and militarism in Germany shall be destroyed, that war criminals shall be justly and swiftly punished, that all German industry capable of military production shall be eliminated or controlled, and that Germany shall make compensation in kind to the utmost of her ability for damage done to allied nations.

Commons, February 27, 1945

Germany, Rearmament of

What is the great new fact which has broken in upon us during the last eighteen months? Germany is rearming. That is the great new fact which rivets the attention of every country in Europe – indeed, in the world – and which throws almost all other issues into the background.

Commons, November 28, 1934

Germany is already well on her way to become, and must become, incomparably the most heavily armed nation in the world and the nation most completely ready for war. *There* is the dominant factor; *there* is the factor which dwarfs all others, and effects the movements of politics and diplomacy in every country throughout Europe; and it is a melancholy reflection in the last hours of this Parliament that we have been the helpless, perhaps even the supine, spectators of this vast transformation, to the acute distress of Europe and to our own grievous disadvantage.

Commons, October 24, 1935

Germany, Reparations

Let me give one striking instance which came to my notice when I was crossing the Atlantic Ocean. We and America took under the Peace Treaty three great liners from Germany. The Germans surrendered them at a valuation and then borrowed the money to build two very much better ones. They immediately captured the Blue Riband of the Atlantic, and they have it still. Now the loans with which the Germans built these ships are subject to a moratorium, while we are unable to go on with our new Cunarder because of our financial crisis. That is typical of what I mean when I say that Germany has not nearly so much reason to complain as some people suppose.

Commons, July 11, 1932

What is the real problem, the real peril? It is not reoccupation of the Rhineland, but this enormous process of the rearmament of Germany. There is the peril. Mr Lansbury says that in the Election I seemed to be haunted by this thought. I confess that I have been occupied with this idea of the great wheels revolving and the great hammers descending day and night in Germany, making the whole of its population into one disciplined war machine. There is the problem that lies before you. There

' "How are we going to stop this war which seems to be moving towards us in so many ways?" '

is what is bringing war nearer. This Rhineland episode is but a step, a stage, an incident in this process. There is fear in every country, all round. Even here, in this island, with some protection from distance, there is fear, deep fear. What is the fear and what is the question which arises from that fear? It is, "How are we going to stop this war which seems to be moving towards us in so many ways?"

Commons, March 26, 1936

Germany, Strength of

Beware. Germany is a country fertile in military surprises. The great Napoleon, in the years after Jena, was completely taken by surprise by the strength of the German army which fought the War of Liberation. Although he had officers all over the place, the German army which fought in the campaign of Leipzig was three or four times as strong as he expected.

Commons, November 28, 1934

Gestapo

No Socialist Government conducting the entire life and industry of the country could afford to allow free, sharp, or worded expressions of public discontent. They would have to fall back on some sort of Gestapo, no doubt very humanely directed in the first instance. And this would nip opinion in the bud; it would stop criticism as it reared its head, and it would gather all the power to the supreme Party and the Party leaders, rising like stately pinnacles above their vast bureaucracies of civil servants, no longer servants and no longer civil. And where would the ordinary simple folk – the common people, as they like to call them in America – where would they be, once this mighty organism had got them in its grip?

London, June 4, 1945

Gettysburg

I was driving the other day not far from the field of Gettysburg, which I know well, like most of your battlefields. It was the decisive battle of the American Civil War. No one after Gettysburg doubted which way the dread balance of war would incline, yet far more blood was shed after the Union victory at Gettysburg than in all the fighting which went before.

The US Congress, Washington, DC, May 19, 1943

I am a child of the House of Commons. I was brought up in my father's house to believe in democracy. "Trust the people" – that was his message. I used to see him cheered at meetings and in the streets by crowds of working men way back in those aristocratic Victorian days when, as Disraeli said, the world was for the few, and for very few. Therefore I have been in full harmony all my life with the tides which have flowed on both sides of the Atlantic against privilege and monopoly, and I have steered confidently towards the Gettysburg ideal of "government of the people, by the people, for the people."

The US Congress, Washington, DC, December 26, 1941

Give and Take

I said last year that our policy was one of moderation, endeavouring to persuade one side to concede and the other to forbear, endeavouring to keep a certain modicum of military force available in order to prevent violent collisions between the two sides [Arabs and Jews in Palestine].

Commons, March 9, 1922

Giving

It is certainly more agreeable to have power to give than to receive. *Commons, April 28, 1949*

Gleam of Victory

The bright gleam has caught the helmets of our soldiers, and warmed and cheered all our hearts.

London, November 10, 1942

Gliders

Gliders are a wonderful means of training pilots, giving them air sense.

Commons, July 30, 1934

Glory, True

Once again the British Commonwealth and Empire emerges safe, undiminished, and united from a mortal struggle. Monstrous tyrannies which menaced our life have been beaten to the ground in ruin, and a brighter radiance illumines the Imperial Crown than any which our annals record. The light is brighter because it comes not only from the fierce but fading glow of military achievements ... but because there mingle with it in mellow splendour the hopes, joys, and blessings of almost all mankind. This is the true glory, and long will it gleam upon our forward path.

Commons, August 15, 1945

Glut of Victory

During the war [1914–1918] we repeatedly asked ourselves the question: How are we going to win? and no one was able to answer it with much precision, until at the end, quite suddenly, quite unexpectedly, our terrible foe collapsed before us, and we were so glutted with victory that in our folly we threw it away.

Commons, June 18, 1940

Gold Standard

We are often told that the gold standard will shackle us to the United States. I will deal with that in a moment. I will tell you what it will shackle us to. It will shackle us to reality. For good or for ill, it will shackle us to reality.

Commons, April 4, 1925

Good Men, Scarcity of

It is sometimes said that good men are scarce. It is perhaps because the spate of events with which we attempt to cope and which we strive to control have far exceeded, in this modern age, the old bounds, that they have been swollen up to giant proportions, while, all the time, the stature and intellect of a man remain unchanged.

Commons, February 6, 1941

Goose

I do not in the least mind being called a goose. I have been called many worse things than that.

Commons, December 3, 1952

Government

Because a government cannot at every moment give an explanation of what it is doing and what is going on, it would be, and it will be, a great mistake to assume that nothing is being done.

Commons, November 11, 1942

His Majesty's Government are bound by the laws which they administer. They are not above the law.

Commons, February 22, 1906

It was always found in the past to be a misfortune to a country when it was governed from one particular point of view, or in the interests of any particular class, whether it was the Court, or the Church, or the Army, or the mercantile or labouring classes. Every country ought to be governed from some central point of view, where all classes and all interests are proportionately represented.

Commons, July 29, 1903

Governments and Rebels

The leader of the Liberal Party speaks of the Government and the rebels. He seems to think that all governments must be infallible and all rebels must be vile. It all depends on what is government, and what are rebels.

Commons, April 14, 1937

Gradualness

In my experience of large enterprises, I have found it is often a mistake to try to settle everything at once. Far off, on the skyline, we can see the peaks of the Delectable Mountains. But we cannot tell what lies between us and them. We know where we want to go; but we cannot foresee all the stages of the journey, nor can we plan our marches as in a military operation.

The Royal Albert Hall, London, May 14, 1947

Gratitude, British

The British public, and the great nation which inherits this somewhat foggy island, are less likely to be grateful for benefits received than they are for evils averted.

Commons, April 13, 1927

Greatheart

It is in the years of peace that wars are prevented and that those foundations are laid upon which the noble structures of the future can be built. But peace will not be preserved without the virtues that make victory possible in war. Peace will not be preserved by pious sentiments expressed in terms of platitudes or by official grimaces and diplomatic correctitude, however desirable this may be from time to time. It will not be preserved by casting aside in dangerous years the panoply of warlike strength. There must be earnest thought. There must also be faithful perseverance and foresight. Greatheart must have his sword and armour to guard the pilgrims on their way. Above all, among the English-speaking peoples, there must be the union of hearts based upon conviction and common ideals. That is what I offer. That is what I seek.

General Assembly of Virginia, Richmond, March 8, 1946

'Above all, among the English-speaking peoples, there must be the union of hearts based upon conviction and common ideals. That is what I offer. That is what I seek'

Greatness, Human

There are many tests by which we may try to measure the greatness of the men who have served high causes, but I shall select only one of them this morning, namely the favourable influence exerted upon the fortunes of mankind.

Commons, October 11, 1946

The price of greatness is responsibility. If the people of the United States had continued in a mediocre station, struggling with the wilderness, absorbed in their own affairs, and a factor of no consequence in the movement of the world, they might have remained forgotten and undisturbed beyond their own protecting oceans: but one cannot rise to be in many ways the leading community in the civilized world without being involved in its problems, without being convulsed by its agonies and inspired by its causes.

Harvard University, September 6, 1943

Great Powers

The world organization cannot be based upon a dictatorship of the great powers. It is their duty to serve the world and not to rule it.

Commons, February 27, 1945

Greece, Invasion of

Without the slightest provocation, with no pretence at parley, Signor Mussolini has invaded Greece, or tried to do so, and his aircraft have murdered an increasing number of Greek civilians, women and children in Salonika and many other open Greek towns. The Greek King, his Government and the Greek people have resolved to fight for life and honour, lest the world should be too easily led in chains.

Commons, November 5, 1940

To the valiant Greek people and their armies – now defending their native soil from the latest Italian outrage, to them we send from the heart of old London our faithful promise that, amid all our burdens and anxieties, we will do our best to aid them in their struggle, and that we will never cease to strike at the foul aggresors in ever-increasing strength from this time forth until the crimes and treacheries which hang around the neck of Mussolini and disgrace the Italian name have been brought to condign and exemplary justice.

Mansion House, London, November 9, 1940

'We gave our guarantee we would not stand by idly and see Poland trampled down by Nazi violence'

Growl

One healthy growl from those benches three years ago – and how different today would be the whole lay-out of our armaments production! Alas, that service was not forthcoming. We have drifted on in general good-natured acquiescence for three whole years – not three whole years of unawareness, but for three whole years with the facts glaring us full in the face.

Commons, November 17, 1938

Growth

The British oak, on which for centuries our navy depended, grows slowly and noiselessly without headlines or sensation, and no one should ever cut one down without planting another. It is very much easier and quicker to cut down trees than to grow them. In cases where bad, oppressive laws warp the free development of human society, much cutting down may be needed, and sometimes the forest itself has to be cleared. Great work was done by the Liberal and Conservative Parties in the nineteenth century, but the twentieth century with its terrible events has brought us problems of a different order, not many of which can be solved merely by passing Acts of Parliament.

Woodford, September 6, 1952

Guarantee

We strove long, too long, for peace, and suffered thereby; but from the moment when we gave our guarantee that we would not stand by idly and see Poland trampled down by Nazi violence, we have never looked back, never flagged, never doubted, never flinched. We were sure of our duty, and we have discharged it, and will discharge it, without swerving or slackening, to the end.

Guildhall, London, June 8, 1943

Guide

The true guide of life is to do what is right.

Huddersfield, October 15, 1951

Guillotine

Those who talk of revolution ought to be prepared for the guillotine.

Commons, October 10, 1902

Gulf

Between us and the orthodox Socialists there is a great doctrinal gulf, which yawns and gapes … There is no such gulf between Conservative and National Governments I have formed, and Liberals. There is scarcely a Liberal sentiment which animated the great Liberal leaders of the past which we do not inherit and defend.

London, June 4, 1945

Gullibility

I have sympathy with, and respect for, the well-meaning, loyal-hearted people who make up the League of Nations Union in this country, but what impresses me most about them is their long-suffering and inexhaustible gullibility. Any scheme of any kind for disarmament put forward by any country, so long as it is surrounded by suitable phraseology, is hailed by them, and the speeches are cheered, and those who speak gain the meed of their applause.

Commons, November 23, 1932

WE CANNOT YET SEE HOW DELIVERANCE WILL COME.

Or when it will come, but nothing is more certain than that every trace of Hitler's footsteps will be sponged and purged.

And, if need be, blasted from the surface of the earth.

St James's Palace, London, June 12, 1941

Hagiology, in Medicine

I have been inclined to feel from time to time that there ought to be a hagiology of medical science and that we ought to have saints' days to commemorate the great discoveries which have been made for all mankind, and perhaps for all time – or for whatever time may be left to us. Nature, like many of our modern statesmen, is prodigal of pain. I should like to find a day when we can take a holiday, a day of jubilation, when we can fête good Saint Anaesthesia and chaste and pure Saint Antiseptic.

Guildhall, London, September 10, 1947

Haile Selassie

It was a satisfaction for me to see for the first time in the flesh Haile Selassie, that historical figure who pleaded the cause of his country amid the storms of the League of Nations, who was the first victim of Mussolini's lust for power and conquest, and who was also the first to be restored to his ancient throne by the heavy exertions of our British and Indian armies in the far-off days of 1940 and 1941.

Commons, February 27, 1945

Handicap

Peaceful Parliamentary nations have more difficulty in transforming themselves into vast warmaking organisms than dictator states who glorify war and feed their youth on dreams of conquest.

London, March 30, 1940

Hard things

Things are not always right because they are hard, but if they are right one must not mind if they are also hard.

Llandudno, October 9, 1948

'Hate is a bad guide. I have never considered myself at all a good hater'

Harrow

Hitler, in one of his recent discourses, declared that the fight was between those who have been through the Adolf Hitler schools and those who have been at Eton. Hitler has forgotten Harrow.

Harrow, December 18, 1940

Harvard

Here, now today, I am once again in academic groves – groves is, I believe, the right word – where knowledge is garnered, where learning is stimulated, where virtues are inculcated and thought encouraged. Here, in the broad United States, with a respectable ocean on either side of us, we can look out upon the world in all its wonder and in all its woe.

Harvard University, September 6, 1943

Hate

Hate is not a good guide in public or in private life. I am sure that class hatred and class warfare, like national revenge, are the most costly luxuries in which anyone can indulge.

Commons, April 24, 1950

Hate is a bad guide. I have never considered myself at all a good hater – though I recognize that from moment to moment it has added stimulus to pugnacity.

Commons, November 6, 1950

Hatred of Germany

It will not be by German hands that the structure of Europe will be rebuilt or the union of the European family achieved. In every country into which the German armies and the Nazi police have broken there has sprung up from the soil a hatred of the German name and a contempt for the Nazi creed which the passage of hundreds of years will not efface from human memory. We cannot yet see how deliverance will come. Or when it will come, but nothing is more certain than that every trace of Hitler's footsteps, every stain of his infected and corroding fingers, will be sponged and purged. And, if need be, blasted from the surface of the earth.

St James's Palace, London, June 12, 1941

185

Headlines

The newspapers, with their alluring headlines, do not do justice to the proportion of current events. Everyone is busy, or is oppressed by the constant cares and difficulties of daily life. Headlines flicker each day before them. Any disorder or confusion in any part of the world, every kind of argument, trouble, dispute, friction or riot – all flicker across the scene. People go tired to bed, at the end of their long, bleak, worrying days, or else they cast care aside, and live for the moment. But, all this time, a tremendous event in Asia is moving towards its culmination, and we should be unworthy of the times in which we live, or of the deeds which we have done if, through unduly careful restraint, we appeared to others unconscious of the gravity, or careless of the upshot, of events which affect the lives of vast numbers of human beings who, up to the present, have dwelt for well or ill beneath our protecting shield.

Commons, December 12, 1946

Healing

The discoveries of healing science must be the inheritance of all. That is clear. Disease must be attacked, whether it occurs in the poorest or the richest man or woman, simply on the ground that it is the enemy; and it must be attacked just in the same way as the fire brigade will give its full assistance to the humblest cottage as readily as to the most important mansion.

Royal College of Physicians, London, March 2, 1944

Hedgehog

Our country should suggest to the mind of a potential paratrooper the back of a hedgehog rather than the paunch of a rabbit.

Commons, December 6, 1951

Heroic Period of History

What a triumph the life of these battered cities is, over the worst that fire and bomb can do. What a vindication of the civilized and decent way of living we have been trying to work for and work towards in our island. What a proof of the virtues of free institutions. What a test of the quality of our local authorities, and of institutions and customs and societies so steadily built. This ordeal by fire has even in a certain sense exhilarated the

'This is indeed the grand heroic period of our history, and the light of glory shines on all'

manhood and womanhood of Britain. The sublime but also terrible and sombre experiences and emotions of the battlefield, which for centuries had been reserved for the soldiers and sailors, are now shared, for good or ill, by the entire population. All are proud to be under the fire of the enemy. Old men, little children, the crippled veterans of former wars, aged women, the ordinary hard-pressed citizen or subject of the King as he likes to call himself, the sturdy workmen who swing the hammers or load the ships, skilful craftsmen, the members of every kind of ARP service, are proud to feel that they stand in the line together with our fighting men, when one of the greatest of causes is being fought out, as fought out it will be, to the end. This is indeed the grand heroic period of our history, and the light of glory shines on all.

London, April 27, 1941

Herrenfolk, Rule of

What is this New Order which they seek to fasten first upon Europe and if possible – for their ambitions are boundless – upon all the continents of the globe? It is the rule of the Herrenfolk – the masterrace – who are to put an end to democracy, to Parliaments, to the fundamental freedoms and decencies of ordinary men and women, to the historic rights of nations; and give them in exchange the iron rule of Prussia, the universal goose-step, and a strict, efficient discipline enforced upon the working-classes by the political police, with the German concentration camps and firing parties, now so busy in a dozen lands, always handy in the background. There is the New Order.

London, August 24, 1941

Hiatus in Air Armaments

There is the same kind of helplessness and hopelessness about dealing with this air problem as there is about dealing with the unemployment

187

problem, or the currency question, or the question of economy. All the evils are vividly portrayed, and the most admirable sentiments are expressed, but as for a practical course of action, solid footholds on which we can tread step by step, there is in this great sphere, as in other spheres of government activity, a gap, a hiatus, a sense that there is no message from the lips of the prophet. There is no use gaping vacuously on the problems of the air. Still less is there any use in indulging in pretence in any form.

Commons, March 14, 1933

Hindsight

Nothing is more easy, nothing is cheaper, nothing is more futile, than to criticize the hazardous and incalculable events and tendencies of war after the event has occurred.

Commons, February 21, 1917

Hiroshima

There are voices which assert that the bomb should never have been used at all. I cannot associate myself with such ideas. Six years of total war have convinced most people that had the Germans or Japanese discovered this new weapon they would have used it upon us to our complete destruction with the utmost alacrity. I am surprised that very worthy people, but people who in most cases had no intention of proceeding to the Japanese front themselves, should adopt the position that rather than throw this bomb, we should have sacrificed a million American and a quarter of a million British lives in the desperate battles and massacres of an invasion of Japan. Future generations will judge these dire decisions, and I believe that if they find themselves dwelling in a happier world from which war has been banished, and where freedom reigns, they will not condemn those who struggled for their benefit amid the horrors and miseries of this gruesome and ferocious epoch.

Commons, August 16, 1945

The bomb brought peace, but men alone can keep that peace, and henceforward they will keep it under penalties which threaten the survival not only of civilization but of humanity itself. I may say that I am in entire agreement with the President that the secrets of the atomic bomb should so far as possible not be imparted at the present time to any other country in the world. This is in no design or wish for arbitrary power, but for the common safety of the world. Nothing can stop the progress of research and experiment in every country, but although research will no doubt proceed in many places, the construction of the immense plants necessary to transform theory into action cannot be improvised in any country.

Commons, August 16, 1945

History

In case at any forthcoming General Election there may be an attempt to revive these former controversies, we are taking steps to have little booklets prepared recording the utterances, at different moments, of all the principal figures involved in those baffling times. For my part, I consider that it will be found much better by all Parties to leave the past to history, especially as I propose to write that history myself.

Commons, January 23, 1948

History with its flickering lamp stumbles along the trail of the past, trying to reconstruct its scenes, to revive its echoes, and kindle with pale gleams the passion of former days.

Commons, November 12, 1940

The right to guide the course of history is the noblest prize of victory. We are still toiling up the hill; we have not yet reached the crest-line of it; we cannot survey the landscape or even imagine what its condition will be when that longed-for morning comes. The task which lies before us immediately is at once practical, more simple and more stern. I hope – indeed I pray – that we shall not be found unworthy of our victory if after toil and tribulation it is granted to us. For the rest we have to gain the victory. That is our task.

Commons, August 20, 1940

It has been said that the dominant lesson of history is that mankind is unteachable.

The General Assembly of Virginia, Richmond, March 8, 1946

When the situation was manageable it was neglected, and now that it is thoroughly out of hand we apply too late the remedies which then might have effected a cure. There is nothing new in the story. It is as old as the sibylline books. It falls into that long, dismal catalogue of the fruitlessness of experience and the confirmed unteachability of mankind. Want of foresight, unwillingness to act when action would be simple and effective, lack of clear thinking, confusion of counsel until the emergency comes, until self-preservation strikes its jarring gong – these are the features which constitute the endless repetition of history.

Commons, May 2, 1935

It may well be that the most glorious chapters of our history are yet to be written. Indeed, the very problems and dangers that encompass us and our country ought to make Englishmen and women of this generation glad to be here at such a time. We ought to rejoice at the responsibilities with which destiny has honoured us, and be proud that we are guardians of our country in an age when her life is at stake.

The Royal Society of St George, London, April 24, 1933

Hitler

So besotted is this man in his lust for blood and conquest, so blasting is the power he wields over the lives of Germans, that he even blurted out the other day that his armies would be better clothed and his locomotives better prepared for their second winter in Russia than they were for their first.

London, May 10, 1942

When Herr Hitler escaped his bomb on July 20th he described his survival as providential; I think that from a purely military point of view we can all agree with him, for certainly it would be most unfortunate if the allies were to be deprived, in the closing phases of the struggle, of that form of warlike genius by which Corporal Schickelgruber has so notably contributed to our victory.

Commons, September 28, 1944

I know of no reason to suppose that Hitler is not in full control of his faculties and the resources of his country. I think he probably repents that he brought appetite unbridled and ambition unmeasured to his dealings with other nations. I have very little doubt that if Hitler could have the past back he would play his hand a little differently. He probably regrets having turned down repeated efforts to avoid war, efforts which almost brought the British Government into disrepute. I should think he now repents that he did not curb his passions before he brought the world to misery.

Washington, DC, May 25, 1943

No one can say how far Herr Hitler's empire will extend before this war is over, but I have no doubt that it will pass away as swiftly as, and perhaps more swiftly than, did Napoleon's empire, although, of course, without any of its glitter or its glory.

Commons, September 5, 1940

Hitler and Napoleon

I always hate to compare Napoleon with Hitler, as it seems an insult to the great Emperor and warrior to connect him in any way with a squalid caucus boss and butcher. But there is one respect in which I must draw a parallel. Both these men were temperamentally unable to give up the tiniest scrap of any territory to which the high water-mark of their hectic fortunes had carried them. Thus, after Leipzig in 1813, Napoleon left all his garrisons on the Rhine, and 40,000 men in Hamburg. He refused to withdraw many other vitally important elements of his armies, and he had to begin the campaign of 1814 with raw levies and a few seasoned troops brought in a hurry from Spain. Similarly, Hitler has successfully scattered the German armies all over

Europe, and by obstinating at every point, from Stalingrad and Tunis down to the present moment, he has stripped himself of the power to concentrate in main strength for the final struggle.

Commons, September 28, 1944

Hitler's Generalship

He has lost, or will lose when the tally is complete, nearly a million men in France and the Low Countries. Other large armies may well be cut off in the Baltic States, in Finland, and in Norway. Less than a year ago, when the relative weakness of Germany was already becoming apparent, he was ordering further aggressive action in the Aegean, and the re-occupation of the islands which the Italians had surrendered, or wished to surrender. He has scattered and squandered a very large army in the Balkan Peninsula, whose escape will be very difficult; 27 divisions, many of them battered, are fighting General Alexander in Northern Italy. Many of these will not be able to recross the Alps to defend the German Fatherland. Such a vast frittering-away and dispersal of forces has never been seen, and is, of course, a prime cause of the impending ruin of Germany.

Commons, September 28, 1944

Hitler's Resolve

Herr Hitler is not thinking only of stealing other people's territories, or flinging gobbets of them to his little confederate. I tell you truly what you must believe when I say this evil man, this monstrous abortion of hatred and defeat, is resolved on nothing less than the complete wiping out of the French nation, and the disintegration of its whole life and future.

London, October 21, 1940

'This evil man, this monstrous abortion of hatred and defeat, is resolved on nothing less than the complete wiping out of the French nation'

Hitler's Strategy

I salute Marshal Stalin, the great champion, and I firmly believe that our twenty years' treaty with Russia will prove one of the most lasting and durable factors in preserving the peace and the good order and the progress of Europe. It may well be that Russian success has been somewhat aided by the strategy of Herr Hitler – of Corporal Hitler. Even military idiots find it difficult not to see some faults in some of his actions. Here he now finds himself with perhaps ten divisions in the north of Finland and 20 or 30 divisions cut off in the Baltic States, all of which three or four months ago could have been transported with their material and their weapons to stand between Germany and the Russian advance. It is far too late for him to achieve that at the present time. Altogether, I think it is much better to let officers rise up in the proper way.

Commons, August 2, 1944

Home and Abroad

When I am abroad I always make it a rule never to criticize or attack the Government of my own country. I make up for lost time when I come home.

Commons, April 18, 1947

Home Guard

Our eyes are fixed upon the future, but we may spare a moment to glance back to those past days of 1940, which are so strangely imprinted upon our memories that we can hardly tell whether they are near or far away. In those days of May, and June, and July, in that terrible summer, when we stood alone, and as the world thought, forlorn, against the all-powerful aggressor with his vast armies and masses of equipment, Mr Anthony Eden, as Secretary of State for War, called upon the local Defence Volunteers to rally round the searchlight positions. Shot-guns, sporting rifles, and staves, were all they could find for weapons; it was not until July that we ferried safely across the Atlantic the 1,000,000 rifles and 1,000 field guns, with ammunition proportionable, which were given to us by the Government and people of the United States by an act of precious and timely succour.

London, May 14, 1943

Honour as Guide

I have thought in this difficult period, when so much fighting and so many critical and complicated manoeuvres are going on, that it is above all things important that our policy and conduct should be upon the highest level, and that honour should be our guide.

London, April 27, 1941

Hour, Their Finest

I expect that the Battle of Britain is about to begin. Upon this battle depends the survival of Christian civilization. Upon it depends our own British life, and the long continuity of our institutions and our Empire. The whole fury and might of the enemy must very soon be turned on us. Hitler knows that he will have to break us in this island or lose the war. If we can stand up to him, all Europe may be free and the life of the world may move forward into broad, sunlit uplands. But if we fail, then the whole world, including the United States, including all that we have known and cared for, will sink into the abyss of a new Dark Age made more sinister, and perhaps more protracted, by the lights of perverted science. Let us therefore brace ourselves to our duties, and so bear ourselves that, if the British Empire and its Commonwealth last for a thousand years, men will say, "This was their finest hour."

Commons, June 18, 1940

'The human story does not always unfold like an arithmetical calculation on the principle that two and two make four. Sometimes they make five or minus three'

House of Commons

There is no situation to which it cannot address itself with vigour and ingenuity. It is the citadel of British liberty. It is the foundation of our laws.

Commons, October 28, 1942

Housing

Houses are built of bricks, mortar and goodwill, not of politics, prejudices and spite.

Cardiff, February 8, 1950

Good housing is the first of the social services. Bad housing makes more disease than the best health service can cure.

Glasgow, May 18, 1951

Human Story, The

The human story does not always unfold like an arithmetical calculation on the principle that two and two make four. Sometimes in life they make five or minus three; and sometimes the black-board topples down in the middle of the sum and leaves the class in disorder and the pedagogue with a black eye. The element of the unexpected and the unforeseeable is what gives some of its relish to life and saves us from falling into the mechanical thraldom of the logicians.

London, May 7, 1946

Humanity, Laws of

Consideration for the lives of others and the laws of humanity, even when one is struggling for one's life and in the greatest stress, does not go wholly unrewarded.

Commons, February 2, 1917

Hydrogen Bomb

The hydrogen bomb carries us into dimensions which have never confronted practical human thought and have been confined to the realms of fancy and imagination.

Commons, April 4, 1954

Hypocrisy

I say frankly that I would rather have a peace-keeping hypocrisy than straightforward, brazen vice, taking the form of unlimited war.

Commons, April 14, 1937

I AM A GREAT ADMIRER OF THE SCOTS.

I am quite friendly with the Welsh, especially one of them.

I must confess to some sentiment about old Ireland, in spite of the ugly mask she tries to wear.

Royal Society of St George, London, April 24, 1933

Ideas, Power of

What is this miracle, for it is nothing less, that called men from the uttermost ends of the earth, some riding twenty days before they could reach their recruiting centres, some armies having to sail 14,000 miles across the seas before they reached the battlefield? What is this force, this miracle which makes governments, as proud and sovereign as any that have ever existed, immediately cast aside all their fears, and immediately set themselves to aid a good cause and beat the common foe? You must look very deep into the heart of man, and then you will not find the answer unless you look with the eye of the spirit. Then it is that you learn that human beings are not dominated by material things, but by ideas for which they are willing to give their lives or their life's work.

Commons, April 21, 1944

Ideologies

We are told we must not involve ourselves in a quarrel about ideologies. If this means we are not to back Communism against Nazism or vice versa, we all agree. Both doctrines are equally obnoxious. Certainly we should not back one against the other. But surely we must have an opinion between Right and Wrong? Surely we must have an opinion between Aggressor and Victim?

Free Trade Hall, Manchester, May 9, 1938

If

I give no guarantee, I make no promise or prediction for the future. But if the next six months, during which we must expect even harder fighting and many disappointments, should find us in no worse position than that in which we stand today; if, after having fought so long alone, single-handed against the might of Germany, and against Italy, and against the intrigues and treachery of Vichy, we should still be found the faithful and unbeaten guardian of the Nile Valley and of the regions that lie about it, then I say that a famous chapter will have been written in the martial history of the British Empire and Commonwealth of Nations.

Commons, June 10, 1941

Illusion

We are going away on our holidays. Jaded ministers, anxious but impotent Members of Parliament, a public whose opinion is more bewildered and

'You must look deep into the heart of man, and then you will not find the answer unless you look with the eye of the spirit. Human beings are dominated by ideas for which they are willing to give their lives'

more expressionless than anything I can recall in my life – all will seek the illusion of rest and peace.

Commons, July 20, 1936

Imagination

You cannot tell from appearances how things will go. Sometimes imagination makes things out far worse than they are; yet without imagination not much can be done. Those people who are imaginative see many more dangers than perhaps exist, certainly many more than will happen; but then they must also pray to be given that extra courage to carry this far-reaching imagination.

Harrow School, Harrow, October 29, 1941

Immunity of Britain

It may be hard for our island people, with their long immunity, to realize this ugly, unpleasant alteration in our position. We are an undefeated people. Nearly a thousand years have passed since we were subjugated by external force. All our outlook for several generations has been influenced by a sense of invincible, inexpugnable security at home. That security is no longer absolute or certain, and we must address our minds courageously, seriously, to the new conditions under which we have now to dwell, and under which Continental nations have always dwelt.

Commons, March 4, 1937

Imperium et Libertas

The maxim of Lord Beaconsfield, *Imperium et Libertas*, is still our guide. This truth has already been proved abundantly since those words were spoken. Without freedom there is no foundation for our Empire; without Empire there is no safeguard for our freedom.

Central Hall, Westminster, March 15, 1945

Incantations

I myself do not believe that we shall come through our difficulties by reliance on any particular logical or doctrinaire theory, I do not believe that there is any way in which, by chanting some incantation, we shall be able to produce a solution of the difficulties with which we are confronted.

Commons, July 24, 1928

Incongruity

To abandon India, with all the dire consequences that would follow therefrom, but to have a war with the Jews in order to give Palestine to the Arabs amid the execration of the world, appears to carry incongruity of thought and policy to levels which have rarely been attained in human history.

Commons, November 12, 1946

Incorruptibility

There is a gulf fixed between private conduct and that of persons in an official, and, above all, in a ministerial position. The abuse or misuse for personal gain of the special powers and privileges which attach to office under the State is rightly deemed most culpable, and, quite apart from any question of prosecution under the law, is decisive in respect of ministers.

Commons, February 3, 1949

Indemnity, German

Germany has paid since the war an indemnity of about one thousand millions sterling, but she has borrowed in the same time about two thousand millions sterling with which to pay that indemnity and to equip her factories.

Commons, November 23, 1932

Independence, Declaration of

We must never cease to proclaim in fearless tones the great principles of freedom and the rights of man which are the joint inheritance of the English-speaking world and which through Magna Carta, the Bill of Rights, the Habeas Corpus, trial by jury, and the English common law, find their most famous expression in the American Declaration of Independence.

Westminster College, Fulton, Missouri, March 5, 1946

India

What has been the effect of our immense act of surrender in India? On the morrow of our victory and of our services, without which human freedom would not have survived, we are divesting ourselves of the mighty and wonderful empire which had been built up in India by two hundred years of effort and sacrifice, and the number of the King's subjects is being reduced to barely a quarter of what it has been for generations. Yet at this very moment and in the presence of this unparalled act of voluntary abdication, we are still ceaselessly abused by the Soviet wireless and by certain unfriendly elements in the United States for being a land-grabbing Imperialistic power seeking expansion and aggrandizement. While Soviet Russia is expanding or seeking to expand in every direction, and has already brought many extra scores of millions of people directly or indirectly under the despotic control of the Kremlin and the rigours of Communist discipline, we, who sought nothing from this war but to do our duty and are in fact reducing ourselves to a fraction of our former size and population, are successfully held up to world censure.

Blackpool, October 5, 1946

> India is a continent as large as and more populous than Europe, and not less deeply divided by racial and religious differences than Europe. India has no more unity than Europe, except that superficial unity which has been created by our rule and guidance in the last 150 years.
>
> *Westminster, May 7, 1946*

All the great countries in this war count their armies by millions, but the Indian Army has a peculiar characteristic not found in the armies of Britain or the United States or Russia or France or in the armies of our foes, in that it is entirely composed of volunteers. No one has been conscripted or compelled. The same thing is broadly true throughout our great Colonial Empire.

Guildhall, London, June 30, 1943

Indignation

It is very easy to say that your opponents have been guilty of a breach of faith, but it is a great mistake to splash the paint about so freely that your words cease to have any real meaning and cease to carry any sense of affront even to those to whom they are applied, and cease to bear any connection with any genuine feeling of indignation on the part of those on whose behalf they are spoken.

Commons, March 27, 1911

Individual Rights

Since the dawn of the Christian era a certain way of life has slowly been shaping itself among the western peoples, and certain standards of conduct and government have come to be esteemed. After many miseries and prolonged confusion, there arose into the broad light of day the conception of the right of the individual; his right to be consulted in the government of his country; his right to invoke the law even against the State itself.

London, October 16, 1938

In moving steadily and steadfastly from a class to a national foundation in the politics and economics of our society and civilization, we must not forget the glories of the past, nor how many battles we have fought for the rights of the individual and for human freedom.

London, March 21, 1943

Inexorable Laws

I am not basing myself on individual promises, but on the working of inexorable laws.

Commons, June 5, 1928

Infantry

This war proceeds along its terrible path by the slaughter of infantry. It is this infantry which is the most difficult to replenish, which is continually worn away on both sides, and though all the other services of the army are necessary to its life, and to its maintenance ... it is this fighting part that is the true measure of your military power, and the only true measure.

Commons, May 23, 1916

Initiative in War

Almost the first of the great principles of war is to seize the initiative, to rivet the attention of the enemy on your action, and to confront him with a series of novel and unexpected situations which leave him no time to pursue a policy of his own.

Commons, February 21, 1917

Innovations

We must beware of needless innovations, especially when guided by logic.

Commons, December 17, 1942

Inquiries

When the House became very anxious a few months ago about our existing granaries being only about half full, and some Hon Members had the audacity to suggest that perhaps it might be just as well to fill them right up and keep them almost filled instead of half empty, the Minister for the Co-ordination of Defence came forward with a plan. It was the kind of plan which is always popular, always acceptable, and always most effective in allaying agitation and staving off Parliamentary questions. His plan was to have an inquiry. There would be an inquiry over which he himself would preside. Of course, once that has been announced, obviously all other questions whenever they are raised can be answered most effectively by saying, "Hush! The inquiry is still proceeding; the case is sub judice. We must not interrupt these most searching toils and studies which are being undertaken. We must wait with patience until the whole matter can be presented." That inquiry is still proceeding.

Commons, July 20, 1936

Inspiration

A wonderful story is unfolding before our eyes. How it will end we are not allowed to know. But on both sides of the Atlantic we all feel, I repeat, all, that we are a part of it, that our future and that of many generations is at stake. We are sure that the character of human society will be shaped by the resolves we take and the deeds we do. We need not bewail the fact that we have been called upon to face such solemn responsibilities. We may be proud, and even rejoice amid our tribulations, that we have been born at this cardinal time for so great an age and so splendid an opportunity of service here below.

London, June 16, 1941

'These dictators on their pedestals are afraid of words and thoughts: words spoken abroad, thoughts stirring at home, terrify them'

It is a message of good cheer to our fighting forces on the seas, in the air, and in our waiting armies in all their posts and stations, that we send them from this capital city. They know that they have behind them a people who will not flinch or weary of the struggle – hard and protracted though it be; but that we shall rather draw from the heart of suffering itself the means of inspiration and survival, and of a victory won not only for ourselves but for all; a victory won not only for our own time, but for the long and better days that are to come.

London, September 11, 1940

Instinctive Urge

The British race is not actuated mainly by the hope of material gain. Otherwise we should long ago have sunk in the ocean of the past. It is stirred on almost all occasions by sentiment and instinct, rather than by programmes or worldly calculations.

Blackpool, October 5, 1946

Instrumentalities

But arms – the instrumentalities, as President Wilson called them – are not sufficient by themselves. We must add to them the power of ideas. People say we ought not to allow ourselves to be drawn into a theoretical antagonism between Nazidom and democracy; but the antagonism is here now. It is this very conflict of spiritual and moral ideas which gives the free countries a great part of their strength. You see these dictators on their pedestals, surrounded by the bayonets of their soldiers and the truncheons of their police. On all sides they are guarded by masses of armed men, cannons, aeroplanes, fortifications, and the like – they boast and vaunt themselves before the world, yet in their hearts there is unspoken fear. They are afraid of words and thoughts: words spoken abroad, thoughts stirring at home – all the more powerful because forbidden – terrify them.

London, October 16, 1938

Insults

Every kind of insult was flung out, not that we seasoned politicians mind what was said about us by people for whom we entertain no respect.

Commons, November 12, 1946

'In all the great crises, the interest of Britain has marched with the progress and freedom of mankind'

Insurance

If I had to sum up the immediate future of democratic politics in a single word I should say "insurance". That is the future – insurance against dangers from abroad, insurance against dangers scarcely less grave and much more near and constant which threaten us here at home in our own island.

Free Trade Hall, Manchester, May 23, 1909

Insurance, National

I personally am very keen that a scheme for the amalgamation and extension of our present incomparable insurance systems should have a leading place in our Four Years' Plan. I have been prominently connected with all these schemes of national compulsory organized thrift from the time when I brought my friend Sir William Beveridge into the public service thirty-five years ago, when I was creating the labour exchanges, on which he was a great authority, and when, with Sir Hubert Llewellyn Smith, I framed the first unemployment insurance scheme. The prime parent of all national insurance schemes is Mr Lloyd George. I was his lieutenant in those distant days, and afterwards it fell to me, as Chancellor of the Exchequer eighteen years ago, to lower the pensions age to sixty-five and to bring in the widows and orphans.

London, March 21, 1943

Insurance Risk

No one is able to forecast the exact moment of his death. That is a mystery which is hidden from us. Still, as the years pass by, and as each of us, in our turn, pass the summit on the way and descend slowly and gradually or rapidly as the case may be, the actuarial position of each taxpayer is definitely and effectively altered.

Commons, June 21, 1926

Insurance, Social

Roughly, I believe it to be no exaggeration to say that the rates to cover a man till seventy are in many cases scarcely half what they would be if they had to cover him till death. Do you see what that means? It is a prodigious fact. It is the sort of fact by the discovery of which people make gigantic fortunes; and I suggest to you that we should make this gigantic fortune for John Bull.

Free Trade Hall, Manchester, May 23, 1909

Insure

If I had my way I would write the word "insure" over the door of every cottage, and upon the blotting book of every public man, because I am convinced that by sacrifices which are conceivably small, which are all within the power of the very poorest man in regular work, families can be secured against catastrophes which otherwise would smash them up for ever.

Manchester, May 23, 1909

Intellectuals

Historians have noticed, all down the centuries, one peculiarity of the English people which has cost them dear. We have always thrown away after a victory the greater part of the advantages we gained in the struggle. The worst difficulties from which we suffer do not come from without. They come from within. They do not come from the cottages of the wage-earners. They come from a peculiar type of brainy people always found in our country, who, if they add something to its culture, take much from its strength.

Royal Society of St George, London, April 24, 1933

Interest

If we in this small island have gradually grown to a considerable estate, and have been able to give our wage-earners some relief from the harder forms of economic pressure, and to build up a decent, tolerant, compassionate, flexible, and infinitely varied society, it is because in all the great crises of our history, the interest of Britain has marched with the progress and freedom of mankind.

Canada Club, London, April 20, 1939

Interference

I sometimes have a feeling, in fact I have it very strongly, a feeling of interference. I want to stress that. I have a feeling sometimes that some guiding hand had interfered. I have a feeling that we have a guardian because we serve a great cause, and that we shall have that guardian so long as we serve that cause faithfully. And what a cause it is! One has only to look at the overwhelming evidence which pours in day by day of the bestial cruelties of the Nazis and the fearful miseries of Europe in all the lands into which they have penetrated; the people ground down, exploited, spied upon, terrorized, shot by platoons of soldiers, day after day the executions, and every kind of petty vexation added to those dark and bloody acts of terrorism. Think what they would do to us if they got here. Think what they would do to us, we who have barred their way to the loot of the whole world, we whom they hate the most because they dread and envy us the most. Think what they would do to us.

Westminster Central Hall, London, October 31, 1942

Internal Combustion Engine

We are not far away – we cannot tell how far – from some form of internal combustion engines for warships of all kinds, and the indirect and wasteful use of oil to generate steam will, in the future, give place to the direct employment of its own explosive force.

Commons, March 26, 1913

I have always considered that the substitution of the internal combustion engine for the horse marked a very gloomy milestone in the progress of mankind.

Commons, June 24, 1952

Internationalist

I am a great admirer of the Scots. I am quite friendly with the Welsh, especially one of them. I must confess to some sentiment about old Ireland, in spite of the ugly mask she tries to wear.

Royal Society of St George, London, April 24, 1933

Interruptions

All the years that I have been in the House of Commons I have always said to myself one thing: "Do not interrupt," and I have never been able to keep to that resolution.

Commons, July 10, 1935

Intuition, Hitler's

I am free to admit that in North Africa we builded better than we knew. The unexpected came to the aid of the design and multiplied the results. For this we have to thank the military intuition of Corporal Hitler. We may notice, as I predicted in the House of Commons three months ago, the touch of the masterhand. The same insensate obstinacy which condemned Field-Marshal von Paulus and his army to destruction at Stalingrad has brought this new catastrophe upon our enemies in Tunisia.

Speech to the US Congress, May 19, 1943

Invasion

Above all, we must not be led by the Lord President [Mr Stanley Baldwin] into this helpless, hopeless mood. Our island is surrounded by the sea. It always has been, and, although the House may not realize it, the sea was in early times a great disadvantage because an invader could come across the sea and no one knew where he would land; very often he did not know himself.

Commons, March 14, 1933

The plain fact that an invasion, planned on so vast a scale, has not been attempted in spite of the very great need of the enemy to destroy us in our citadel, and that all these anxious months, when we stood alone and the whole of the world wondered, have passed safely away – that fact constitutes in itself one of the historic victories of the British Isles and is a monumental milestone on our onward march.

Commons, November 5, 1940

The difficulties of the invader are not ended when he sets foot on shore. A new chapter of perils opens upon him. I am confident that we shall succeed in defeating and largely destroying this most tremendous onslaught by which we are now threatened, and anyhow, whatever happens, we will all go down fighting to the end. I feel as sure as the sun will rise tomorrow that we shall be victorious.

Commons, September 17, 1940

The shipping available and now assembled is sufficient to carry in one voyage nearly half a million men. We should, of course, expect to drown a great many on the way over, and to destroy a large proportion of their vessels. But when you reflect upon the many points from which they could start, and upon the fact that even the most likely sector of invasion, i.e. the sector in which enemy fighter support is available for their bombers and dive-bombers, extending from the Wash to the Isle of Wight, is nearly as long as the whole front in France from the Alps to the sea, and also upon the dangers of fog or artificial fog, one must expect many lodgements or attempted lodgements to be made on our island simultaneously. These we shall hope to deal with as they occur, and also to cut off the supply across the sea by which the enemy will seek to nourish his lodgements.

Commons, September 17, 1940

Inversion

The Romans had a maxim: "Shorten your weapons and lengthen your frontiers." But our maxim seems to be "Diminish your weapons and increase your obligations." Aye, and "diminish the weapons of your friends."

Commons, March 14, 1934

Invitations

It is a very fine thing to refuse an invitation, but it is a good thing to wait till you get it first.

Commons, February 22, 1911

Ireland and England

The discontent that prevailed between England and Ireland arose not so much from differencies of religion and race as from the belief that the English connection was not a profitable nor paying one. If Ireland were more prosperous she would be more loyal, and if more loyal more free.

Commons, May 19, 1904

I defy respectfully, and I dialectically defy, you, by the utmost exercise of your imagination to conjure up or picture even any set of circumstances in which the ruin of England would not mean the ruin of Ireland also.

Commons, April 30, 1912

The fact that we cannot use the south and west coasts of Ireland to refuel our flotillas and aircraft and thus protect the trade by which Ireland as well as Great Britain lives, is a most heavy and grievous burden and one which should never have been placed on our shoulders, broad though they be.

Commons, November 5, 1940

In the case of the Irish ports, in the spring of 1938, absolutely wrong political data, in my opinion, were put before the Chiefs of Staff – another set of Chiefs of Staff – and another set of Chiefs of Staff – and they gave advice which nearly brought us to our ruin. [Laughter.] I have heard all this mocking laughter before in the time of a former government. I remember being once alone in the House, protesting against the cession of the Southern Irish ports. I remember the looks of incredulity, the mockery, derision and laughter I had to encounter on every side, when I said that Mr de Valera might declare Ireland neutral.

Commons, May 24, 1946

Irish Character

No people in the world are really less likely to turn Bolshevik than the Irish. Their strong sense of personal possession, their respect for the position of women, their love of country and their religious convictions constitute them in a peculiar sense the most sure and unyielding opponents of the withering and levelling doctrines of Russia.

Commons, February 16, 1922

'No people in the world are really less likely to turn Bolshevik than the Irish'

Irish Feuds

The British Empire cannot afford to be drawn continually by these brutal Irish feuds into a position dishonouring to its general and long-maintained reputation.

Commons, April 12, 1922

Irish Prosperity

Under complete fiscal freedom England holds Irish prosperity in the hollow of her hand.

Commons, December 15, 1921

Irishism

As I said the other night in the small hours of the morning – [Laughter] – that is an Irishism; I mean the other day in the small hours of the morning.

Commons, June 12, 1925

Iron Cross

At the start of the last war the Iron Cross was a highly prized decoration, but by 1918 it had been granted so freely that it was little valued except, I believe, by Herr Hitler, who, it is alleged, gave it to himself some time later.

Commons, March 22, 1944

After the Armistice, the Germans, who are the most adaptive people, manufactured large numbers of Iron Crosses for sale to the French troops as souvenirs. In the present war they have already some fifteen new medals and twenty-nine new distinctive badges. They have not yet reached the stage of manufacturing them for sale to the allies.

Commons, March 22, 1944

Iron Curtain

From Stettin in the Baltic to Trieste in the Adriatic an iron curtain has descended across the Continent. Behind that line lie all the capitals of the ancient states of central and eastern Europe. Warsaw, Berlin, Prague, Vienna, Budapest, Belgrade, Bucharest and Sofia, all these famous cities and the populations around them lie in what I must call the Soviet sphere, and all are subject in one form or another, not only to Soviet influence but to a very high and in many cases increasing measure of control from Moscow.

Westminster College, Fulton, Missouri, March 5, 1946

Let there be sunshine on both sides of the Iron Curtain; and if ever the sunshine should be equal on both sides, the curtain will be no more.

Blenheim, August 4, 1947

Ten ancient capitals of Europe are behind the Iron Curtain. A large part of this continent is held in bondage. They have escaped from Nazism only to fall into the other extreme of Communism. It is like making a long and agonizing journey to leave the North Pole only to find out that, as a result, you have woken up in the South Pole. All around are only ice and snow and bitter piercing winds.

Strasbourg, August 17, 1949

Israel

The coming into being of a Jewish State in Palestine is an event in world history to be viewed in the perspective not of a generation or a century, but in the perspective of a thousand, two thousand or even three thousand years.

Commons, January 26, 1949

Italian Empire, Fall of

The events in Libya are only part of the story: they are only part of the story of the decline and fall of the Italian Empire, that will not take a future Gibbon so long to write as the original work.

London, February 9, 1941

Italian Navy

We are also told that the Italian navy is to come out and gain sea superiority in these waters.

If they seriously intend it, I shall only say that we shall be delighted to offer Signor Mussolini a free and safeguarded passage through the Straits of Gibraltar in order that he may play the part to which he aspires. There is a general curiosity in the British fleet to find out whether the Italians are up to the level they were at in the last war or whether they have fallen off at all.

Commons, June 18, 1940

Italy

The Italian surrender was a windfall, but it had nothing to do with the date fixed for harvesting the orchard. The truth is that the Armistice announcement was delayed to fit in with the attack, and not the attack delayed to fit in with the announcement.

Commons, September 21, 1943

We have never been your foes till now. In the last war against the barbarous Huns we were your comrades. For fifteen years after that war we were your friends. Although the institutions which you adopted after that war were not akin to ours, and diverged, as we think, from the sovereign impulses which had commanded the unity of Italy, we could still march forward in peace and good will.

London, December 23, 1940

The fate of Italy is indeed terrible, and I personally find it very difficult to nourish animosity against the Italian people. The overwhelming mass of the nation rejoiced in the idea of being delivered from the subtle tyranny of the Fascists, and they wished, when Mussolini was overthrown, to take their place as speedily as possible by the side of the British and American armies who, it was expected, would quickly rid the country of the Germans.

Commons, May 24, 1944

As we stand today there is no doubt that a cloud has come over the old friendship between Great Britain and Italy, a cloud which may very easily not pass away, although undoubtedly it is everyone's desire that it should. It is an old friendship, and we must not forget, what is a little-known fact, that at the time Italy entered into the Triple Alliance in the last century she stipulated particularly that in no circumstances should her obligations under the Alliance bring her into armed conflict with Great Britain.

Commons, July 11, 1935

It is for the Italian people, forty millions of them, to say whether they want this terrible thing to happen to their country or not. One man, and one man alone, has brought them to this pass. There was no need for them to go to war; no one was going to attack them. We tried our best to induce them to remain neutral, to enjoy peace and prosperity in a world of storm. But Mussolini could not resist the temptation of stabbing prostrate France, and what he thought was helpless Britain, in the back. Mad dreams of imperial glory, the lust of conquest and of booty, the arrogance of long-unbridled tyranny, led him to his fatal, shameful act. In vain I warned him: he would not harken. The hyena in his nature broke all bounds of decency and even common sense. Today his empire is gone. We have over a hundred Italian generals and nearly three hundred thousand of his soldiers in our hands as prisoners of war. Agony grips the fair land of Italy. This is only the beginning, and what have the Italians to show for it? A brief promenade by German permission along the Riviera; a flying visit to Corsica; a bloody struggle with the heroic patriots of Yugoslavia; a deed of undying shame in Greece; the ruins of Genoa, Turin, Milan. One man and the regime he has created have brought these measureless calamities upon the hard-working, gifted and once happy Italian people, with whom, until the days of Mussolini, the English-speaking world had so many sympathies and never a quarrel.

London, November 29, 1942

Italy, Liberation of

We must be careful not to get ourselves into the kind of position into which the Germans have blundered in so many countries – that of having to hold down and administer in detail, from day to day, by a system of gauleiters, the entire life of very large populations. Such a course might well, in practice, turn the sense of liberation, which it may soon be in our power to bestow upon the Italian people, into a sullen discontent against us and all our works. The rescuers might soon, indeed, be regarded as tyrants; they might even be hated by the Italian people as much or almost as much as their German allies. I certainly do not wish, in the case of Italy, to tread a path which might lead to execution squads and concentration camps, and above all having to carry on our shoulders a lot of people who ought to be made to carry themselves.

Commons, July 17, 1943

HUMAN JUDGMENT MAY FAIL.

You may act very wisely, you think, but it may turn out a great failure.

I have seen many things happen, but the fact remains that human life is presented to us as a simple choice between right and wrong.

Hotel Bristol, Oslo, May 12, 1948

Japan

Japan, with all her treachery and greed, remains unsubdued. The injury she has inflicted ... and her detestable cruelties call for justice and retribution ...

London, May 8, 1945

I must admit that, having voted for the Japanese alliance nearly 40 years ago, in 1902, and having always done my very best to promote good relations with the Island Empire of Japan, and always having been a sentimental well-wisher to the Japanese and an admirer of their many gifts and qualities, I should view with keen sorrow the opening of a conflict between Japan and the English-speaking world.

Mansion House, London, November 10, 1941

In our conferences in January 1942, between the President and myself, and between our high expert advisers, it was evident that, while the defeat of Japan would not mean the defeat of Germany, the defeat of Germany would infallibly mean the ruin of Japan.

US Congress, Washington, DC, May 19, 1943

I do not believe that Japan, deeply entangled in China, nay, bleeding at every pore in China, her strength ebbing away in a wrongful and impossible task, and with the whole weight of Russia upon her in the north of China, will wish to make war upon the British Empire until she sees how matters go in Europe.

City Carlton Club, London, June 28, 1939

No one must underrate any more the gravity and efficiency of the Japanese war machine. Whether in the air or upon the sea, or man to man on land, they have already proved themselves to be formidable, deadly, and, I am sorry to say, barbarous antagonists. This proves a hundred times over that there never was the slightest chance, even though we had been much better prepared in many ways than we were, of our standing up to them alone while we had Nazi Germany at our throat and Fascist Italy at our belly.

London, February 15, 1942

'The Japanese, whose game is what I may call to make hell while the sun shines…'

Japanese Game

The Japanese, whose game is what I may call to make hell while the sun shines… .

Commons, January 27, 1942

Japanese Madness

Another mistake of our foes was made by Japan when they attacked the United States at Pearl Harbor instead of attacking us alone who were already busy with Italy and Germany in Europe. It was most fortunate that, led away by their dark conspiracies and schemes, dizzy and dazzled from poring over plans, they sprang out upon a peaceful nation with whom they were at that time in peaceful parley, and were led away and tottered over the edge and, for the sake of sinking half a dozen ships of war and beating up a naval port, brought out against them the implacable energies and the measureless power of the 130 million educated people who live in the United States. We have much to be thankful for.

Westminister Central Hall, London, October 31, 1942

Jewish Brigade

The Government have decided to accede to the request of the Jewish Agency for Palestine that a Jewish Brigade group should be formed to take part in active operations. I know there are vast numbers of Jews serving with our forces and the American forces throughout all the armies, but it seems to me indeed appropriate that a special Jewish unit, a special unit of that race which has suffered indescribable torments from the Nazis, should be represented as a distinct formation amongst the forces gathered for their formal overthrow, and I have no doubt they will not only take part in the struggle but also in the occupation which will follow.

Commons, September 28, 1944

Journalism

I have been a journalist and half my lifetime I have earned my living by selling words and I hope thoughts.

Ottawa, January 12, 1952

Joy

Soberness and restraint do not necessarily prevent the joyous expression of the human heart.

Commons, May 1, 1945

Judges, British

Judges had to maintain, and did in fact maintain, though free from criticism, a far more vigorous standard than was required from any class I knew in the realm. What would be thought of a Lord Chief Justice if he won the Derby? [Laughter.] Yet I could cite a solid precedent where such an act had been perpetrated by a Prime Minister who, on the whole, had got away with it all right. [Laughter.]

Commons, March 23, 1954

Judgment, Human

Human judgment may fail. You may act very wisely, you think, but it may turn out a great failure. On the other hand, one may do a foolish thing which may turn out well. I have seen many things happen, but the fact remains that human life is presented to us as a simple choice between

'Soberness and restraint do not necessarily prevent the joyous expression of the human heart'

right and wrong. If you obey that law you will find that that way is far safer in the long run than all calculation which can ever be made.

Hotel Bristol, Oslo, May 12, 1948

Judiciary, The British

The British judiciary, with its traditions and record, was one of the greatest living assets of our race and people, and its independence was part of our message to the ever-growing world that was rising so swiftly around us.

Commons, March 23, 1954

Juggernaut, German

The monstrous juggernaut engine of German might and tyranny has been beaten and broken, outfought and outmanoeuvred by Russian valour, generalship and science, and it has been beaten to an extent which may well prove mortal.

Mansion House, London, November 9, 1943

Julius Caesar

Julius Caesar gained far more by his clemency than by his prowess.

Commons, July 1, 1952

Jury, Trial by

The ancient Anglo-Saxon foundation of all our system of criminal justice is trial by jury.

Commons, July 15, 1948

We regard it as a fundamental safeguard of our democratic liberties and life, and a principle which has been woven into the whole history of our judicial system, that the supreme question, "Guilty or Not Guilty?" shall be decided by ordinary folk.

Commons, July 15, 1948

> **Justice**
> Justice moves slowly and remorselessly upon its path, but it reaches its goal eventually.
>
> *Commons, July 23, 1929*

Justice first

One ought to be just before one is generous.

Belle Vue, Manchester, December 6, 1947

Justice, Sword of

When we remind ourselves of the frightful tyrannies and cruelties with which the German armies, their gauleiters and subordinate tormentors, are now afflicting almost all Europe; when we read every week of the mass executions of Poles, Norwegians, Dutchmen, Czechoslovaks, Frenchmen, Yugoslavs and Greeks; when we see these ancient and honoured countries, of whose deeds and traditions Europe is the heir, writhing under the merciless alien yoke, and when we see their patriots striking back with every week a fiercer and more furious desperation, we may feel sure that we bear the sword of justice, and we resolve to use that sword with the utmost severity to the full and to the end.

Guildhall, London, June 30, 1943

THE PRIVILEGE OF UNIVERSITY EDUCATION IS A GREAT ONE.

The more widely it is extended the better for any country.

It should not be looked upon as something to end with youth but as a key to open many doors of thought and knowledge.

University of London, November 18, 1948

Kent, Duke of

There is something about death on active service which makes it different from common or ordinary death in the normal course of nature. It is accepted without question by the fighting men. Those they leave behind them are also conscious of a light of sacrifice and honour which plays around the grave or the tomb of the warrior. They are for the time being uplifted. This adds to their fortitude, but it does not in any way lessen their pain. Nothing can fill the awful gap, nothing can assuage or comfort the loneliness and deprivation which fall upon wife and children when the prop and centre of their home is suddenly snatched away. Only faith in a life after death in a brighter world where dear ones will meet again – only that and the measured tramp of time can give consolation.

Commons, September 8, 1942

King George VI, Kindness of

I do not think that any Prime Minister has ever received so much personal kindness and encouragement from his sovereign as I have. Every week I have my audience, the greater part of which occurs most agreeably at luncheon, and I have seen the King at close quarters in every phase of our formidable experiences. I remember well how in the first months of this administration the King would come in from practising with his rifle and his tommy-gun in the garden at Buckingham Palace, and if it had come to a last stand in London, a matter which had to be considered at one time, I have no doubt that His Majesty would have come very near departing from his usual constitutional rectitude by disregarding the advice of his ministers.

Commons, May 15, 1945

Knights of the Air

The great French army was very largely, for the time being, cast back and disturbed by the onrush of a few thousands of armoured vehicles. May it not also be that the cause of civilization itself will be defended by the skill and devotion of a few thousand airmen? There never had been, I suppose, in all the world, in all the history of war, such an opportunity for youth. The Knights of the Round Table, the Crusaders, all fall back into the past: not only distant but prosaic; these young men, going forth every morn to guard their native land and all that we stand for, holding in their hands these instruments of colossal and shattering power, of whom it may be said that "Every morn brought forth a noble chance, and every chance brought forth a noble knight," deserve our gratitude, as do all of the brave men who, in so many ways and on so many occasions, are ready, and continue ready, to give life and all for their native land.

Commons, June 4, 1940

Knock at the Door

At the present time – I trust a very fleeting time – "police governments" rule over a great number of countries. It is a case of the odious 18B, carried to a horrible excess. The family is gathered round the fireside to enjoy the scanty fruits of their toil and to recruit their exhausted strength by the little food that they have been able to gather. There they sit. Suddenly there is a knock at the door, and a heavily armed policeman appears. He is not, of course, one who resembles in any way those functionaries whom we honour and obey in the London streets. It may be that the father or son, or a friend sitting in the cottage, is called out and taken off into the dark, and no one knows whether he will ever come back again, or what his fate has been. All they know is that they had better not inquire. There are millions of humble homes in Europe at the moment, in Poland, in Czechoslovakia, in Austria, in Hungary, in Yugoslavia, in Rumania, in Bulgaria – where this fear is the main preoccupation of the family life.

Commons, August 16, 1945

Knock Down

You don't want to knock a man down except to pick him up in a better frame of mind.

Ritz-Carlton Hotel, New York, March 25, 1949

'We must all learn how to support ourselves, but we must also learn how to live'

Knowledge

While all knowledge continues to expand, as Lord Balfour said today, the human faculty remains stationary, and that has induced an experimental mood in all our studies and sciences, a desire to test matters and not to yield oneself completely to clear-cut and logical definitions.

Commons, July 24, 1928

Gradually, as I have passed through life, I have developed a strong feeling that a university training should not be too practical in its aims. Young people study at universities to achieve knowledge, and not to learn a trade. We must all learn how to support ourselves, but we must also learn how to live. We need a lot of engineers in the modern world, but we do not want a world of modern engineers. Great events have come to pass during our lifetime.

University of Oslo, May 12, 1948

The privilege of university education is a great one. The more widely it is extended the better for any country. It should not be looked upon as something to end with youth but as a key to open many doors of thought and knowledge.

University of London, November 18, 1948

SOMEONE SAYS IT'S A LIE.

Well, I am reminded by that of the remark of the witty Irishman who said:

"There are a terrible lot of lies going about the world, and the worst of it is that half of them are true."

Commons, February 22, 1906

Labour, Rights of

The Trade Unions are a long-established and essential part of our national life. Like other human institutions they have their faults and their weaknesses. At the present time they have more influence upon the Government of the country, and less control over their own members, than ever before. But we take our stand by these pillars of our British society as it has gradually been developed and evolved itself, of the right of individual labouring men or women to adjust their wages and conditions by collective bargaining, including the right to strike; and the right of everyone, with due notice and consideration for others, to choose or change his occupation if he thinks he can better himself and his family.

Brighton, October 4, 1947

Landing Operation

It is quite impossible for those who do not know the facts and figures of the American assembly in Britain, or of our own powerful expeditionary armies now preparing here, who do not know the dispositions of the enemy on the various fronts, who cannot measure his reserves and resources and his power to transfer large forces from one front to another over the vast railway system of Europe, who do not know the state and dimensions of our fleet and landing craft of all kinds – and this must be proportionate to the work they have to do – who do not know how the actual processes of a landing take place, or what are the necessary steps to build it up, or what has to be thought out beforehand in relation to what the enemy can do in days or weeks – it is impossible for those who do not know the facts, which are the study of hundreds of skilful officers day after day and month after month, to pronounce a useful opinion upon this operation.

Commons, September 21, 1943

Language, Strong

I do not think any expression of scorn or severity which I have heard used by our critics has come anywhere near the language which I have been myself accustomed to use, not only orally, but in a stream of written minutes. In fact, I wonder that a great many of my colleagues are on speaking terms with me.

Commons, June 25, 1941

I have no objection to a proper use of strong language, but a certain amount of art and a certain amount of selective power is needed, if the effect is to be produced.

Commons, December 9, 1925

Lap, The Last

This is just the moment not to slacken. All the races which the calendar holds, or nearly all of them, are won in the last lap; and it is then, when it is most hard, when one is most tired, when the sense of boredom seems to weigh upon one, when even the most glittering events, exciting, thrilling events, are, as it were, smothered by satiation, when headlines in the newspapers, though perfectly true, succeed one another in their growing emphasis, and yet the end seems to recede before us – like climbing a hill when there is another peak beyond – it is at that very moment that we in this island have to give that extra sense of exertion, of boundless, inexhaustible, dynamic energy that we have shown, as the records now made public have emphasized in detail. Tirelessness is what we have to show now.

Commons, November 29, 1944

Laws, Economic

On questions of economic law it does not matter at all what the electors think or vote or say. The economic laws proceed.

Commons, July 16, 1929

Lawyers

I could not help feeling impressed with how easy it must be for a very distinguished lawyer to procure the conviction of an innocent man.

Commons, March 30, 1914

Leadership

Nothing is more dangerous in wartime than to live in the temperamental atmosphere of a Gallup Poll, always feeling one's pulse and taking one's temperature. I see it said that leaders should keep their ears to the ground. All I can say is that the British nation will find it very hard to look up to the leaders who are detected in that somewhat ungainly posture.

Commons, September 30, 1941

Anyone leading a Party must have a brain larger than his own, must have numbers of people through whom he can operate.

Commons, July 20, 1936

It is no use leading other nations up the garden and then running away when the dog growls.

Commons, June 11, 1937

If today I am very kindly treated by the mass of the people of this country, it is certainly not because I have followed public opinion in recent years. There is only one duty, only one safe course, and that is to try to be right and not to fear to do or to say what you believe to be right. That is the only way to deserve and to win the confidence of our great people in these days of trouble.

Commons, September 30, 1941

Do not, whatever be the torrent of abuse which may obstruct the necessary action, think too poorly of the greatness of our fellow countrymen. Let the House do its duty. Let the Government give the lead, and the nation will not fail in the hour of need.

Commons, November 28, 1934

League of Nations

I have sympathy with, and respect for, the well-meaning, loyal-hearted

'Let the House do its duty. Let the Government give the lead, and the nation will not fail in the hour of need'

people who make up the League of Nations Union in this country, but what impresses me most about them is their long-suffering and inexhaustible gullibility. Any scheme of any kind for disarmament put forward by any country, so long as it is surrounded by suitable phraseology, is hailed by them, and the speeches are cheered, and those who speak gain the need of their applause.

Commons, November 23, 1932

Legality in War

There can be no justice if in a mortal struggle the aggressor tramples down every sentiment of humanity, and if those who resist him remain entangled in the tatters of violated legal conventions.

London, March 30, 1940

Legislation

I do not take the view that every Bill must be rammed through Parliament exactly in the form that the Cabinet of the day thinks fit. I believe in Parliamentary discussion and I hold strongly that the elected representatives of the people, and the House of Lords, in its relation established by the Parliament Act, should both share in the shaping of legislation.

Scarborough, October 11, 1952

Legislation and Charity

I object on principle to doing by legislation what properly belongs to charity.

Commons, July 31, 1901

Lend and Lease

By very severe measures we had been able to gather and spend in America about £500,000,000 sterling, but the end of our financial resources was in sight – nay, had actually been reached. All we could do at that time a year ago was to place orders in the United States without being able to see our way through, but on a tide of hope and not without important encouragement.

Then came the majestic policy of the President and Congress of the United States in passing the Lend and Lease Bill, under which in two successive enactments about £3,000,000,000 sterling were dedicated to the cause of world freedom without – mark this, for it is unique – the setting up of any account in money. Never again let us hear the taunt that money is the ruling thought or power in the hearts of the American democracy. The Lend and Lease Bill must be regarded without question as the most unsordid act in the whole of recorded history.

Mansion House, London, November 10, 1941

He [President Roosevelt] devised the extraordinary measure of assistance called Lend-Lease, which will stand forth as the most unselfish and unsordid financial act of any country in all history.

Commons, April 17, 1945

Lenin

Lenin was sent into Russia by the Germans in the same way that you might send a phial containing a culture of typhoid or cholera to be poured into the water supply of a great city, and it worked with amazing accuracy.

Commons, November 5, 1919

No sooner did Lenin arrive than he began beckoning a finger here and a finger there to obscure persons in sheltered retreats in New York, in Glasgow, in Berne and other countries, and he gathered together the leading spirits of a formidable sect, the most formidable sect in the world, of which he was the high priest and chief. With these spirits around him he set to work with demoniacal ability to tear to pieces every institution on which the Russian State and nation depended. Russia was laid low. Russia had to be laid low. She was laid low to the dust.

Commons, November 5, 1919

Leopold, King

At the last moment, when Belgium was already invaded, King Leopold called upon us to come to his aid, and even at the last moment we came. He and his brave, efficient army, nearly half a million strong, guarded our left flank and thus kept open our only line of retreat to the sea. Suddenly, without the advice of his ministers and upon his own personal act, he sent a plenipotentiary to the German command, surrendered his army, and exposed our whole flank and means of retreat.

Commons, June 4, 1940

Liberals

In my judgment, a Liberal is a man who ought to stand as a restraining force against an extravagant policy. He is a man who ought to keep cool in the presence of Jingo clamour. He is a man who believes that confidence between nations begets confidence, and that the spirit of peace and good-will makes the safety it seeks. And, above all, I think a Liberal is a man who should keep a sour look for scaremongers of every kind and of every size, however distinguished, however ridiculous – and sometimes the most distinguished are the most ridiculous – a cold, chilling, sour look for all of them, whether their panic comes from the sea or from the air or from the earth or from the waters under the earth.

Free Trade Hall, Manchester, May 23, 1909

Liberalism

Liberalism supplies at once the higher impulse and the practicable path; it appeals to persons by sentiments of generosity and humanity; it proceeds by courses of moderation; by gradual steps, by steady effort from day to day, from year to year. Liberalism enlists hundreds of thousands upon the side of progress and popular democratic reform whom militant Socialism would drive into violent Tory reaction.

St Andrew's Hall, Glagsow, October 11, 1906

Liberalism is a quickening spirit – it is immortal. It will live on through all the days, be they good days or be they evil days. No! I believe it will even burn stronger and brighter and more helpful in evil days than in good – just like your harbour-lights, which shine out across the sea, and which on a calm night gleam with soft refulgence, but through the storm flash a message of life to those who toil on the rough waters.

Kinnaird Hall, Dundee, May 14, 1908

Liberalism and Socialism

Liberalism has its own history and its own tradition. Socialism has its own formulas and aims. Socialism seeks to pull down wealth; Liberalism seeks to raise up poverty. Socialism would destroy private interests; Liberalism would preserve private interests in the only way in which they can be safely and justly preserved, namely by reconciling them with public right. Socialism would kill enterprise; Liberalism would rescue enterprise from the trammels of privilege and preference. Socialism assails the pre-eminence of the individual; Liberalism seeks, and shall seek more in the future, to build up a minimum standard for the mass. Socialism exalts the rule; Liberalism exalts the man. Socialism attacks capital; Liberalism attacks monopoly.

Kinnaird Hall, May 14, 1908

Liberation of Europe

We have one principle about the liberated countries or the repentant satellite countries which we strive for according to the best of our ability and resources. Here is the principle. I will state it in the broadest and most familiar terms: Government of the people, by the people, for the people, set up on a basis of election by the free and universal suffrage, with secrecy of the ballot and no intimidation. That is and has always been the policy of this Government in all countries. That is our only aim, our only interest, and our only care. It is to that goal that we try to make our way across all the difficulties, obstacles, and perils of the long road. Trust the people, make sure they have a fair chance to decide their destiny without being terrorized from either quarter or regimented. There is our policy for Italy, for Yugoslavia, and for Greece. What other interest have we than that? For that we shall strive, and for that alone.

Commons, January 18, 1945

Liberty, Struggle for

We know that other hearts in millions and scores of millions beat with ours; that other voices proclaim the cause for which we strive; other strong hands wield the hammers and shape the weapons we need; other clear and gleaming eyes are fixed in hard conviction upon the tyrannies that must and shall be destroyed.

London, March 18, 1941

Lies

Someone says it's a lie. Well, I am reminded by that of the remark of the witty Irishman who said: "There are a terrible lot of lies going about the world, and the worst of it is that half of them are true."

Commons, February 22, 1906

Life

Those whose minds are attracted or compelled to rigid and symmetrical systems of government should remember that logic, like science, must be the servant and not the master of man. Human beings and human societies are not structures that are built or machines that are forged. They are plants that grow and must be tended as such. Life is a test and this world a place of trial. Always the problems, or it may be the same problem, will be presented to every generation in different forms.

Massachusetts Institute of Technology, Boston, March 31, 1949

What is the use of living, if it be not to strive for noble causes and to make this muddled world a better place for those who will live in it after we are gone? How else can we put ourselves in harmonious relation with the great verities and consolations of the infinite and the eternal? And I avow my faith that we are marching towards better days. Humanity will not be cast down. We are going on – swinging bravely forward along the grand high road – and already behind the distant mountains is the promise of the sun.

Kinnaird Hall, Dundee, October 10, 1908

Liquidation of Persons

It is part of the established technique of the "cold war" the Soviets have begun against us all, that, in any country which has fallen into their power, people of character and men of heart and personality outstanding in any walk of life, from the manual worker to the university professor, shall be what is called in their savage jargon "liquidated".

Llandudno, October 9, 1948

Lloyd, Lord

Lord Lloyd and I have been friends for many years and close political associates during the last twelve years. We championed several causes together which did not command the applause of large majorities; but it is just in that kind of cause, where one is swimming against the stream, that one learns the worth and quality of a comrade and friend.

Commons, February 6, 1941

London can take it

It is the practice and in some cases the duty of many of my colleagues and many Members of the House to visit the scenes of destruction as promptly as possible, and I go myself from time to time. In all my life, I have never

'We are marching towards better days. Humanity will not be cast down. And already behind the distant mountains is the promise of the sun'

'London, which is so vast and strong that she is like a prehistoric monster into whose armoured hide showers of arrows can be shot in vain'

been treated with so much kindness as by the people who have suffered most. One would think one had brought some great benefit to them, instead of the blood and tears, the toil and sweat, which is all I have ever promised. On every side, there is the cry, "We can take it," but with it, there is also the cry, "Give it 'em back."

Commons, October 8, 1940

London, Defence of

Take the astounding admission that modern guns available for the defence of London would have been doubled in number but for the bankruptcy of a small firm charged with an essential part. I beg the Prime Minister to face the force of that admission. He is a business man of high competence himself. Is it not shocking that such a thing should have happened?

Commons, November 17, 1938

Statisticians may amuse themselves by calculating that after making allowance for the working of the law of diminishing returns, through the same house being struck twice and three times over, it would take ten years, at the present rate, for half the houses of London to be demolished. After that, of course, progress would be much slower.

Commons, October 8, 1940

When after the enemy wearied of his attack upon the capital and turned to other parts of the country, many of us in our hearts felt anxiety lest the weight of attack concentrated in those smaller organisms should prove more effective than when directed on London, which is so vast and strong that she is like a prehistoric monster into whose armoured hide showers of arrows can be shot in vain.

County Hall, London, July 14, 1941

237

'It is, however, my sure belief that we are getting the better of this menace to our life. We are buffeted by the waves, but the ocean tides flow steady and strong in our favour'

We would rather see London laid in ruins and ashes than that it should be tamely and abjectly enslaved.

Commons, July 14, 1940

Londoners

I remember one winter evening travelling to a railway station – which still worked – on my way north to visit troops. It was cold and raining. Darkness had almost fallen on the blacked-out streets. I saw everywhere long queues of people, among them hundreds of young girls in their silk stockings and high-heeled shoes, who had worked hard all day and were waiting for bus after bus, which came by already overcrowded, in the hope of reaching their homes for the night. When at that moment the doleful wail of the siren betokened the approach of the German bombers, I confess to you that my heart bled for London and the Londoner.

County Hall, London, July 14, 1941

Lords, Function of the House of

It is not the function of the House of Lords to govern the people but to make sure that the people have the right to govern themselves.

Commons, November 16, 1949

Losses at Sea

I must again repeat the warning which I gave to the House in September, that a steady flow of losses must be expected, that occasional disasters will occur, and that any failure upon our part to act up to the level of circumstances would immediately be attended by grave dangers. It is, however, my sure belief that we are getting the better of this menace to our life. We are buffeted by the waves, but the ocean tides flow steady and strong in our favour.

Commons, December 6, 1939

A MEDAL GLITTERS, BUT IT ALSO CASTS A SHADOW.

It is not possible to satisfy everybody.

All that is possible is to give the greatest satisfaction to the greatest number and to hurt the feelings of the fewest.

Commons, March 22, 1944

MacArthur's Generalship

The ingenious use of aircraft to solve the intricate tactical problems, by the transport of reinforcements, supplies, and munitions, including field guns, is a prominent feature of MacArthur's generalship, and should be carefully studied in detail by all concerned in the technical conduct of the war.

Commons, February 11, 1943

MacDonald, Ramsay

I remember, when I was a child, being taken to the celebrated Barnum's Circus, which contained an exhibition of freaks and monstrosities, but the exhibit on the programme which I most desired to see was the one described as "The Boneless Wonder". My parents judged that that spectacle would be too revolting and demoralizing for my youthful eyes, and I have waited fifty years to see the Boneless Wonder sitting on the Treasury Bench.

Commons, January 28, 1931

Magnetic Mines

A strident effort has been made by German propaganda to persuade the world that we have laid these magnetic mines ourselves in the fairways of our own harbours, in order, apparently, to starve ourselves out. When this inanity expired amid general derision, the alternative claim was made that the sinking of the neutrals by mine was another triumph of German science and seamanship, and should convince all nations that the German mastery of the seas was complete.

Commons, December 6, 1939

The magnetic mine, and all the other mines with which the narrow waters, the approaches to this island, are strewn, do not present us with any problem which we deem insoluble. It must be remembered that in

'I have waited fifty years to see the Boneless Wonder sitting on the Treasury Bench'

'The only guide to a man is his conscience; the only shield to his memory is the rectitude and sincerity of his actions'

the last war we suffered very grievous losses from mines, and that at the climax more than six hundred British vessels were engaged solely upon the task of minesweeping. We must remember that. We must always be expecting some bad things from Germany, but I will venture to say that it is with growing confidence that we await the further developments or variants of their attack.

London, January 20, 1940

Malta

For now nearly two years Malta has stood against the enemy. What a thorn it has been in their side! What toll it has taken of their convoys! Can we wonder that a most strenuous effort has been made by Germany and Italy to rid themselves of this fierce aggressive foe? For the last six weeks over 450 German first-line strength in aircraft, and perhaps 200 Italian, have been venting their fury on Malta. An unending intermittent bombardment has fallen upon the harbour and city, and sometimes as many as 300 aircraft have attacked in a single day. The terrific ordeal has been borne with exemplary fortitude by the garrison and people. Very heavy losses have been inflicted upon the enemy's air strength.

Commons, April 23, 1942

Man

The only guide to a man is his conscience. The only shield to his memory is the rectitude and sincerity of his actions. It is very imprudent to walk through life without this shield, because we are so often mocked by the failure of our hopes; but with this shield, however the fates may play, we march always in the ranks of honour.

Commons, November 12, 1940

'The nature of man is a dual nature. The character of the organization of human society is dual. Man is at once a unique being and a gregarious animal'

No man can be a collectivist alone or an individualist alone. He must be both an individualist and a collectivist. The nature of man is a dual nature. The character of the organization of human society is dual. Man is at once a unique being and a gregarious animal. For some purposes he must be collectivist, for others he is, and he will for all time remain, an individualist.

St Andrew's Hall, Glasgow, October 11, 1906

Man-Power

Man-power – and when I say that I include of course woman-power – is at a pitch of intensity at the present time in this country which was never reached before, not even in the last war, and certainly not in this. I believe our man-power is not only fully extended, but applied on the whole to the best advantage. I have a feeling that the community in this island is running at a very high level, with a good rhythm, and that if we can only keep our momentum – we cannot increase our pace – that very fact will enable us to outclass our enemies and possibly even our friends.

Commons, October 13, 1943

Management, Bureaucratic

Bureaucratic management cannot compare in efficiency with that of well-organized private firms. We are told that the management by officials is disinterested management. That may be true. The bureaucrats suffer no penalties for wrong judgment; so long as they attend their offices punctually and do their work honestly and behave in a polite manner towards their political masters they are sure of their jobs and their pensions. They are completely disinterested in the directness of their judgment. But the ordinary private trader, as you know in your own lives, faces impoverishment or perhaps bankruptcy if he cannot measure things right from day to day, and those who show themselves unable to do this are replaced by more capable men and organizers.

Perth, May 28, 1948

Mankind

I have always taken the view that the fortunes of mankind in its tremendous journey are principally decided for good or ill – but mainly for good, for the path is upward – by its greatest men and its greatest episodes.

London, January 9, 1941

Market, Black

If you destroy a free market you create a black market.

Commons, February 3, 1949

Martial Law

Martial law is no law at all. Martial law is brute force. Of course all martial law is illegal, and an attempt to introduce illegalities into martial law, which is not military law, is like attempting to add salt water to the sea.

Commons, April 2, 1906

'Martial law is brute force. All martial law is illegal, and an attempt to introduce illegalities into martial law, which is not military law, is like attempting to add salt water to the sea'

> **Massacres**
>
> I must say that I had no idea, when the war came to an end, of the horrible massacres which had occurred; the millions and millions that have been slaughtered. That dawned on us gradually after the struggle was over.
>
> *Commons, August 1, 1946*

Maxim

The Romans had a maxim, "Shorten your weapons and lengthen your frontiers." But our maxim seems to be, "Diminish your weapons and increase your obligations." Aye, and diminish the weapons of your friends.

Commons, March 14, 1934

Medals

The object of giving medals, stars, and ribbons is to give pride and pleasure to those who have deserved them. At the same time a distinction is something which everybody does not possess. If all have it, it is of less value. There must, therefore, be heartburnings and disappointments on the border line. A medal glitters, but it also casts a shadow. The task of drawing up regulations for such awards is one which does not admit of a perfect solution. It is not possible to satisfy everybody without running the risk of satisfying nobody. All that is possible is to give the greatest satisfaction to the greatest number and to hurt the feelings of the fewest.

Commons, March 22, 1944

Medicinal Personalities

Science, prodded on by the urge of the age, has presented to us in the last decade a wonderful bevy of new and highly attractive medicinal personalities. We have M and B, penicillin, tetramycin, aureomycin and several others that I will not hazard my professional reputation in mentioning, still less in trying to place in order.

Royal College of Physicians, London, July 10, 1951

Mediterranean

To gain and hold command of the Mediterranean in case of war is a high duty of the fleet. Once that is achieved all European land forces on the shores of North Africa will be decisively affected. Those that have command of the Mediterranean behind them can be reinforced to any extent and supplied to any extent. Those that have no such command will be like cut flowers in a vase.

Commons, March 16, 1939

Megalomania

At the beginning of this war megalomania was the only form of sanity.

Commons, November 15, 1915

Mercy

Long before the Christian revelation, the world had found out by practice that mercy towards a beaten enemy was well worth while, and that it was much easier to gain control over wide areas by taking prisoners than by making everyone fight to the death against you.

Commons, July 1, 1952

Middle East

In the Middle East you have arid countries. In East Africa you have dripping countries. There is the greatest difficulty to get anything to grow

'Long before the Christian revelation, the world had found out by practice that mercy towards a beaten enemy was well worth while'

on the one place, and the greatest difficulty to prevent things smothering and choking you by their hurried growth in the other. In the African Colonies you have a docile, tractable population, who only require to be well and wisely treated to develop great economic capacity and utility; whereas the regions of the Middle East are unduly stocked with peppery, pugnacious, proud politicians and theologians, who happen to be at the same time extremely well armed and extremely hard up.

Commons, July 14, 1921

Militarism

Nazi tyranny and Prussian militarism are the two main elements in German life which must be absolutely destroyed. They must be absolutely rooted out if Europe and the world are to be spared a third and still more frightful conflict.

Commons, September 21, 1943

Millionaires

Nor should it be supposed as you would imagine, to read some of the Leftwing newspapers, that all Americans are multi-millionaires of Wall Street. If they were all multi-millionaires that would be no reason for condemning a system which has produced such material results.

The Royal Albert Hall, London, April 21, 1948

Milk

There is no finer investment for any community than putting milk into babies.

BBC, March 21, 1943

Miners at War

I am very sorry that we have had to debar so many miners from going to the war in the armed forces. I respect their feelings, but we cannot afford it; we cannot allow it. Besides the need for their services in the pits, there is danger in the pits too, and where there is danger there is honour. "Act well thy part, there all the honour lies," and that is the motto I want to give out to all those who in an infinite variety of ways are playing an equally worthy part in the consummation of our high purpose.

Westminster Central Hall, London, October 31, 1942

Mischief-Makers

I appeal to all patriotic men on both sides of the Atlantic Ocean to stamp their feet on mischief-makers and sowers of tares wherever they may be found, and let the great machines roll into battle under the best possible conditions for their success.

Commons, February 11, 1943

'I am very sorry that we have had to debar so many miners from going to the war in the armed forces. I respect their feelings, but we cannot afford it'

'Remember we have a missing generation, we must never forget that – the flower of the past, lost in the great battles of the last war'

Miseries, Sharing of

I do not wonder that British youth is in revolt against the morbid doctrine that nothing matters but the equal sharing of miseries: that what used to be called the submerged tenth can only be rescued by bringing the other nine-tenths down to their level; against the folly that it is better that everyone should have half rations rather than that any, by their exertions or ability, should earn a second helping.

London, June 22, 1948

Missing Generation, The

Remember we have a missing generation, we must never forget that – the flower of the past, lost in the great battles of the last war. There ought to be another generation in between these young men and us older figures who are soon, haply, to pass from the scene. There ought to be another generation of men, with their flashing lights and leading figures. We must do all we can to try to fill the gap, and, as I say, there is no safer thing to do than to run risks in youth.

Commons, November 29, 1944

Mistakes

I am sure that the mistakes of that time [concerning German Reparations] will not be repeated; we shall make another set of mistakes.

Commons, June 8, 1944

I would rather make mistakes in propaganda than in action. Events are the final rulers and time is needed for them to make their pronouncements clear.

Scarborough, October 11, 1952

When we reflect upon the magnitude of modern events compared with the men who have to try to control or cope with them, and upon the frightful consequences of these events on hundreds of millions, the importance of not making avoidable mistakes grows impressively upon the mind.

Commons, September 30, 1941

Dictators, as well as democratic and Parliamentary governments, make mistakes sometimes. Indeed, when the whole story is told, I believe it will be found that the dictators, for all their preparations and prolonged scheming, have made greater mistakes than the democracies they have assailed.

London, May 10, 1942

Mistakes in War

Anyone who supposes that there will not be mistakes in war is very foolish. I draw a distinction between mistakes. There is the mistake which comes through daring, what I call a mistake towards the enemy, in which you must always sustain your commanders, by sea, land or air. There are mistakes from the "safety first" principle, mistakes of turning away from the enemy; and they require a far more acid consideration.

Commons, May 7, 1941

Mob Law

I do not allow a Party or a body to call themselves democrats because they are stretching farther and farther into the most extreme forms of revolution. I do not accept a Party as necessarily representing democracy because it becomes more violent as it becomes less numerous. One must have some respect for democracy, and not use the word too lightly. The last thing which resembles democracy is mob law, with bands of gangsters,

'Anyone who supposes that there will not be mistakes in war is very foolish'

'If it be true that every country gets the form of government it deserves, we may certainly flatter ourselves'

armed with deadly weapons, forcing their way into great cities, seizing the police stations and key points of government, endeavouring to introduce a totalitarian régime.

Commons, December 8, 1944

Moderation

Disagreement is much more easy to express, and often much more exciting to the reader, than agreement. The highest common factor of public opinion is not a fertile ground for lively epigrams and sharp antithesis. The expression of broad and simple principles likely to command the assent and not to excite the dissent of vast communities must necessarily be in guarded terms. I should not myself fear even the accusation of platitude in such a statement if it only sought the greatest good of the greatest number.

Commons, July 12, 1954

Monarchy, Blessings of

These are the days when in other countries ignorant people are often disposed to imagine that progress consists in converting oneself from a monarchy into a republic. In this country we have known the blessings of limited monarchy. Great traditional and constitutional chains of events have come to make an arrangement, to make a situation, unwritten, which enables our affairs to proceed on what I believe is a superior level of smoothness and democratic progress.

London, May 18, 1944

Monarchy, Constitutional

If it be true, as has been said, that every country gets the form of government it deserves, we may certainly flatter ourselves. The wisdom of our ancestors has led us to an envied and enviable situation. We have the strongest Parliament in the world. We have the oldest, the most famous, the most honoured, the most secure, and the most serviceable, monarchy in the world. King and Parliament both safely and solidly based upon the will of the people expressed by free and fair election on the principle of universal suffrage.

Commons, May 15, 1945

Money

A government can easily raise money and can always print it, but the labour and materials represented by the money come in a different category. Labour and the savings of the community are the key.

Commons, December 6, 1945

Monopolies

There is a growing feeling, which I entirely share, against allowing those services which are in the nature of monopolies to pass into private hands.

St Andrew's Hall, Glasgow, October 11, 1906

I believe that the monopoly by the State of all the means of production, distribution, and exchange would be fatal both to our national well-being and to our personal freedom, as we have long enjoyed them. The cost of State management takes more from the workers than will ever be taken by the profits of private enterprise. It is not the interest of the wage-earners to have to deal with all powerful State employer rather than with the flexibility of private business. When losses are made, under the present system these losses are borne by the individuals who sustained them and took the risk and judged things wrongly, whereas under State management all losses are quartered upon the tax-payers and the community as a whole. The elimination of the profit motive and of self-interest as a practical guide in the myriad transactions of daily life will

'The cost of State management takes more from the workers than private enterprise'

restrict, paralyse and destroy British ingenuity, thrift, contrivance and good housekeeping at every stage in our life and production, and will reduce all our industries from a profit-making to a loss-making process.

Belle Vue, Manchester, December 6, 1947

Monroe Doctrine

For at least two generations we were, as the American writer Walter Lippman has reminded us, a guardian, and almost a guarantor, of the Monroe doctrine upon which, as Canning's eye foresaw, the free development of South America was founded. We and the civilized world owe many blessings to the United States, but we have also in later generations made our contribution to their security and splendour.

London, May 7, 1946

Montgomery, Field-Marshal

Let me also pay my tribute to this vehement and formidable General Montgomery, a Cromwellian figure, austere, severe, accomplished, tireless, his life given to the study of war, who has attracted to himself in an extraordinary measure the confidence and the devotion of his army.

Commons, February 11, 1943

Field-Marshal Montgomery is one of the greatest living masters of the art of war. Like Stonewall Jackson, he was a professor and teacher of the military science before he became an actor on the world stage. It has been my fortune and great pleasure often to be with him at important moments in the long march from Mersa Matruh to the Rhine. Either on the eve of a great battle, or while the struggle was actually in progress, always I have found the same buoyant, vigorous, efficient personality with every aspect of the vast operation in his mind, and every unit of mighty armies in his grip.

Commons, October 22, 1945

Moods of the British

In a long and varied life I have constantly watched and tried to measure the moods and inspirations of the British people. There is no foe they will not face. There is no hardship they cannot endure. Whether the test be sharp and short or long and wearisome, they can take it. What they do not forgive is false promises and vain boastings.

Brighton, October 4, 1947

Moon, Crying for the

What is the point in crying out for the moon when you have the sun, when you have the bright orb of day in whose refulgent beams all the lesser luminaries hide their radiance?

Commons, February 16, 1938

Mourning

Only faith in a life after death in a brighter world where dear ones will meet again – only that and the measured tramp of time can give consolation.

Commons, September 8, 1942

Munich

We are in the presence of a disaster of the first magnitude which has befallen Great Britain and France. Do not let us blind ourselves to that. It must now be accepted that all the countries of central and eastern Europe will make the best terms they can with the triumphant Nazi power. The system of alliances in central Europe upon which France has relied for her safety has been swept away, and I can see no means by which it can be reconstituted.

Commons, October 5, 1938

The Chancellor of the Exchequer [Sir John Simon] said it was the first time Herr Hitler had been made to retract – I think that was the word – in any degree. We really must not waste time after all this long debate upon the difference between the positions reached at Berchtesgaden, at Godesberg and at Munich. They can be very simply epitomized, if the

House will permit me to vary the metaphor. £1 was demanded at the pistol's point. When it was given, £2 were demanded at the pistol's point. Finally, the dictator consented to take £1 17s. 6d. and the rest in promises of goodwill for the future.

Commons, October 5, 1938

Many people, no doubt, honestly believe that they are only giving away the interests of Czechoslovakia, whereas I fear we shall find that we have deeply compromised, and perhaps endangered, the safety and even the independence of Great Britain and France. This is not merely a question of giving up the German colonies, as I am sure we shall be asked to do. Nor is it a question only of losing influence in Europe. It goes far deeper than that. You have to consider the character of the Nazi movement and the rule which it implies.

Commons, October 5, 1938

Do not suppose that this is the end. This is only the beginning of the reckoning. This is only the first sip, the first foretaste of a bitter cup which will be proffered to us year by year unless, by a supreme recovery of moral health and martial vigour, we arise again and take our stand for freedom as in the olden time.

Commons, October 5, 1938

I do not grudge our loyal, brave people, who were ready to do their duty no matter what the cost, who never flinched under the strain of

'Terrible words have for the time being been pronounced against the western democracies: "Thou art weighed in the balance and found wanting"'

last week – I do not grudge them the natural, spontaneous outburst of joy and relief when they learned that the hard ordeal would no longer be required of them at the moment; but they should know the truth. They should know that there has been gross neglect and deficiency in our defences; they should know that we have sustained a defeat without a war, the consequences of which will travel far with us along our road; they should know that we have passed an awful milestone in our history, when the whole equilibrium of Europe has been deranged, and that the terrible words have for the time being been pronounced against the western democracies: "Thou art weighed in the balance and found wanting."

Commons, October 5, 1938

Mussolini

Italians, I will tell you the truth. It is all because of one man. One man and one man alone has ranged the Italian people in deadly struggle against the British Empire, and has deprived Italy of the sympathy and intimacy of the United States of America. That he is a great man I do not deny, but that after eighteen years of unbridled power he has led your country to the horrid verge of ruin can be denied by none. It is one man who, against the Crown and Royal Family of Italy, against the Pope and all the authority of the Vatican and of the Roman Catholic Church, against the wishes of the Italian people, who had no lust for this war, has arrayed the trustees and inheritors of ancient Rome upon the side of the ferocious pagan barbarians.

London, December 23, 1940

255

The successful campaign in Sicily brought about the fall of Mussolini and the heartfelt repudiation by the Italian people of the Fascist creed. Mussolini indeed escaped, to eat the bread of affliction at Hitler's table, to shoot his son-in-law, and help the Germans wreak vengeance upon the Italian masses whom he had professed to love, and over whom he had ruled for more than twenty years. This fate and judgment, more terrible than death, has overtaken the vainglorious dictator who stabbed France in the back and thought his crime had gained him the empire of the Mediterranean.

London, March 26, 1944

Mysteries of the Future

I have no fear of the future. Let us go forward into its mysteries, let us tear aside the veils which hide it from our eyes, and let us move onward with confidence and courage. All the problems of the post-war world, some of which seem so baffling now, will be easier of solution once decisive victory has been gained, and once it is clear that victory won in arms has not been cast away by folly or by violence when the moment comes to lay the broad foundations of the future world order, and it is time to speak great words of peace and truth to all.

The Royal Albert Hall, London, September 29, 1943

Mystic Link

We fought alone against tyranny for a whole year, not purely from national motives. It is true that our lives depended upon our doing so, but we fought the better because we felt with conviction that it was not only our own cause but a world cause for which the Union Jack was kept flying in 1940 and 1941. The soldier who laid down his life, the mother who wept for her son, and the wife who lost her husband, got inspiration and comfort and felt a sense of being linked with the universal and the eternal by the fact that we fought for what was precious not only for ourselves but for mankind.

Commons, June 27, 1950

THE ANCIENT ATHENIANS

overpowered a tribe in the Peloponnesus

and when they had the hostile army herded on a beach naked for slaughter, they set them free and said: "This was not because they were men; it was done because of the nature of Man."

Commons, January 18, 1945

Napoleon

Some have compared Hitler's conquests with those of Napoleon. It may be that Spain and Russia will shortly furnish new chapters to that theme. It must be remembered, however, that Napoleon's armies carried with them the fierce, liberating and equalitarian winds of the French Revolution, whereas Hitler's empire has nothing behind it but racial self-assertion, espionage, pillage, corruption, and the Prussian boot.

Commons, May 7, 1941

National Service

It is arguable even that we tried to play too large a part in European affairs between the wars and before the first war, while not being able or willing to accept the same conditions of service, or put up the same manpower, as our allies or potential allies were forced to do. We should have carried far more weight in the councils of peace if we had had national service.

Commons, March 31, 1947

'In dealing with nationalities, nothing is more fatal than a dodge'

National Unity

What does national unity mean? It surely means that reasonable sacrifices of Party opinions, personal opinion, and Party interest, should be made by all in order to contribute to the national security.

Commons, August 2, 1939

Nationalism

Where nationalism means the lust for pride and power, the craze for supreme domination by weight or force; where it is the senseless urge to be the biggest in the world, it is a danger and a vice. Where it means love of country and readiness to die for country; where it means love of tradition and culture and the gradual building up across the centuries of a social entity dignified by nationhood, then it is the first of virtues.

States-General of the Netherlands, The Hague, May 9, 1946

Nationalities

In dealing with nationalities, nothing is more fatal than a dodge. Wrongs will be forgivcn, sufferings and losses will be forgiven or forgotten, battles will be remembered only as they recall the martial virtues of the combatants; but anything like chicane, anything like a trick, will always rankle.

Commons, April 5, 1906

Nationalization

Nationalization of industry is the doom of trade unionism.

Blackpool, October 14, 1950

National Guilt

It may well be that those guilty races who trumpeted the glories of war at the beginning will be extolling the virtues of peace before the end. It would certainly seem right, however, that those who fix, on their own terms, the moment for beginning wars should not be the same men who fix, on their own terms, the moment for ending them. These observations are of a general character, but not without their particular application.

Commons, June 8, 1943

When peaceful nations like the British and the Americans, very careless in peacetime about their defences, care-free, unsuspecting nations, peoples who have never known defeat – improvident nations I will say, feckless nations, nations who despise the military art and thought war so wicked that it could never happen again – when nations like these are set upon by highly-organized, heavily-armed conspirators, planning and calculating in secret for years on end, exalting war as the highest form of human effort, glorifying slaughter and aggression, prepared and trained to the last point science and discipline can carry them, is it not natural that the peaceful, unprepared, improvident peoples should suffer terribly and that the wicked, scheming aggressors should have their reign of savage exaltation?

Usher Hall, Edinburgh, October 12, 1942

Nature

Man in this moment of his history has emerged in greater supremacy over the forces of nature than has ever been dreamed of before. He has it in his power to solve quite easily the problems of material existence. He has conquered the wild beasts, and he has even conquered the insects and the microbes. There lies before him, as he wishes, a golden age of peace and progress. All is in his hand. He has only to conquer his last and worst enemy – himself. With vision, faith and courage, it may be within our power to win a crowning victory for all.

Commons, March 28, 1950

Nature of Man

I read somewhere that when the ancient Athenians, on one occasion, overpowered a tribe in the Peloponnesus which had wrought them great injury by base, treacherous means, and when they had the hostile army herded on a beach naked for slaughter, they forgave them and set them free, and they said: "This was not because they were men; it was done because of the nature of Man."

Commons, January 18, 1945

Naval Treaty with Germany

We have, however unintentionally, nullified and stultified the League of Nations condemnation of treaty-breaking in respect of armaments, in which we were ourselves concerned, in which, indeed, we took a leading part. We have, it seems to me, revealed, again quite unintentionally, a very considerable measure of indifference to the interests of other powers, particularly powers in the Baltic, who were encouraged by our example to join with us in the League of Nations in condemning treaty-breaking. In the name of what is called practical realism we have seemed to depart from the principle of collective security in a very notable fashion. [By concluding the Treaty with Germany.]

Commons, July 11, 1935

Navies

I have always thought that the union of these two great forces [the British and American navies], not for purposes of aggression or narrow selfish interests, but in an honourable cause, constitutes what I may call the sheet-anchor of human freedom and progress.

Corn Exchange, Cambridge, May 19, 1939

Navy in Action

Wonderful exertions have been made by our Navy and Air Force; by the hundreds of mine-sweeping vessels which with their marvellous appliances keep our ports clear in spite of all the enemy can do; by the men who build and repair our immense fleets of merchant ships; by the men who load and unload them; and, need I say, by the officers and men of the Merchant Navy who go out in all weathers and in the teeth of all dangers to fight for the life of their native land and for a cause they comprehend and serve.

BBC, April 27, 1941

The Navy has a dual function. In war it is our means of safety; in peace it sustains the prestige, repute and influence of this small island; and it is a major factor in the cohesion of the British Empire and Commonwealth. The tasks which the Navy has performed in peacetime are hardly less magnificent than those it has achieved in war. From Trafalgar onwards, for more than 100 years Britannia ruled the waves. There was a great measure of peace, the freedom of the seas was maintained, the slave trade was extirpated, the Monroe doctrine of the United States found its sanction in British naval power.

Commons, March 8, 1948

The Royal Navy, especially after the toning-up which it has received, is unsurpassed in the world and is still the main bulwark of our security; and even at this eleventh hour, if the right measures are taken and if the right spirit prevails in the British nation and the British Empire, we may surround ourselves with other bulwarks equally sure, which will protect us against whatever storms may blow.

Commons, March 19, 1936

'The Royal Navy, especially after the toning-up which it has received, is unsurpassed in the world'

Nazi Power

You must have diplomatic and correct relations, but there can never be friendship between the British democracy and the Nazi power, that power which spurns Christian ethics, which cheers its onward course by a barbarous paganism, which vaunts the spirit of aggression and conquest, which derives strength and perverted pleasure from persecution, and uses, as we have seen, with pitiless brutality the threat of murderous force. That power cannot ever be the trusted friend of the British democracy.

Commons, October 5, 1938

All over the world men and women, under every sky and climate, of every race, creed and colour, all have the feeling that in the casting-down of this monstrous Nazi engine of tyranny, cruelty, greed and aggression – in the casting of it down shattered in pieces, something will have been achieved by the whole human race which will affect in a decisive manner its future destinies, and which will even in our own time be marked by very sensible improvement in the conditions under which the great masses of the people live.

The Royal Albert Hall, London, September 29, 1943

Nazism in Europe

We cannot afford to see Nazidom in its present phase of cruelty and intolerance, with all its hatreds and all its gleaming weapons, paramount in Europe.

Commons, October 24, 1935

Neck of England

When I warned them [the French Government] that Britain would fight on alone whatever they did, their generals told their Prime Minister and his divided Cabinet: "In three weeks England will have her neck wrung like a chicken." Some chicken! Some neck!

Canadian Parliament, Ottawa, December 30, 1941

Nelson Breed

The spirit of all our forces serving on the salt water has never been more strong and high than now. The warrior heroes of the past may look down, as Nelson's monument looks down upon us now, without any feeling that the island race has lost its daring or that the examples they set in bygone centuries have faded as the generations have succeeded one another. It was not for nothing that Admiral Harewood, as he instantly and at full speed attacked an enemy which might have sunk any one of his ships by a single successful salvo from its far heavier guns, flew Nelson's immortal signal, of which neither the new occasion, nor the conduct of all ranks and ratings, nor the final result, were found unworthy.

Guildhall, London, February 23, 1940

Nerves, War of

If, as was suggested in a recent oration, there is to be a contest of nerve, will-power, and endurance in which the whole British and German peoples are to engage, be it sharp or be it long, we shall not shrink from it. We believe that the spirit and temperament bred under institutions of freedom will prove more enduring and resilient than anything that can be got out of the most efficiently enforced mechanical discipline.

Commons, September 5, 1940

Netherlands, Fate of the

I shall not attempt to prophesy whether the frenzy of a cornered maniac will drive Herr Hitler into the worst of all his crimes; but this I will say without a doubt, that the fate of Holland and Belgium, like that of Poland, Czechoslovakia and Austria, will be decided by the victory of the British Empire and the French Republic. If we are conquered, all will be enslaved, and the United States will be left single-handed to guard the rights of man. If we are not destroyed, all these countries will be rescued and restored to life and freedom.

Commons, November 8, 1939

Neutrality

One of the most extraordinary things that I have ever known in my experience is the way in which German illegalities, atrocities and brutalities, are coming to be accepted as if they were part of the ordinary day-to-day conditions of war. Why, Sir, the neutral Press makes more fuss when I make a speech telling them what is their duty than they have done when hundreds of their ships have been sunk and many thousands of their sailors have been drowned or murdered, for that is the right word, on the open sea. Apparently, according to the present doctrine of neutral states, strongly endorsed by the German Government, Germany is to gain one set of advantages by breaking all the rules and committing foul outrages upon the seas, and then go on and gain another set of advantages through insisting, whenever it suits her, upon the strictest interpretation of the International Code she has torn to pieces. It is not at all odd that His Majesty's Government are getting rather tired of it. I am getting rather tired of it myself.

Commons, February 27, 1940

Only yesterday, while the sailors from a British submarine were carrying ashore on stretchers eight emaciated Dutchmen whom they had rescued from six days' exposure in an open boat, Dutch aviators in Holland, in the name of strict and impartial neutrality, were shooting down a British aircraft which had lost its way. I do not reproach the Dutch, our valiant allies of bygone centuries; my heart goes out to them in their peril and distress, dwelling as they do in the cage with the tiger. But when we are

'If we are conquered, all will be enslaved, and the United States will be left single-handed to guard the rights of man'

264

'To stand still would be to fall; to fall would be to perish. We must go forward'

asked to take as a matter of course interpretations of neutrality which give all the advantages to the aggressor and inflict all the disadvantages upon the defenders of freedom, I recall a saying of the late Lord Balfour: "This is a singularly ill-contrived world, but not so ill-contrived as that."

London, March 30, 1940

They [the neutral nations] bow humbly and in fear to German threats of violence, comforting themselves meanwhile with the thought that the allies will win, that Britain and France will strictly observe all the laws and conventions, and that breaches of these laws are only to be expected from the German side. Each one hopes that if he feeds the crocodile enough, the crocodile will eat him last. All of them hope that the storm will pass before their turn comes to be devoured. But I fear – I fear greatly – the storm will not pass. It will rage and it will roar, ever more loudly, ever more widely. It will spread to the south; it will spread to the north. There is no chance of a speedy end except through united action; and if at any time Britain and France, wearying of the struggle, were to make a shameful peace, nothing would remain of the smaller states of Europe with their shipping and their possessions, but to be divided between the opposite, though similar, barbarisms of Nazidom and Bolshevism.

London, January 20, 1940

New Age

The wonderful century which followed the Battle of Waterloo and the downfall of the Napoleonic domination, which secured to this small island so long and so resplendent a reign, has come to an end. We have arrived at a new time. Let us realize it. And with that new time strange methods, huge forces, larger combinations – a Titanic world – have sprung up around us. The foundations of our power are changing. To stand still would be to fall; to fall would be to perish. We must go forward. We will go forward. We will go forward into a way of life more earnestly viewed, more scientifically organized, more consciously national, than any we have known. Thus alone shall we be able to sustain and to renew, through the generations which are to come, the fame and the power of the British race.

Free Trade Hall, Manchester, May 23, 1909

Next Best

In other days I used to say that when the ace is out the king is the best card.

Commons, March 16, 1939

Niagara

The gravity of the general situation is in no way diminished by the fact that it has become less exciting than it was two or three weeks ago. When you are drifting down the stream of Niagara, it may easily happen that from time to time you run into a reach of quite smooth water, or that a bend in the river or a change in the wind may make the roar of the falls seem far more distant; but your hazard and your preoccupation are in no way affected thereby.

Commons, April 6, 1936

No!

Alexander the Great remarked that the people of Asia were slaves because they had not learned to pronounce the word "No". Let that not be the epitaph of the English-speaking peoples or of Parliamentary democracy, or of France, or of the many surviving liberal States of Europe.

London, October 16, 1938

Normandy

It is the wish and also the desire of General Eisenhower that the battle for Normandy should be viewed as a whole and as one single set of operations conducted by an allied force, linked in brotherhood and intermingled in every manner that may seem convenient. But this should certainly not prevent the British House of Commons from expressing its unstinted admiration for the splendid and spectacular victories gained by the United States troops under General Bradley, both at Cherbourg and in the southward march, now become almost a gallop, down the peninsula. The Germans have certainly had remarkable opportunities of revising the mocking and insulting estimate which they put upon the military value of the American army at the time they declared war upon the great Republic.

Commons, August 2, 1944

This vast operation is undoubtedly the most complicated and difficult that has ever taken place. It involves tides, wind, waves, visibility, both from the air and the sea standpoint, and the combined employment of land, air and sea forces in the highest degree of intimacy and in contact with conditions which could not and cannot be fully foreseen.

Commons, June 6, 1944

Norway

I here must say a word about Norway. We have the most profound sympathy with the Norwegian people. We have understood the terrible dilemma in which they have been placed. Their sentiments, like those of every other small country, were with the Allies. They writhed in helpless anger while scores of their ships were wantonly sunk and many hundreds of their sailors cruelly drowned. They realize fully that their future independence and freedom are bound up with the victory of the allies. But the feeling of powerlessness in the ruthless grip of Nazi wrath made them hope against hope until the last moment that at least their soil and their cities would not be polluted by the trampling of German marching columns or their liberties and their livelihood stolen away by foreign tyrants. But this hope has been in vain. Another violent outrage has been perpetrated by Nazi Germany against a small and friendly power, and the Norwegian Government and people are today in arms to defend their hearths and homes.

Commons, April 11, 1940

Nuremberg Trials

The Nuremberg trials are over, and the guilty leaders of the Nazi regime have been hanged by the conquerors. We are told that thousands yet remain to be tried, and that vast categories of Germans are classed as potentially guilty because of their association with the Nazi regime. After all, in a country which is handled as Germany was, the ordinary people have very little choice about what to do. I think some consideration should always be given to ordinary people. Everyone is not a Pastor Niemoller or a martyr, and when ordinary people are hurled this way and that, when the cruel hands of tyrants are laid upon them and vile systems of regimentation are imposed and enforced by espionage and other forms of cruelty, there are great numbers of people who will succumb.

Commons, November 12, 1946

Nuts

Except for our fighting services, we have been driven back to a large extent from the carnivore to the herbivore. That may be quite satisfactory to the dietetic scientists who would like to make us all live on nuts, but undoubtedly it has produced, and is producing, a very definite effect upon the energetic output of the heavy worker.

Commons, July 29, 1941

THE BRITISH PEOPLE ARE GOOD ALL THROUGH.

You can test them as you would put a bucket into the sea, and always find it salt.

The genius of our people springs from every class and from every part of the land.

London, June 13, 1945

Obligations

There are two supreme obligations which rest upon a British government. They are of equal importance. One is to strive to prevent a war, and the other is to be ready if war should come.

City Carlton Club, London, June 28, 1939

Odds Against

Certainly it is true that we are facing numerical odds; but that is no new thing in our history. Very few wars have been won by mere numbers alone. Quality, will-power, geographical advantages, natural and financial resources, the command of the sea, and, above all, a cause which rouses the spontaneous surgings of the human spirit in millions of hearts – these have proved to be the decisive factors in the human story. If it were otherwise, how would the race of men have risen above the apes; how otherwise would they have conquered and extirpated dragons and monsters; how would they have ever evolved the moral theme; how would they have marched across the centuries to broad conceptions of compassion, of freedom, and of right? How would they ever have discerned those beacon lights which summon and guide us across the rough dark waters, and presently will guide us across the flaming lines of battle towards better days which lie beyond?

London, January 20, 1940

Offer, The only

I would say to the House, as I said to those who have joined this Government: "I have nothing to offer but blood, toil, tears and sweat."

Commons, May 13, 1940

'I have nothing to offer but blood, toil, tears and sweat'

Officialdom

Will not the daily toil of the actual producing worker have a heavier burden thrust upon it by the enormous hordes of disinterested and largely uninterested officials than would be the case under private management? And will not these officials be less efficient, more costly, and far more dictatorial than the private employers?

Ayr, May 16, 1947

One Man

The people of Italy were never consulted, the army of Italy was never consulted. No one was consulted. One man, and one man alone, ordered Italian soldiers to ravage their neighbour's vineyard. Surely the time has come when the Italian monarchy and people, who guard the sacred centre of Christendom, should have a word to say upon these awe-inspiring issues? Surely the Italian army, which has fought so bravely on many occasions in the past, but now evidently has no heart for the job, should take some care of the life and future of Italy?

London, December 23, 1940

Opinions

It is curious that, while in the days of my youth I was much reproached with inconsistency and being changeable, I am now scolded for adhering to the same views I had in early life and even for repeating passages from speeches which I made long before most of you were born. Of course the world moves on and we dwell in a constantly changing climate of opinion. But the broad principles and truths of wise and sane political actions do not necessarily alter with the changing moods of a democratic electorate. Not everything changes. Two and two still make four, and I could give you many other instances which go to prove that all wisdom is not new wisdom.

Belle Vue, Manchester, December 6, 1947

Opponents

The spectacle of a number of middle-aged gentlemen who are my political opponents being in a state of uproar and fury is really quite exhilarating to me.

Commons, May 21, 1952

> **Opportunities**
>
> With opportunities comes responsibility. Strength is granted to us all when we are needed to serve great causes.
>
> *New York, March 15, 1946*

Opportunity

The British people are good all through. You can test them as you would put a bucket into the sea, and always find it salt. The genius of our people springs from every class and from every part of the land. You cannot tell where you will not find a wonder. The hero, the fighter, the poet, the master of science, the organizer, the artist, the engineer, the administrator, or the jurist – he may spring into fame. Equal opportunity for all, under free institutions and equal laws – there is the banner for which we will do battle against all rubber-stamp bureaucracies or dictatorships.

London, June 13, 1945

How proud we ought to be, young and old alike, to live in this tremendous, thrilling, formative epoch in the human story, and how fortunate it was for the world that when these great trials came upon it there was a generation that terror could not conquer and brutal violence could not enslave. Let all who are here remember, as the words of the hymn we have just sung suggest, let all of us who are here remember that we are on the stage of history, and that whatever our station may be, and whatever part we have to play, great or small, our conduct is liable to be scrutinized not only by history but by our own descendants.

Let us rise to the full level of our duty and of our opportunity, and let us thank God for the spiritual rewards He has granted for all forms of valiant and faithful service.

Harvard University, September 6, 1943

Opposition

No one should be deterred in wartime from doing his duty merely by the fact that he will be voting against the Government, and still less because the Party Whips are acting as tellers.

Commons, July 29, 1941

No one need be mealy-mouthed in debate, and no one should be chicken-hearted in voting. I have voted against governments I have been elected to support, and, looking back, I have sometimes felt very glad that I did so. Everyone in these rough times must do what he thinks is his duty.

Commons, January 27, 1942

'We are fighting by ourselves alone; but we are not fighting for ourselves alone'

Ordeal by Battle

And now it has come to us to stand alone in the breach, and face the worst that the tyrant's might and enmity can do. Bearing ourselves humbly before God, but conscious that we serve an unfolding purpose, we are ready to defend our native land against the invasion by which it is threatened. We are fighting by ourselves alone; but we are not fighting for ourselves alone. Here in this strong City of Refuge which enshrines the title-deeds of human progress and is of deep consequence to Christian civilization; here, girt about by the seas and oceans where the navy reigns; shielded from above by the prowess and devotion of our airmen – we await undismayed the impending assault. Perhaps it will come tonight. Perhaps it will come next week. Perhaps it will never come. We must show ourselves equally capable of meeting a sudden violent shock, or what is perhaps a harder test, a prolonged vigil. But be the ordeal sharp or long, or both, we shall seek no terms, we shall tolerate no parley; we may show mercy – we shall ask for none.

Commons, July 14, 1940

Ordeals

I have seen many painful scenes of havoc, and of the fine buildings and acres of cottage homes blasted into rubble-heaps of ruin. But it is just in those very places where the malice of the savage enemy has done its worst, and where the ordeal of the men, women and children has been most severe, that I found their morale most high and splendid. Indeed, I felt encompassed by an exaltation of spirit in the people which seemed to lift mankind and its troubles above the level of material facts into that joyous serenity we think belongs to a better world than this.

London, April 27, 1941

It may be that great ordeals are coming to us in this island from the air. We shall do our best to give a good account of ourselves; and we must always remember that the command of the seas will enable us to bring the immense resources of Canada and the New World into play as a decisive ultimate air factor, a factor beyond the reach of what we have to give and take over here.

London, October 1, 1939

Outlandish Ideas

No idea is so outlandish that it should not be considered with a searching, but at the same time with a steady, eye.

Commons, May 23, 1940

"Outwith"

I must thank the Hon Gentleman for making me acquainted with the word "outwith", with which I had not previously had the pleasure of making acquaintance. For the benefit of English Members I may say that it is translated, "outside the scope of". I thought it was a misprint at first.

Commons, December 5, 1944

P

IT IS THE SAME IN POLITICS AS IT IS IN WAR.

When one crest has been left, it is necessary to go to the next.

To halt half-way in the valley between is to court swift and certain destruction.

Commons, April 5, 1906

Pain

By a blessed dispensation, human beings forget physical pain much more quickly than they do their joyous emotions and experiences. A merciful Providence passes the sponge of oblivion across much that is suffered and enables us to cherish the great moments of life and honour which come to us in our march through life.

Empress Hall, London, October 21, 1949

Palestine

The idea that the Jewish problem could be solved or even helped by a vast dumping of the Jews of Europe into Palestine is really too silly to consume our time in the House this afternoon.

Commons, August 1, 1946

Panacea

I do not believe in looking about for some panacea or cure-all on which we should stake our credit and fortunes trying to sell it like a patent medicine to all and sundry. It is easy to win applause by talking in an airy way about great new departures in policy, especially if all detailed proposals are avoided.

Blackpool, October 5, 1946

Panic

It is very much better sometimes to have a panic feeling beforehand, and then be quite calm when things happen, than to be extremely calm beforehand and to get into a panic when things happen.

Commons, May 22, 1935

Parliament

It must be remembered that the function of Parliament is not only to pass good laws, but to stop bad laws.

Commons, April 4, 1944

The object of Parliament is to substitute arguments for fisticuffs.

Commons, June 6, 1951

The time-honoured ceremonial and procedure in which Crown and Parliament have played their part today carry with them to anxious minds the balm of confidence and serenity. When our beloved Sovereign and the Queen come from their battered palace to a building which is not without evidence of the strokes of war, when the Sovereign comes to open Parliament in person and calls his faithful Commons to the discharge of their duties, at every step, in every measure, in every formality, and in every resolution that we pass, we touch customs and traditions which go back far beyond the great Parliamentary conflicts of the seventeenth century; we feel the inspiration of old days, we feel the splendour of our political and moral inheritance.

Commons, November 21, 1940

Parliament can compel people to obey or to submit, but it cannot compel them to agree.

Commons, September 27, 1926

Parliament at War

During the last two hundred and fifty years the British Parliament has fought several great and long European wars with unwearied zeal and tenacity, and carried them all to a successful conclusion. In this war they are fighting not only for themselves, but for Parliamentary institutions wherever they have been set up all over the globe.

Free Trade Hall, Manchester, January 27, 1940

Partisans, Tito's

In the autumn of 1941, Marshal Tito's Partisans began a wild and furious war for existence against the Germans. They wrested weapons from the Germans' hands, they grew rapidly in numbers; no reprisals, however bloody, whether upon hostages or the villages, deterred them. For them, it was death or freedom. Soon they began to inflict heavy injury upon the Germans and became masters of wide regions. Led with great skill, organized on the guerilla principle, they were at once elusive and deadly. They were here, they were there, they were everywhere. Large scale offensives have been launched against them by the Germans, but in every case the Partisans, even when surrounded, have escaped, after inflicting great losses and toil upon the enemy.

Commons, February 22, 1944

Past, The

We are not in a position to say tonight, "The past is the past." We cannot say, "The past is the past," without surrendering the future.

Commons, March 14, 1938

Patience, Christian

There is, I gather, in some quarters the feeling that the way to win the war is to knock the Government about, keep them up to the collar, and harry them from every side; and I find that hard to bear with Christian patience.

Commons, February 22, 1944

Patriotism

Patriotic men and women, especially those who understand the high causes in human fortunes which are now at stake, must not only rise above fear; they must also rise above inconvenience and, perhaps most difficult of all, above boredom.

London, October 1, 1939

PAYE

The extension of the income tax to the wage-earners was a very remarkable step. That it should have gained the assent of this House, elected on universal suffrage, is also a remarkable fact, showing how extremely closely the wage-earning masses of the country and those who represent them feel associated with the vital issues now being fought out in the field.

Commons, September 22, 1943

Peace

I say quite frankly, though I may shock the House, that I would rather see another ten or twenty years of one-sided armed peace than see a war between equally well-matched powers or combinations of powers – and that may be the choice.

Commons, November 23, 1932

Patience and perseverance must never be grudged when the peace of the world is at stake.

Commons, February 25, 1954

'We cannot say, "The past is the past," without surrendering the future'

Persia

It is a very melancholy thing to contemplate the possibility of an ancient capital of a monarchy like that of Persia being engulfed in the tides of barbarism, and a culture which, though primitive in many respects, is nevertheless ancient, being swamped and beaten down under the heel of a Bolshevik invasion, but there must be some limit to the responsibilities of Britain.

Commons, December 15, 1920

Phlegm

Here we are gathered in academic robes to go through a ceremonial and repeat formulas associated with the giving of university degrees. Many of those here today have been all night at their post, and all have been under the fire of the enemy in heavy and protracted bombardment. That you should gather in this way is a mark of fortitude and phlegm, of a courage and detachment from material affairs, worthy of all that we have learned to believe of ancient Rome or of modern Greece.

Bristol University, April 12, 1941

Physicians, College of

This college, on whose past you, Lord Moran, have descanted, on whose past you have opened some windows which cast a view upon its former glories, was, I am assured, founded by a man of wide experience of human nature – and of both sexes – King Henry VIII, in 1518. It is claimed that he thus created medicine as a profession and cast a stern Tudor frown upon quackery of all kinds.

Royal College of Physicians, London, March 2, 1944

Pillage

We are a rich and easy prey. No country is so vulnerable, and no country would better repay pillage than our own. With our enormous Metropolis here, the greatest target in the world, a kind of tremendous, fat, valuable cow tied up to attract the beast of prey, we are in a position in which we have never been before, and in which no other country in the world is at the present time.

Commons, July 30, 1934

Pinnacle of Power

The United States stands at this time at the pinnacle of world power. It is a solemn moment for the American Democracy. For with primacy in power is also joined an awe-inspiring accountability to the future. If you look around you, you must feel not only the sense of duty done but also you must feel anxiety lest you fall below the level of achievement.

Westminster College, Fulton, Missouri, March 5, 1946

Piracy

It is true that the *Deutschland* escaped the clutches of our cruisers by the skin of her teeth, but the *Spee* still sticks up in the harbour of Montevideo as a grisly monument and as a measure of the fate in store for any Nazi warship which dabbles in piracy on the broad waters.

London, January 20, 1940

Planning

It is the habit of architects and builders to be more sanguine when putting forward their plans than is subsequently found to be justified by the actual facts.

Commons, October 28, 1943

There is nothing new in planning. Every government, ancient or modern, must look ahead and plan. Did not Joseph advise Pharaoh to build granaries and fill them for the lean years when the Nile waters failed?

Empress Hall, London, October 14, 1949

Planning, State

I do not believe in the capacity of the State to plan and enforce an active high grade economic productivity upon its members or subjects. No matter how numerous are the committees they set up, or the ever-growing hordes of officials they employ, or the severity of the punishments they inflict or threaten, they cannot approach the high level of internal economic production which, under free enterprise, personal initiative, competitive selection, the profit motive corrected by failure, and the infinite processes of good house-keeping and personal ingenuity, constitutes the life of a free society.

Commons, October 28, 1947

Platitudes

This is no time for windy platitudes and glittering advertisements. The Conservative Party had far better go down telling the truth and acting in accordance with the verities of our position than gain a span of shabbily-bought office by easy and fickle froth and chatter.

Central Hall, Westminster, March 15, 1945

Plimsoll

No man could have offended more against the rules of the House than Mr Plimsoll, for he used violent language, was disorderly in debate, preferred a serious charge against another Hon Member which was found afterwards to be baseless, shook his fist in the face of Mr Disraeli, and left the House stating that he would not withdraw one single word of what he had said. ... Mr Plimsoll was given a week to consider his position, and on returning he declined to withdraw the substance of what he said, but he made amends for his disorderly conduct, which showed that a respectful apology was not incompatible even with the most strenuous protest. But although Mr Plimsoll's apology was of a qualified nature, the House was disposed to be generous, and he was allowed to resume his seat, and the mark of his work was set upon every ship that went to sea.

Commons, February 11, 1902

Poise and Temper

Having, at the end of my life, acquired some influence on affairs, I wish to make it clear that I would not needlessly prolong this war by a single day; and my hope is that if and when British people are called by victory to share in the august responsibilities of shaping the future, we shall show the same poise and temper as we did in the hour of our mortal peril.

Commons, September 21, 1943

Poland

We have never weakened in any way in our resolve that Poland shall be restored and stand erect as a sovereign, independent nation, free to model her social institutions or any other institutions in any way her people chose, provided, I must say, that these are not on Fascist lines, and provided that Poland stands loyally as a barrier and friend of Russia against German aggression from the west.

Commons, December 15, 1944

All over Europe, races and states whose culture and history made them a part of the general life of Christendom in centuries when the Prussians were no better than a barbarous tribe, and the German Empire no more than an agglomeration of pumpernickel principalities, are now prostrate under the dark, cruel yoke of Hitler and his Nazi gang. Every week his firing parties are busy in a dozen lands, Monday he shoots Dutchmen; Tuesday, Norwegians; Wednesday, French and Belgians stand against the wall; Thursday it is the Czechs who must suffer. And now there are the Serbs and the Greeks to fill his repulsive bill of executions. But always, all the days, there are the Poles. The atrocities committed by Hitler upon the Poles, the ravaging of their country, the scattering of their homes, the affronts to their religion, the enslavement of their man-power, exceed in severity and in scale the villainies perpetuated by Hitler in any other conquered land.

London, May 3, 1941

There are few virtues that the Poles do not possess – and there are few mistakes they have ever avoided.

Commons, August 16, 1945

Polish Home Army

I am sure I am expressing the feelings of the House, as well as those of His Majesty's Government, in paying tribute to the heroic stand of the Polish Home Army and of the Polish civilian population of Warsaw. Their resistance to overwhelming odds, under inconceivable conditions of hardship, came to an end on October 3rd, after a fight which lasted 63 days. Despite all the efforts of the Soviet army, the strong German positions on the Vistula could not be taken, and relief could not come in

'It is hard enough to understand the politics of one's own country; it is almost impossible to understand those of foreign countries'

time. British, American, Polish and Soviet airmen did what they could to succour the Poles at Warsaw, but although this sustained the Polish resistance beyond what could have seemed possible, it could not turn the tide. In the battle for Warsaw, terrible damage has been inflicted upon that noble city, and its heroic population has undergone sufferings and privations unsurpassed even among the miseries of this war.

Commons, October 5, 1944

Politics

Politics is not a game. It is an earnest business.

National Liberal Club, London, October 9, 1909

Politics, Understanding

It is hard enough to understand the politics of one's own country; it is almost impossible to understand those of foreign countries.

Commons, February 22, 1944

Politics and War

It is the same in politics as it is in war. When one crest has been left, it is necessary to go to the next. To halt half-way in the valley between is to court swift and certain destruction.

Commons, April 5, 1906

Pomp and Power

On the whole it is wise in human affairs, and in the government of men, to separate pomp from power.

Ottawa, January 14, 1952

Population, Transfer of

The transference of several millions of people would have to be effected from the east to the west or north, as well as the expulsion of the Germans – because that is what is proposed: the total expulsion of the Germans – from the areas to be acquired by Poland in the west and the north. For expulsion is the method which, so far as we have been able to see, will be the most satisfactory and lasting. There will be no mixture of populations to cause endless trouble, as has been the case in Alsace-Lorraine. A clean sweep will be made. I am not alarmed by the prospect of the disentanglement of populations, nor even by these large transferences, which are more possible in modern conditions than they were ever before.

Commons, December 15, 1944

Population, Trend of

There is no branch of human knowledge in which we can pierce the mysteries of the future so clearly as in the trend of population. Here you have prophecies which rest on certainty; here the searchlight of statistics ranges with accuracy for thirty or forty years ahead. The destiny of our country, which after all has rendered notable services to mankind in peace and latterly in war, depends upon an ever-flowing fountain of healthy children, born into what we trust will be a broader society and a less distracted world. Science, now so largely perverted to destruction, must raise its glittering shield not only over the children but over the mothers, not only over the family, but over the home.

Royal College of Physicians, London, March 2, 1944

Power, Balance of

The whole history of the world is summed up in the fact that when nations are strong they are not always just, and when they wish to be just they are often no longer strong. I desire to see the collective forces of the world invested with overwhelming power. If you are going to depend on a slight margin, one way or the other, you will have war. But if you get five or ten to one on one side, all bound rigorously by the covenant and the conventions which they own, then you may have an opportunity of a settlement which will heal the wounds of the world. Let us have this blessed union of power and justice: "Agree with thine

'Great wars come when both sides believe they are more or less equal'

adversary quickly, while thou art in the way with him." Let us free the world from the reproach of a catastrophe carrying with it calamity and tribulation beyond the tongue of man to tell.

Commons, March 26, 1936

Great wars come when both sides believe they are more or less equal, when each thinks it has a good chance of victory.

New York, October 14, 1947

From what I have seen of our Russian friends and allies during the war, I am convinced that there is nothing they admire so much as strength, and there is nothing for which they have less respect than weakness, especially military weakness. For that reason the old doctrine of a balance of power is unsound. We cannot afford, if we can help it, to work on narrow margins, offering temptations to a trial of strength.

Westminster College, Fulton, Missouri, March 5, 1946

Power, Division of

The wisdom of our ancestors for more than 300 years has sought the division of power in the Constitution: Crown, Lords and Commons have been checks and restraints upon one another.

Huddersfield, October 15, 1951

Both here and across the ocean, over the generations and the centuries, the idea of the division of powers has lain deep at the root of our development. We do not want to live in a system dominated either by one man or one theme. Like nature, we follow in theme the paths of variety and change and our faith that in the mercy of God things will get better and better if we all try our best.

Coronation Luncheon, Westminster Hall, May 27, 1953

Power, Limits of

Parliament can compel people to obey or to submit, but it cannot compel them to agree.

Commons, September 27, 1926

Power and Mercy

The finest combination in the world is power and mercy. The worst combination in the world is weakness and strife.

Commons, March 3, 1919

Power, Overbalance of

As I look upon the future of our country in the changing scene of human destiny I feel the existence of three great circles among the free nations and democracies. I almost wish I had a blackboard. I would make a picture for you. I don't suppose it would get hung in the Royal Academy, but it would illustrate the point I am anxious for you to hold in your minds. The first circle for us is naturally the British Commonwealth and Empire, with all that that comprises. Then there is also the English-speaking world in which we, Canada, and the other British Dominions and the United States play so important a part. And finally there is United Europe. These three majestic circles are co-existent and if they are linked together there is no force or combination which could overthrow them or even challenge them.

Llandudno, October 9, 1948

'You have to run risks. There are no certainties in war. There is a precipice on either side of you'

Power Politics

I have anxiously asked the question, "What are power politics?" I know some of our friends across the water so well that I am sure I can always speak frankly without causing offence. Is having a navy twice as big as any other navy in the world power politics? Is having the largest air force in the world with bases in every part of the world power politics? Is having all the gold in the world power politics? If so, we are certainly not guilty of these offences, I am sorry to say. They are luxuries that have passed away from us.

Commons, January 18, 1945

Power and Responsibility

Where there is great power there is great responsibility, where there is less power there is less responsibility, and where there is no power there can, I think, be no responsibility.

Commons, February 28, 1952

Powers, Great and Small

We may deplore, if we choose, the fact that there is a difference between great and small, between the strong and the weak in the world, but there undoubtedly is such a difference, and it would be foolish to upset good arrangements which are proceeding on a broad front for the sake of trying to obtain immediately what is a hopeless ideal.

Commons, March 15, 1945

Precipices

You have to run risks. There are no certainties in war. There is a precipice on either side of you – a precipice of caution and a precipice of over-daring.

Commons, September 21, 1942

Predictions

Most of all shall I refrain from making any prediction upon the future. It is a month ago that I remarked upon the long silence of Herr Hitler, a remark which apparently provoked him to make a speech in which he told the German people that Moscow would fall in a few days. That shows, as everyone I am sure will agree, how much wiser he would have been to go on keeping his mouth shut.

Commons, November 12, 1941

Preparedness

Mark you, in time of peace, in peace politics, in ordinary matters of domestic affairs and class struggles, things blow over, but in these great matters of defence, and still more in the field of actual hostilities, the clouds do not roll by. If the necessary measures are not taken, they turn into thunderbolts and fall on your heads.

Commons, May 31, 1935

The more you are prepared and the better you are known to be prepared, the greater is the chance of staving off war and of saving Europe from the catastrophe which menaces it.

Commons, May 25, 1938

Press, The

We sneer at the Press, but they give an extremely true picture of a great deal that is going on, a very much fuller and more detailed picture than we are able to receive from ministers of the Crown.

Commons, April 13, 1939

Priority

I have always been very much struck by the advantage enjoyed by people who lived at an earlier period of the world than one's own. They had the first opportunity of saying the right thing. Over and over again it had happened to me to think of something which I thought was worth saying, only to find that it had been already exploited, and very often spoiled, before I had an opportunity of saying it.

Commons, May 19, 1927

Priority among Virtues

Compassion, charity and generosity are noble virtues, but the Government should be just before they are generous.

Commons, March 12, 1947

Principles

It is vain to imagine that the mere perception or declaration of right principles, whether in one country or in many countries, will be of any value unless they are supported by those qualities of civic virtue and manly courage – aye, and by those instruments and agencies of force and science which in the last resort must be the defence of right and reason.

University of Bristol, July 2, 1938

In critical and baffling situations it is always best to recur to first principles and simple action.

London, March 17, 1951

Prisoners of War

What is a prisoner of war? He is a man who has tried to kill you and, having failed to kill you, asks you not to kill him. Long before the Christian revelation, the world had found out by practice that mercy towards a beaten enemy was well worth while and that it was much easier to gain control over wide areas by taking prisoners than by making everyone fight to the death against you.

Commons, July 1, 1952

Private Property

Personally I think that private property has a right to be defended. Our civilization is built up on private property, and can only be defended by private property.

Commons, August 11, 1947

Prize, The Last

If I remain in public life at this juncture it is because, rightly or wrongly, but sincerely, I believe that I may be able to make an important contribution to the prevention of a third world war and to bringing nearer that lasting peace settlement which the masses of the people of every race and in every land fervently desire. I pray indeed that I may have this opportunity. It is the last prize I seek to win. I have been blessed with so much good fortune throughout my long life, and I am treated with so much kindness by my fellow countrymen far outside the ranks of Party, and indeed also in the United States and in Europe, that all the daydreams of my youth have been surpassed.

Plymouth, October 23, 1951

If I stay on for the time being, bearing the burden of my age, it is not because of love for power or office. I have had an ample feast of both. If I stay it is because I have the feeling that I may, through things that have happened, have an influence on what I care about above all else – the building of a sure and lasting peace.

Margate, October 10, 1953

Procrastination

The era of procrastination, of half-measures, of soothing and baffling expedients, of delays, is coming to its close. In its place we are entering a period of consequences.

Commons, November 12, 1936

Programme

I stand by my original programme – blood, toil, tears and sweat … to which I added five months later many shortcomings, mistakes and disappointments!

Commons, January 27, 1942

'Progress and reaction are relative terms. What one man calls progress another will call reaction'

Progress

Alone among the nations of the world we have found the means to combine empire and liberty. Alone among the peoples we have reconciled democracy and tradition; for long generations, nay, over several centuries, no mortal clash or religious or political gulf has opened in our midst. Alone we have found the way to carry forward the glories of the past through all the storms, domestic and foreign, that have surged about, and thus to bring the labours of our forebears as a splendid inheritance for modern progressive democracy to enjoy.

Caxton Hall, London, October 9, 1940

I cannot doubt we have the strength to carry a good cause forward, and to break down the barriers which stand between the wage-earning masses of every land and the free and more abundant daily life which science is ready to afford.

Commons, October 1, 1939

Progress and Reaction

Progress and reaction are no doubt relative terms. What one man calls progress another will call reaction. If you have been rapidly descending the road to ruin and you suddenly check yourself, stop, turn back and retrace your steps, that is reaction, and no doubt your former guide will have every reason to reproach you with inconsistency.

St Andrew's Hall, Glasgow, October 11, 1906

Progress, Social

I have always been a bit shy of defining war aims, but if these great communities, now struggling not only for their own lives but for the freedom and progress of the world, emerge victorious, there will be an electric atmosphere in the world which may render possible an advance towards a greater and broader social unity and justice than could otherwise have been achieved in peacetime in a score of years. We are no theorists or doctrinaires. Trade unionists are practical men aiming at practical results. I might say that our aim will be to build a society in which there will be wealth and culture, but where wealth shall not prey on commonwealth nor culture degenerate into class and pride.

Speech at a luncheon in London, March 27, 1941

Prohibition

I do not think we are likely to learn much from the liquor legislation of the United States.

Commons, April 11, 1927

'I do not think we are likely to learn much from the liquor legislation of the United States'

Promises

I am resolved not to give or to make all kinds of promises and tell all kinds of fairy tales to you who have trusted me and gone with me so far, and marched through the valley of the shadow, till we have reached the upland regions on which we now stand with firmly planted feet.

London, March 21, 1943

Nothing would be easier for me than to make any number of promises and to get the immediate response of cheap cheers and glowing leading articles. I am not in any need to go about making promises in order to win political support or to be allowed to continue in office.

Commons, February 11, 1943

Propaganda

There is an extraordinary volume of German propaganda in this country, of mis-statements made on the highest authority – which everyone knows could be easily disproved – but which obtain currency, and which, because they are not contradicted, are accepted as part of the regular facts on which the public rely. Ministers and Members who are in agreement with the policy of the Government must exert themselves to explain these matters to an anxious, but loyal and courageous, public.

Commons, March 26, 1936

Prophecy

The whole tribe of highly intellectual left-wing scribblers assure us that the Socialist Administration will rule for 20 years.

Blackpool, October 5, 1946

Prophets, Qualification of

A hopeful disposition is not the sole qualification to be a prophet.

Commons, April 30, 1927

Proportion, Sense of

The curious fact that the House prefers to give two days to the television White Paper and only one day to foreign affairs may be noted by future historians as an example of a changing sense of proportion in modern thought.

Commons, December 17, 1953

Proportional Representation

It is quite true that I expressed a view many years ago, which I have seen no reason to dismiss from the region of theoretical principle, in favour of proportional representation in great cities. I have not expressed any views in favour of proportional representation as a whole, on account of the proved ill effects it has had on so many Parliaments.

Commons, February 17, 1953

Prospect, 1942

We have reached a period in the war when it would be premature to say that we have topped the ridge, but now we see the ridge ahead. We see that perseverance, unflinching, dogged, inexhaustible, tireless, valiant, will surely carry us and our allies, the great nations of the world, and the unfortunate nations who have been subjugated and enslaved, on to one of the most deepfounded movements of humanity, which have ever taken place in our history. We see that they will come to the top of the ridge, and then they will have a chance not only of beating down and subduing those evil forces which have withstood us so long, which have twice let ruin and havoc loose on the world, but they will have that further and grander prospect that beyond the smoke of battle and the confusion of the fight we shall have the chance to settle our countries and the whole world together, moving forward together on the high road. That is the prospect that lies before us if we do not fail. And we shall not fail.

Town Hall, Leeds, May 16, 1942

Prosperity

The idea that a nation can tax itself into prosperity is one of the crudest delusions which has ever fuddled the human mind.

The Royal Albert Hall, London, April 21, 1948

Prostration of Germany

In the forefront of any survey of the world stands Germany, a vanquished nation. "Stands," I said – no, prostrate, shattered. Seventy or eighty millions of men and women of an ancient, capable and terribly efficient race are in a ruined famished condition in the heart of Europe.

Commons, November 12, 1946

The real essential fallacy of the protectionist proposal is the idea that taxation is a good thing in itself, that it should be imposed for the fun of the thing, and then, having done it for amusement, we should go round afterwards and look for attractive methods of expenditure in order to give support to the project.

Commons, July 15, 1907

Public Speaking during War

It has been aptly remarked that ministers, and indeed all other public men, when they make speeches at the present time, have always to bear in mind three audiences, one our own fellow countrymen, secondly, our friends abroad, and thirdly, the enemy. This naturally makes the task of public speaking very difficult.

Commons, November 12, 1941

'We are resolved to destroy Hitler and every vestige of the Nazi regime. From this nothing will turn us – nothing'

Pugnacity

There are all sorts of matters which are extremely important upon which we might expend a great deal of energy and pugnacity, but at present we must do our best to keep our pugnacity for export purposes.

Commons, October 6, 1944

Purblindness

Although the fate of Poland stares them in the face, there are thoughtless dilletanti or purblind wordlings who sometimes ask us: "What is it that Britain and France are fighting for?" To this I answer: "If we left off fighting you would soon find out."

London, March 30, 1940

Purpose

We have but one aim and one single, irrevocable purpose. We are resolved to destroy Hitler and every vestige of the Nazi regime. From this nothing will turn us – nothing. We will never parley, we will never negotiate with Hitler or any of his gang. We shall fight him by land, we shall fight him by sea, we shall fight him in the air, until with God's help we have rid the earth of his shadow and liberated its peoples from his yoke. Any man or state who fights on against Nazidom will have our aid. Any man or state who marches with Hitler is our foe.

London, June 22, 1941

Pursuit in War

It is nearly always right to pursue a beaten foe with all one's strength, and even to run serious risks in doing so; of course, there comes a time when the pursuers outstrip the utmost limits of their own supplies, and where the enemy, falling back on his own depots, is able once again to form a front.

Commons, November 9, 1944

Puzzle

During the last three months an element of baffling dualism has complicated every problem of policy and administration. We had to plan for peace and war at the same time. Immense armies were being demobilized; another powerful army was being prepared and dispatched to the other side of the globe. All the personal stresses among millions of men eager to return to civil life, and hundreds of thousands of men who would have to be sent to new and severe campaigns in the Far East, presented themselves with growing tension. This dualism affected also every aspect of our economic and financial life. How to set people free to use their activities in reviving the life of Britain, and at the same time to meet the stern demands of the war against Japan, constituted one of the most perplexing and distressing puzzles that in a long life-time of experience I have ever faced.

Commons, August 16, 1945

BY TRIAL AND ERROR, AND BY PERSEVERANCE ACROSS THE CENTURIES,

we have found out a very good plan.

Here it is: The Queen can do no wrong.

Coronation Luncheon, Westminster Hall, May 27, 1953

Quagmire

There are some general propositions now in vogue which deserve scrutiny. Let me state them in terms of precision: "All oppression from the left is progress. All resistance from the right is reactionary. All forward steps are good, and all backward steps are bad. When you are getting into a horrible quagmire, the only remedy is to plunge in deeper and deeper."

Commons, June 5, 1946

Quebec

Here at the gateway of Canada, in mighty lands which have never known the totalitarian tyrannies of Hitler and Mussolini, the spirit of freedom has found a safe and abiding home. Here that spirit is no wandering phantom. It is enshrined in Parliamentary institutions based on universal suffrage and evolved through the centuries by the English-speaking peoples. It is inspired by the Magna Carta and the Declaration of Independence. It is guarded by resolute and vigilant millions, never so strong or so well armed as today.

London, August 31, 1943

Queen, The

In our island, by trial and error, and by perseverance across the centuries, we have found out a very good plan. Here it is: The Queen can do no wrong. Bad advisers can be changed as often as the people like to use their rights for that purpose. A great battle is lost: Parliament turns out the Government. A great battle is won – crowds cheer the Queen.

Coronation Luncheon, Westminster Hall, May 27, 1953

Queuetopia

The Socialist dream is no longer Utopia but Queuetopia. And if they have the power this part of their dream will certainly come true.

Woodford, January 28, 1950

I CANNOT FORECAST TO YOU THE ACTION OF RUSSIA.

It is a riddle wrapped in a mystery inside an enigma; but perhaps there is a key.

That key is Russian national interest.

London, October 1, 1939

Radar

During the war we imparted many secrets to the Russians especially in connection with radar, but we were not conscious of any adequate reciprocity. Even in the heat of the war both countries acted under considerable reserve.

Commons, November 7, 1945

Range

The British Empire has been built up by running risks. If we had never moved an inch beyond the range of our heavy artillery, our empire would probably have been limited by that same scope.

Commons, March 21, 1922

Rationing

In war-time rationing is the alternative to famine. In peace it may well become the alternative to abundance.

Devonport, February 9, 1950

Reactionary

In Russia a man is called a reactionary if he objects to having his property stolen and his wife and children murdered.

Commons, November 5, 1919

Rearmament

I am strongly of opinion that we require to strengthen our armaments in the air and upon the seas in order to make sure that we are still judges of our own fortunes, our own destinies, and our own action.

Commons, March 14, 1933

The German munition factories are working practically under war conditions, and war material is flowing out from them, and has been for the last twelve months, in an ever broadening flow. Much of this is undoubtedly in violation of the treaties which were signed. Germany is rearming on land; she is rearming also to some extent at sea; but what concerns us most of all is the rearmament of Germany in the air.

Commons, November 28, 1934

Mr Lansbury said just now that he and the Socialist Party would never consent to the rearming of Germany. But is he quite sure that the Germans will come and ask him for his consent before they rearm? Does he not think they might omit that formality and go ahead without even taking a card vote of the TUC?

Commons, November 7, 1933

Recognition

Recognizing a person is not necessarily an act of approval. I will not be personal, or give instances. One has to recognize lots of things and people in this world of sin and woe that one does not like.

Commons, November 17, 1949

Recrimination

Of this I am sure, that if we open a quarrel between the past and the present, we shall find that we have lost the future.

Commons, June 18, 1940

Regimentation

I warn you solemnly, if you submit yourselves to the totalitarian compulsion and regimentation of our national life and labour, there lies before you an almost measureless prospect of misery and tribulation of which a lower standard of living will be the first result, hunger the second, and a dispersal or death of a large proportion of our population the third.

Blenheim Palace, August 16, 1947

Reign of Law

The future towards which we are marching, across bloody fields and frightful manifestations of destruction, must be based upon the broad and simple virtues and upon the nobility of mankind. It must be based upon a reign of law which upholds the principles of justice and fair play, and protects the weak against the strong if the weak have justice on their side. There must be an end to predatory exploitation and nationalistic ambitions.

Commons, May 24, 1944

'We shall defend our island, whatever the cost may be … we shall never surrender'

Reiteration

One must never be afraid or ashamed of ramming home a point. It is reiteration which is important. One must never be shy of pressing home the great points of public controversy which make their appeal to the common sense and conscience of the nation.

The Royal Albert Hall, London, April 30, 1948

The Russian Bolsheviks have discovered that truth does not matter so long as there is reiteration. They have no difficulty whatever in countering a fact by a lie which, if repeated often enough and loudly enough, becomes accepted by the people.

Brighton, October 4, 1947

Religion

Religion has been the rock in the life and character of the British people upon which they have built their hopes and cast their cares. This fundamental element must never be taken from our schools, and I rejoice to learn of the enormous progress that is being made among all religious bodies in freeing themselves from sectarian jealousies and feuds, while preserving fervently the tenets of their own faith.

London, March 21, 1943

Reprisals

The question of reprisals is being discussed in some quarters as if it were a moral issue. What are reprisals? What we are doing now is to batter continuously, with forces which steadily increase in power, each one of those points in Germany which we believe will do the Germans most injury and will most speedily lessen their power to strike at us. Is that a reprisal? It seems to me very like one.

Commons, October 8, 1940

Reproof

I must find the narrow line between reproof of complacency at home and encouragement of the enemy abroad.

Commons, February 22, 1944

Rescue of Europe

Even though large tracts of Europe and many old and famous states have fallen or may fall into the grip of the Gestapo and all the odious apparatus of Nazi rule, we shall not flag or fail. We shall go on to the end, we shall fight in France, we shall fight on the seas and oceans, we shall fight with growing confidence and growing strength in the air, we shall defend our island, whatever the cost may be, we shall fight on the beaches, we shall fight on the landing grounds, we shall fight in the fields and in the streets, we shall fight in the hills; we shall never surrender, and even if, which I do not for a moment believe, this island or a large part of it were subjugated and starving, then our empire beyond the seas, armed and guarded by the British fleet, would carry on the struggle, until, in God's good time, the New World, with all its power and might, steps forth to the rescue and the liberation of the Old.

Commons, June 4, 1940

Resistance

Again and again, it has been proved that fierce and stubborn resistance, even against heavy odds and under exceptional conditions of local disadvantage, is an essential element in victory.

Commons, June 10, 1941

Resistance, Line of Least

It always looks so easy to solve problems by taking the line of least resistance. Again and again in my life I have seen this course lead to the most unexpected result, and what looks like being the easy road turns out to be the hardest and most cruel.

Commons, May 24, 1946

Respect

We do not covet anything from any nation except their respect.

London, October 21, 1940

Responsibility

There is a great deal of difference between being responsible for giving an order on which the loss of several valuable ships might swiftly follow, and merely expressing an opinion, however well-informed, however sincere, however courageous, without such responsibility.

Commons, May 8, 1940

Responsibility, Sense of

When Herr Goebbels's Nazi propaganda blares and blethers upon the ether that Britain and France have lost the capacity to make war if it is forced upon them, we do not get angry because we know it is not true. We know that our sufferings will be very hard and we are determined not to be guilty of bringing about a crash the consequences of which no man can measure. We know also that we could only throw ourselves into such a struggle if our consciences were clear. In this free, old, independent island we are not living in the Middle Ages. We see great hopes for the future of all the world. We see the opportunity of lifting, through the aid of science, all the men in all the lands to a far higher level of well-being and culture than was ever possible before. It is an opportunity which has never come to mankind before, and which may not come to them again, if it is cast away, till generations and perhaps centuries have passed. We are determined that there shall not rest upon us the guilt and the shame of standing between

'In this free, old, independent island we are not living in the Middle Ages. We see great hopes for the future of all the world'

the toiling masses of the world and the ever-brightening prospects which are at last within their reach. It is this sense of responsibility before the high monuments of history which has governed our policy and conduct, and no taunts or insults will move us from this determination.

Commons, June 28, 1939

Restrictions

The whole enterprise, contrivance, and genius of the British nation is being increasingly paralysed by the wartime restrictions from which all other free nations have shaken themselves clear, but these are still imposed upon our people here in the name of a mistaken political philosophy and a largely obsolete mode of thought.

London, January 21, 1950

Retirement

It would be easy for me to retire gracefully in an odour of civic freedom.

Brighton, September 7, 1946

Retribution

The great liner is sinking in a calm sea. One bulkhead after another gives way; one compartment after another is bilged, the list increases; she is sinking, but the captain and the officers and the crew are all in the saloon dancing to the jazz band. But wait till the passengers find out what is their position!

Commons, January 26, 1931

The air power was the weapon which both the marauding States selected as their main tool of conquest. This was the sphere in which they were to triumph. This was the method by which the nations were to be subjugated to their rule. I shall not moralize further than to say that there is a strange, stern justice in the long swing of events.

Commons, February 22, 1944

Revenge

Revenge is, of all satisfactions, the most costly and long drawn out; retributive persecution is, of all policies, the most pernicious.

Commons, October 28, 1948

Rhine

I thought that the Prime Minister's remark which he made some years ago about our frontier being the Rhine was liable at the time to be misunderstood; but if he meant that it was a mortal danger to Britain to have the Low Countries in the fortified grip of the strongest military power upon the Continent, and now, in these days, to have all the German aviation bases established there, he was only repeating the lesson taught in four centuries of history.

Commons, April 6, 1936

Rhineland

We have managed to secure the disadvantages of all the courses without the advantages of any. We have pressed France into a course of action which did not go far enough to help the Abyssinians, but went far enough to sever her from Italy, with the result that the occasion was given to Herr Hitler to tear up treaties and reoccupy the Rhineland.

Commons, April 6, 1936

Rich, The

It is very easy for rich people to preach the virtues of self-reliance to the poor. It is also very foolish, because, as a matter of fact, the wealthy, so far from being self-reliant, are dependent on the constant attention of scores, and sometimes even hundreds, of persons who are employed in waiting upon them and ministering to their wants.

Norwich, July 26, 1909

Rich Men

Rich men, although valuable to the revenue, are not vital to a healthy state of society, but a society in which rich men are got rid of from motives of jealousy is not a healthy state.

Commons, April 24, 1950

Rifle

Nothing is more vital to the self-respect of a soldier than to have his rifle and bayonet, by which he can defend his life and honour.

Commons, December 1, 1948

Right, Victory of

We cannot tell what the course of that struggle will be, into what regions it will carry us, how long it will last, or who will fall by the way. But we are sure that in the end right will win, that freedom will not be trampled down, that a truer progress will open, and a broader justice will reign. And we are determined to play our part worthily, faithfully, and to the end.

Manchester, January 27, 1940

Right and Wrong

Perhaps it is better to be irresponsible and right than to be responsible and wrong.

London, August 26, 1950

Rights of Man

This is not a question of fighting for Danzig or fighting for Poland. We are fighting to save the whole world from the pestilence of Nazi tyranny and in defence of all that is most sacred to man. This is no war of domination or imperial aggrandizement or material gain; no war to shut any country out of its sunlight and means of progress. It is a war, viewed in its inherent quality, to establish, on impregnable rocks, the rights of the individual, and it is a war to establish and revive the stature of man.

Commons, September 3, 1939

Roads

If I had proposed to take £12,000,000 from the navy, all the Liberal Party would have been bound to rise up and say: "Hosanna! Let us, if you will, have a second- or third-class navy, but, whatever happens, we must have first-class roads!"

Commons, April 4, 1927

Rocket, The

The rocket contains approximately the same quantity of high explosive as the flying bomb. However, it is designed to penetrate rather deeper before exploding. This results in somewhat heavier damage in the immediate vicinity of the crater, but rather less extensive blast effect around. The rocket flies through the stratosphere, going up to sixty or seventy miles, and outstrips sound. Because of its high speed, no reliable or sufficient public warning can, in present circumstances, be given.

Commons, November 10, 1944

Roosevelt, President

That great man whom destiny has marked for this climax of human fortune.

Ottawa, December 30, 1941

I conceived an admiration for him as a statesman, a man of affairs, and a war leader. I felt the utmost confidence in his upright, inspiring character and outlook, and a personal regard – affection I must say – for him beyond my power to express today. His love of his own country, his respect for its constitution, his power of gauging the tides and currents of its mobile public opinion, were always evident; but added to these were the beatings of that generous heart which was always stirred to anger and to action by spectacles of aggression and oppression by the strong against the weak. It is, indeed, a loss, a bitter loss to humanity that those heart-beats are, stilled for ever.

Commons, April 17, 1945

When we come to speak of Franklin Roosevelt, however, we enter the sphere of British history and of world history, far above the ebb and flow of Party politics on either side of the Atlantic. And I shall not hesitate to affirm, and indeed to repeat, that he was the greatest American friend that Britain ever found, and the foremost champion of freedom and justice who has ever stretched strong hands across the oceans to rescue Europe and Asia from tyranny or destruction.

London, April 12, 1948

Russia

I cannot forecast to you the action of Russia. It is a riddle wrapped in a mystery inside an enigma; but perhaps there is a key. That key is Russian national interest.

London, October 1, 1939

The inpression I brought back from the Crimea, and from all my other contacts, is that Marshal Stalin and the Soviet leaders wish to live in honourable friendship and equality with the western democracies. I feel also that their word is their bond. I know of no government which stands to its obligations even in its own despite, more solidly than the Russian Soviet Government. I decline absolutely to embark here on a discussion about Russian good faith. It is quite evident that these matters touch the whole future of the world. Sombre indeed would be the fortunes of mankind if some awful schism arose between the western democracies and the Russian Soviet Union, if the future world organization were rent asunder, and if new cataclysms of inconceivable violence destroyed all that is left of the treasures and liberties of mankind.

Commons, February 27, 1945

The Nazi regime is indistinguishable from the worst features of Communism. It is devoid of all theme and principle except appetite and racial domination. It excels all forms of human wickedness in the efficiency of its cruelty and ferocious aggression. No one has been a more consistent opponent of Communism than I have for the last twenty-five years. I will unsay no word that I have spoken about it. But all this fades

'I see also the dull, drilled, docile, brutish masses of the Hun soldiery plodding on like a swarm of crawling locusts'

away before the spectacle which is now unfolding. The past with its crimes, its follies and its tragedies, flashes away. I see the Russian soldiers standing on the threshold of their native land, guarding the fields which their fathers have tilled from time immemorial. I see them guarding their homes where mothers and wives pray – ah yes, for there are times when all pray – for the safety of their loved ones, the return of the breadwinner, of their champion, of their protector. I see the ten thousand villages of Russia, where the means of existence was wrung so hardly from the soil, but where there are still primordial human joys, where maidens laugh and children play. I see advancing upon all this in hideous onslaught the Nazi war machine, with its clanking, heel-clicking, dandified Prussian officers, its crafty expert agents fresh from the cowing and tying-down of a dozen countries. I see also the dull, drilled, docile, brutish masses of the Hun soldiery plodding on like a swarm of crawling locusts. I see the German bombers and fighters in the sky, still smarting from many a British whipping, delighted to find what they believe is an easier and a safer prey.

London, June 22, 1941

ALL THE GREAT THINGS ARE SIMPLE,

and many can be expressed in a single word:

Freedom; justice; honour; duty; mercy; hope.

The Royal Albert Hall, London, May 14, 1947

Sabotage

Can you doubt that times are grave when the word "sabotage" is used in accusation of one of the greatest powers of the world, both by Mr Marshall in the United States and by the Foreign Secretary in this House? Such language in any previous period would have been incompatible with the maintenance of any form of diplomatic relations between the countries affected.

Commons, January 23, 1948

Safety First

There is no less likely way of winning a war than to adhere pedantically to the maxim "safety first".

Commons, April 10, 1941

Sailors

I think it is a safe rule to treat the sailors of every country as equally brave and skilful.

Commons, March 16, 1939

The ultimate strategy of the British navy consists in basing contented men upon prosperous and healthy homes from which the children, generation after generation, can return to the ships which their fathers have taught them to honour.

Commons, March 26, 1913

Saint George

I have to speak to you about St George and the Dragon. I have been wondering what would happen if that legend were repeated under modern conditions.

St George would arrive in Cappadocia, accompanied not by a horse, but by a secretariat. He would be armed not with a lance, but with several flexible formulas. He would, of course, be welcomed by the local branch of the League of Nations Union. He would propose a conference with the dragon – a Round Table Conference, no doubt – that would be more convenient for the dragon's tail. He would make a trade agreement with the dragon. He would lend the dragon a lot of money of the Cappadocian taxpayers. The maiden's release would be referred to Geneva, the dragon reserving all his rights meanwhile. Finally, St George would be photographed with the dragon (inset – the maiden).

Royal Society of St George, London, April 24, 1933

Salvation

To work from weakness and fear is ruin. To work from wisdom and power may be salvation.

Saltram Park, Plymouth, July 15, 1950

Salvation of England

Nothing can save England if she will not save herself. If we lose faith in ourselves, in our capacity to guide and govern, if we lose our will to live, then indeed our story is told.

Royal Society of St George, London, April 24, 1933

Satellites of Germany

One by one, in rapid succession, the satellite states have writhed or torn themselves free from the Nazi tyranny, and, as is usual in such cases, the process has not been one from alliance with Germany to neutrality, but from alliance with Germany to war. This has taken place in Rumania and Bulgaria. Already there is fighting between the Finns and the Germans. The Germans, in accordance with their usual practice and character, are leaving a trail of burnt and blackened villages behind them, even in the land of their unhappy Finnish dupes.

Commons, September 28, 1944

Scandinavia, Invasion of

I consider that Hitler's action in invading Scandinavia is as great a strategic and political error as that which was committed by Napoleon in 1807, when he invaded Spain. Hitler has violated the independence and soil of virile peoples dwelling in very large and expansive countries capable of maintaining, with British and French aid, prolonged resistance to his soldiers and his Gestapo. He has almost doubled the efficiency of the allied blockade. He has made a whole series of commitments upon the Norwegian coast for which he will now have to fight, if necessary, during the whole summer, against powers possessing vastly superior naval forces and able to transport them to the scenes of action more easily than he can.

Commons, April 11, 1940

Schadenfreude

It is a strange and un-Christian habit of mind which makes it easier to endure misfortunes because one sees that others are having them inflicted on them too.

Liverpool, October 2, 1951

Scharnhorst and Gneisenau

I have read this document [Admiralty Report on the German battleships] to the House because I am anxious that Members should realize that our affairs are not conducted entirely by simpletons and dunderheads.

Commons, April 23, 1942

Schism

Sombre indeed would be the fortunes of mankind if some awful schism arose between the western democracies and the Russian Soviet Union, if the future world organization were rent asunder, and if new cataclysms of inconceivable violence destroyed all that is left of the treasures and liberties of mankind.

Commons, February 27, 1945

'Hitler has violated the independence and soil of virile peoples dwelling in very large and expansive countries'

Science

My experience – and it is somewhat considerable – is that in these matters when the need is clearly explained by military and political authorities, science is always able to provide something. "Seek and ye shall find" has been borne out.

Commons, June 7, 1935

Scientistic Government

On many occasions in the past we have seen attempts to rule the world by experts of one kind and another. There have been theocratic governments, military governments, and aristocratic governments. It is now suggested that we should have scientistic – not scientific – governments. It is the duty of scientists, like all other people, to serve the State and not to rule it because they are scientists. If they want to rule the State they must get elected to Parliament or win distinction in the Upper House and so gain access to some of the various administrations which are formed from time to time.

Commons, November 7, 1945

Scone, Stone of

The old quarrels, the age-old feuds which rent our island, have been ended centuries ago by the Union of the Crowns, and by the happy fulfilment of the prophecy, that wherever the Stone of Scone shall rest the Scottish race shall reign.

Usher Hall, Edinburgh, October 12, 1942

Sea, Command of the

So long as we keep command of the sea no descent upon Ireland is possible, and if ever we lost command of the sea it would not be upon Ireland that the descent would be made.

Commons, February 15, 1911

Sea-Power

For more than 300 years we alone amongst the nations have wielded that mysterious and decisive force which is called sea-power. What have we done with it? We have suppressed the slaver. We have charted the seas. We have made them a safe highway for all.

Commons, March 26, 1913

From Trafalgar and Waterloo to the first German war the British navy was supreme upon the seas. Our sea-power during the greater part of the nineteenth century equalled that of all other nations put together. Did we misuse that power? On the contrary, there never were so few warships afloat. History, which has been my guide and inspiration, will show the future ages that the control of the seas which the British held so long was used not for the exercise of warlike ambition, but to keep the peace, to suppress the slave trade and to make the seas safe for the commerce of all nations. All our ports, even our own coastwise trade, were opened to the entry and competition of men and goods from every land.

London, May 7, 1946

Searchlight Company

A friend of mine the other day saw a number of persons engaged in peculiar evolutions, genuflections and gestures ... He wondered whether it was some novel form of gymnastics, or a new religion ... or whether they were a party of lunatics out for an airing. They were a searchlight company of London Territorials, who were doing their exercises as well as they could without having the searchlight.

Commons, November 12, 1936

Security

We have never lived at anybody's mercy. We have never lived upon the good pleasure of any Continental nation in regard to our fundamental requirements. We have never entrusted the home defence of this country to any foreign power. We have never asked for any help from anyone. We have given help to many, but to make good the security of our own island we have asked for help from none.

Commons, March 8, 1934

Self-Reliance

There is no chance of making people self-reliant by confronting them with problems and with trials beyond their capacity to surmount. You do not make a man self-reliant by crushing him under a steam roller.

Norwich, July 26, 1909

Senior Service

It is always easier for the navy to get money than for the army.

Commons, May 17, 1916

Sense of Unity

Whether it be the ties of blood on my mother's side, or the friendships I have developed here over many years of active life, or the commanding sentiment of comradeship in the common cause of great peoples who speak the same language, who kneel at the same altars and, to a very large extent, pursue the same ideals, I cannot feel myself a stranger here in the centre and at the summit of the United States. I feel a sense of unity and fraternal association which, added to the kindliness of your welcome, convinces me that I have a right to sit at your fireside and share your Christmas joys.

The White House, Washington, DC, December 24, 1941

Sikorski, General

General Sikorski's name will long be remembered in history. His faith sustained Poland's spirit in her darkest hour. His courage inspired the Polish people to continue their long and relentless struggle against the German invader. His statesmanship had always in view allied unity in common action against Germany, and the restoration of Poland's independence and greatness. So long as his memory is cherished the accomplishment of the great work for which he gave his life will be assured.

London, July 5, 1944

Simplicity

All the great things are simple, and many can be expressed in a single word: Freedom; justice; honour; duty; mercy; hope.

The Royal Albert Hall, London, May 14, 1947

Singapore, Fall of

Singapore has fallen ... other dangers gather about us ... This, therefore, is one of those moments when the British race and nation can show the sheer quality of their genius. This is one of those moments when they can draw from the heart of misfortune the vital impulses of victory.

BBC, February 15, 1942

Tonight the Japanese are triumphant. They shout their exultation round the world. We suffer. We are taken aback. We are hard pressed. But I am sure even in this dark hour that "criminal madness" will be the verdict which history will pronounce upon the authors of Japanese aggression.

Commons, February 15, 1942

Sirens, Air-raid Warning

There is really no good sense in having these prolonged banshee howlings from sirens two or three times a day over wide areas, simply because hostile aircraft are flying to or from some target which no one can possibly know or even guess. All our precaution regulations have hitherto been based on this siren call, and I must say that one must admire the ingenuity of those who devised it as a means of spreading alarm. Indeed, most people now see how very wise Ulysses was when he stopped the ears of his sailors from all siren songs and had himself tied up firmly to the mast of duty.

Commons, September 5, 1940

Slavery, Ancient

The Greek and Latin philosophers often seem to have been unaware that the society in which they lived was founded upon slavery. They spoke of freedom and political institutions, but they were quite unaware that their culture was built upon detestable foundations.

University of Oslo, May 12, 1948

Smuts, Field-Marshal

In every way he seemed to be one of the most enlightened, courageous, and noble-minded men that we have known in these first fifty years of the twentieth century.

Commons, June 7, 1951

He and I are old comrades. I cannot say there has ever been a kick in our gallop. I was examined by him when I was a prisoner of war, and I escaped; but we made an honourable and generous peace on both sides, and for the last forty years we have been comrades working together.

Westminster Central Hall, London, October 31, 1942

Social Betterment

When I first became Lloyd George's friend and active associate, now more than forty years ago, this deep love of the people, the profound knowledge of their lives and of the undue and needless pressures under which they lived, impressed itself indelibly upon my mind.

Commons, March 28, 1945

Social Justice

At this moment in history the broad, toiling masses in every country have for the first time the opportunity of a fuller and less burdened life. Science is at hand to spread a more bountiful table than has ever been offered to the millions and to the tens of millions. Shorter hours of labour, greater assurances against individual misfortune: a wider if a simpler culture: a more consciously realized sense of social justice: an easier and a more equal society – these are the treasures which, after all these generations and centuries of impotence and confusion, are now within the reach of mankind.

Commons, May 9, 1938

Socialism

Socialism is inseparably interwoven with Totalitarianism and the abject worship of the State. ... This State is to be the arch-employer, the arch-

319

planner, the arch-administrator and ruler, and the arch-caucus-boss.

London, June 4, 1945

Socialism is the philosophy of failure, the creed of ignorance, and the gospel of envy.

Perth, May 28, 1948

Socialism is based on the idea of an all-powerful State which owns everything, which plans everything, which distributes everything, and thus through its politicians and officials decides the daily life of the individual citizen.

London, January 21, 1950

Socialists

A good many of those gentlemen who have delightful rosy views of a noble and brilliant future for the world are so remote from hard facts of daily life and of ordinary politics that I am not very sure that they will bring any useful or effective influence to bear upon the immediate course of events.

Kinnaird Hall, Dundee, May 14, 1908

Society

We must beware of trying to build a society in which nobody counts for anything except a politician or an official, a society where enterprise gains no reward and thrift no privileges.

BBC, March 21, 1943

The scheme of society for which Conservatives and National Liberals stand is the establishment and maintenance of a basic standard of life and labour below which a man or a woman, however old or weak, shall not be allowed to fall.

London, January 21, 1950

Solidarity

You would not expect the three great powers, so differently circumstanced as Britain, the United States, and Soviet Russia, not to have many different views about the treatment of the various and numerous countries into which their victorious arms have carried

'Socialism is the philosophy of failure, the creed of ignorance, and the gospel of envy'

them. The marvel is that all has hitherto been kept so solid, sure, and sound between us all. But this process does not arise of itself. It needs constant care and attention. Moreover, there are those problems of distance, occasion, and personalities which I have so often mentioned to the House, and which make it extremely difficult to bring the heads of the three principal Allies together in one place at one time. I have, therefore, not hesitated to travel from court to court like a wandering minstrel, always with the same song to sing – or the same set of songs.

Commons, October 27, 1944

Solidarity with America

Should the United States become involved in war with Japan, the British declaration will follow within the hour.

Commons, November 10, 1941

Solidarity of good people

When good people get into trouble because they are attacked and heavily smitten by the vile and wicked, they must be very careful not to get at loggerheads with one another. The common enemy is always trying to bring this about, and, of course, in bad luck a lot of things happen which play into the enemy's hands. We must just make the best of things as they come along.

BBC, October 21, 1940

Solutions

Perfect solutions of our difficulties are not to be looked for in an imperfect world.

Sheffield, April 17, 1951

Soul of Man

Laws just or unjust may govern men's actions. Tyrannies may restrain or regulate their words. The machinery of propaganda may pack their minds with falsehood and deny them truth for many generations of time. But the soul of man thus held in trance or frozen in a long night can be awakened by a spark coming from God knows where, and in a moment the whole structure of lies and oppression is on trial for its life.

Massachusetts Institute of Technology, Boston, March 31, 1949

Sovereignty

I am strongly of opinion that we require to strengthen our armaments in the air and upon the seas in order to make sure that we are still judges of our own fortunes, our own destinies, and our own action.

Commons, March 14, 1933

Soviet Russia

Here we have a State whose subjects are so happy that they have to be forbidden to quit its bounds under the direst penalties; whose diplomatists and agents sent on foreign missions have often to leave their wives and children at home as hostages to ensure their eventual return.

Commons, July 29, 1919

Profound changes have taken place in Soviet Russia. The Trotskyite form of Communism has been completely wiped out. The victories of the Russian armies have been attended by a great rise in the strength of the Russian State, and a remarkable broadening of its views. The religious side of Russian life has had a wonderful rebirth. The discipline and military etiquette of the Russian armies are unsurpassed. There is a new National Anthem, the music of which Marshal Stalin sent me, which I asked the BBC to play on the frequent occasions when there are great Russian victories to celebrate.

Commons, May 24, 1944

Spain

The Spaniards are a proud and morose people, and they have long memories. They have not forgotten Napoleon and the attempted French subjugation of Spain 130 years ago. Besides this, they have had a civil war which has cost them a million lives. Even the Communists in Spain will not thank foreign governments for trying to start another civil war, and anything more silly than to tell the Spaniards that they ought to overthrow Franco, while, at the same time, assuring them that there will be no military intervention by the Allies, can hardly be imagined.

Commons, June 5, 1946

There is no doubt that if Spain had yielded to German blandishments and pressure at that juncture our burden would have been much heavier. The Straits of Gibraltar would have been closed, and all access to Malta would have been cut off from the west. All the Spanish coast would have become the nesting-place of German U-boats. I certainly did not feel at the time that I should like to see any of these things happen, and none of them did happen.

Commons, May 24, 1944

Some people think that our foreign policy towards Spain is best expressed by drawing comical or even rude caricatures of General Franco; but I think there is more in it than that.

Commons, May 24, 1944

Spaniards

They do not want to go on killing each other for the entertainment of foreigners.

Commons, April 14, 1937

Speaker, The

The Speaker represents and embodies the spirit of the House of Commons; and that spirit, which has transported itself to so many lands and climates and to countries far outside our sphere, is one of the gleaming and enduring glories of the British and in a special way ... of the English message to the world.

Commons, November 15, 1951

Speech in Wartime

No sensible person in wartime makes speeches because he wants to. He makes them because he has to, and to no one does this apply more than to the Prime Minister. I have repeatedly called attention to the disadvantages of my having to give too frequent reviews of the war, and I have always declined to be drawn into discussions about strategy or tactics so far as they may have relation to current or pending events.

Commons, November 12, 1941

Speed

In the modern world everything moves quickly. Tendencies which 200 or 300 years ago worked out over several generations, may now reach definite decisions in a twelvemonth.

Commons, April 24, 1950

Spion Kop, Battle of

Rather more than three years previously I was present at the battle of Spion Kop and the fact that had struck me was on what tiny trifles the fortunes of battles depended. Had there been, on the morning of the battle of Spion Kop, a few good maps of the country with the troops, they could have taken up a position on Spion Kop as nearly impregnable as the one they did take up was untenable. The hill was held all day at a great sacrifice of life, and had there been a little oil to work the signalling lamps at night, so that communications might be kept up between Sir Charles Warren's headquarters and Colonel Thorneycroft on the hill, that sacrifice might have been taken advantage of and reinforcements sent up. I was very much impressed by that.

Commons, February 24, 1903

Spirit of Britain

Little does he [Hitler] know the spirit of the British nation, or the tough fibre of the Londoners, whose forebears played a leading part in the establishment of Parliamentary institutions and who have been bred to value freedom far above their lives. This wicked man, the repository and embodiment of many forms of soul-destroying hatred, this monstrous product of former wrongs and shame, has now resolved to try to break our famous island race by a process of indiscriminate slaughter and destruction. What he has done is to kindle a fire in British hearts, here and all over the world, which will glow long after all traces of the conflagration he has caused in London have been removed. He has lighted a fire which will burn with a steady and consuming flame until the last vestiges of Nazi tyranny have been burnt out of Europe, and until the Old World – and the New – can join hands to rebuild the temples of man's freedom and man's honour, upon foundations which will not soon or easily be overthrown.

London, September 11, 1940

Spur of Necessity

Many things which were attempted in the war we were told were technically impossible, but patience, perseverance, and above all, the spur of necessity under war conditions made men's brains act with greater vigour, and science responded to the demand. That being so, I venture to set the research side of air defence in a position of primary importance. I agree that there is nothing which can offer any substitute for an equal or superior force, a readiness to retaliate, but if you could discover some new method the whole of our affairs would be greatly simplified.

Commons, June 7, 1935

Squandermania

The Right Hon Member for Caernarvon Boroughs [Mr David Lloyd George] is going to borrow £200,000,000 and to spend it … upon paying the unemployed to make racing tracks for well-to-do motorists to make the ordinary pedestrian skip; and we are assured that the mere prospect of this has entirely revivified the Liberal Party. At any rate, it has brought

'What he [Hitler] has done is to kindle a fire in British hearts which will glow long after the conflagration he has caused'

one notable recruit. Lord Rothermere, chief author of the anti-waste campaign, has enlisted under the Happy Warrior of Squandermania.

Commons, April 15, 1929

Stability

One side claims to be the party of progress, as if progress was bound to be right, no matter in what direction. The other side emphasizes stability, which is also very important in this changing world.

Commons, November 11, 1947

Stake, The

If the co-operation between the United States and the British Empire in the task of extirpating the spirit and regime of Totalitarian intolerance, wherever it may be found, were to fail, the British Empire, rugged and embattled, might indeed hew its way through and preserve the life and strength of our own country and our own empire for the inevitable renewal of the conflict on worse terms, after an uneasy truce. But the chance of setting the march of mankind clearly and surely along the high roads of human progress would be lost, and might never return.

Speech in London at a Luncheon of the Pilgrims, January 9, 1941

Stalin

He is a man of massive outstanding personality, suited to the sombre and stormy times in which his life has been cast; a man of inexhaustible courage and will-power, and a man direct and even blunt in speech, which, having been brought up in the House of Commons, I do not mind at all, especially when I have something to say of my own. Above all, he is a man with that saving sense of humour which is of high importance to all men and all nations, but particularly to great men and great nations. Stalin also left upon me the impression of a deep, cool wisdom, and a complete absence of illusions of any kind.

Commons, September 8, 1942

Standard Bearer

I have naturally considered very carefully what is my own duty in these times. It would be easy for me to retire gracefully in an odour of civic freedoms, and this plan crossed my mind frequently some months ago. I feel now however that the situation is so serious and what may have to come so grave, that I am resolved to go forward carrying the flag as long as I have the necessary strength and energy, and have your confidence. It is of the highest importance to our name and endurance as a great power, and to the cohesion of our national and imperial life, that there should be re-established at the earliest moment some poise and balance between the political forces in our island, and that those who were so unexpectedly clad with overwhelming Parliamentary power should be made to realize that they are the servants, and not the masters, of the British nation.

Blackpool, October 5, 1946

State Buying

State buying has provoked State selling. It has brought national feelings into what ought to be ordinary commercial dealings. Governments flourish their national flag at each other before they can even buy or sell a pig or a cow.

Liverpool, October 2, 1951

State Socialists

Collective ideologists – those professional intellectuals who revel in decimals and polysyllables.

Margate, October 10, 1953

States, Small

I do not take the view which was fashionable some time ago that the day of the small States is ended, and that the modern world can only adapt itself to great empires.

Brussels, November 16, 1952

Statesmen, Victorian

The statesmen whom I saw in those days seemed to tower above the general level in a most impressive way. The tests were keener, the standards were higher, and those who surmounted them were men it was a treat and honour to meet. They were the representatives of an age of ordered but unceasing movement. Liberalism had stricken the shackles off the slave and broken down the barriers of privilege. The road was open to those of the highest natural quality and ability who chose to tread it.

Commons, December 6, 1950

Steel Helmets

The story of the steel helmets is one which reflects very little credit upon the perspicacity of our administration. We were about six months behind the French and even the Belgian army in the general adoption of this valuable means of protection.

Commons, July 24, 1916

Step, Wrong

It is not very easy to retrace a wrong step in politics.

Commons, February 22, 1906

Strain

To maintain 50,000 or 60,000 men as we have done for nearly 100 years in India has been an extraordinary strain upon this island. It is like holding a dumbbell at arm's length.

Commons, December 1, 1948

Strong, The

It is better for the strong to help the weak than for the weak to hinder the strong.

Huddersfield, October 15, 1951

Sublime Hour

This is one of the most awe-striking periods in the long history of France and Britain. It is also beyond doubt the most sublime. Side by side, unaided except by their kith and kin in the great Dominions and by the wide empires which rest beneath their shield – side by side, the British and French peoples have advanced to rescue not only Europe but mankind from the foulest and most soul-destroying tyranny which has ever darkened and stained the pages of history. Behind them – behind us – behind the armies and fleets of Britain and France – gather a group of shattered states and bludgeoned races: the Czechs, the Poles, the Norwegians, the Danes, the Dutch, the Belgians – upon all of whom the long night of barbarism will descend, unbroken even by a star of hope, unless we conquer, as conquer we must; as conquer we shall.

London, May 19, 1940

Sublime Task

To rebuild Europe from its ruins and make its light shine forth again upon the world, we must first of all conquer ourselves. It is in this way only that the sublime, with its marvellous transmutations of material things, can be brought into our daily life.

The Hague, May 7, 1948

Submarine Service

There is no branch of His Majesty's Forces which in this war has suffered the same proportion of fatal loss as our submarine service. It is the most dangerous of all the services. That is perhaps the reason why the First Lord tells me that entry into it is keenly sought by officers and men.

Commons, September 9, 1941

British submarines suffer from the serious disadvantage that they have very few targets to attack. They are not allowed, by the custom of the sea and by the conventions to which we have subscribed, to sink merchant ships without warning, or without being able to provide for the safety of the merchant crews. British submarines do not wage war on neutral vessels. They do not attack humble fishing boats.

London, December 18, 1939

'British submarines do not wage war on neutral vessels. They do not attack humble fishing boats'

Submission

Can peace, goodwill, and confidence be built upon submission to wrong-doing backed by force? One may put this question in the largest form. Has any benefit or progress ever been achieved by the human race by submission to organized and calculated violence?

London, October 16, 1938

Sudetenland

We in this country, as in other Liberal and democratic countries, have a perfect right to exalt the principle of self-determination, but it comes ill out of the mouths of those in Totalitarian States who deny even the smallest element of toleration to every section and creed within their bounds. But, however you put it, this particular block of land, this mass of human beings to be handed over, has never expressed the desire to go into the Nazi rule. I do not believe that even now, if their opinion could be asked, they would exercise such an opinion.

Commons, October 5, 1938

Suez Canal

The strategic importance of Egypt and the Canal has been enormously reduced by modern developments of war.

Commons, July 14, 1954

Sunlight

We shall go forward together. The road upward is strong. There are upon our journey dark and dangerous valleys through which we have to make and fight our way. But it is sure and certain that if we persevere, and we shall persevere, we shall come through these dark and dangerous valleys into a sunlight broader and more genial and more lasting than mankind has ever known.

Leeds, May 16, 1942

T

WE SHALL NOT FAIL OR FALTER.

We shall not weaken
or tire. Neither the
sudden shock of battle,
nor the long-drawn trials
of vigilance and exertion
will wear us down.

Give us the tools, and we will finish
the job.

London, February 9, 1941

Tank, The

In the last war, tanks were built to go three or four miles an hour and to stand up to rifle or machine-gun bullets. In the interval the process of mechanical science had advanced so much that it became possible to make a tank which could go 15, 20, or 25 miles an hour and stand up to cannon fire. That was a great revolution, by which Hitler has profited. That is a simple fact which was perfectly well known to the military and technical services three or four years before the war. It did not spring from German brains. It sprang from British brains, and from brains like those of General de Gaulle in France, and it has been exploited and turned to our grievous injury by the uninventive but highly competent and imitative Germans.

Commons, May 7, 1941

How do you make a tank? People design it, they argue about it, they plan it and make it, and then you take the tank and test and re-test it. When you have got it absolutely settled then, and only then, you go into production. But we have never been able to indulge in the luxury of that precise and leisurely process. We have had to take it straight off the drawing-board and go into full production, and take the chance of the many errors which the construction will show coming out after hundreds and thousands of them have been made.

Commons, July 2, 1942

Teaching

I am always ready to learn, although I do not always like being taught.

Commons, November 4, 1952

Technicians

We want a lot of engineers in the modern world, but we do not want a world of engineers. We want some scientists, but we must keep them in their proper place.

University of London, November 18, 1948

Tempest of War

When I look back on the perils which have been overcome, upon the great mountain waves through which the gallant ship has driven, when I remember all that has gone wrong, and remember also all that has gone right, I feel sure we have no need to fear the tempest. Let it roar, and let it rage. We shall come through.

Commons, May 7, 1941

Territory, Transference of

The sentence I myself contributed to the Atlantic Charter, about no transference of territory apart from the will of the local inhabitants, has proved, in many cases, to be an unattainable ideal and, in any case, did not, in my experience, apply to enemy countries.

Commons, June 5, 1946

Terror and Peace

Moralists may find it a melancholy thought that peace can find no nobler foundations than mutual terror.

Commons, March 5, 1952

Terrorists, Dealing with

No country in the world is less fit for a conflict with terrorists than Great Britain. That is not because of her weakness or cowardice; it is because of her restraint and virtues, and the way of life in which we have lived so long in this sheltered island.

Commons, January 31, 1947

Teutonic Urge

We war against tyranny, and we seek to preserve ourselves from destruction. I am convinced that the British, American, and Russian peoples, who have suffered measureless waste, peril and bloodshed twice in a quarter of a century through the Teutonic urge of domination, will this time take steps to put it beyond the power of Prussia or of all Germany to come at them again with pent-up vengeance and long-nurtured plans.

Commons, September 21, 1943

Thanksgiving

It is a poor heart that never rejoices; but our thanksgiving, however fervent, must be brief.

US Congress, Washington, DC, May 19, 1943

Third Front, The

Personally, I always think of the Third Front as well as the Second Front. I have always thought that the western democracies should be like a boxer who fights with two hands and not one.

I firmly believe that the great flanking movement into North Africa, made under the authority of President Roosevelt and of His Majesty's Government, for whom I am a principal agent, will be regarded in the after time as quite a good thing to do in all the circumstances.

London, August 31, 1943

Thirty Years War

We are faced, not with the prospect of a new war, but with something very like the possibility of a resumption of the war which ended in November 1918.

Commons, March 19, 1935

Thrall, German

Now we are reaching a period when the Germans will be conquered completely, and Europe will be entirely liberated from their thrall.

The brutal hosts which marched so enthusiastically upon us, their eyes alive with greed and the passion of war and the earnest desire for mastery over others, have reached a time when they will be added to those long, melancholy, and humiliating streams of prisoners who, having done the worst to the world, have no hope but in its mercy.

Bristol University, April 21, 1945

Tidiness

Tidiness is a virtue, symmetry is often a constituent of beauty.

Commons, October 22, 1945

Time

Up to the present, time has been on our side, but time is a changeable ally. He may be with you in one period and against you in another, and then if you come through that other, he may return again more faithful than before.

Commons, March 30, 1940

Time of Fear

When danger is at a distance, when there is plenty of time to make the necessary preparations, when you can bend twigs instead of having to break massive boughs – it is right, indeed it is a duty, to sound the alarm. But when danger comes very near, when it is plain that not much more can be done in the time that may be available, it is no service to dwell upon the shortcomings or neglects of those who have been responsible. The time to be frightened is when evils can be remedied; when they cannot be fully remedied they must be faced with courage. When danger is far off we may think of our weakness; when it is near we must not forget our strength.

City Carlton Club, London, June 28, 1939

Time, March of

Things happen so quickly nowadays, and there are such a lot of them going on, that one finds it somewhat difficult to measure evenly the march of time. For myself, I can say there are weeks which seem to pass in a flash and then again there are others which are unutterably long and slow. At times it is almost difficult to believe that so much has happened and at another that so little time has passed.

Mansion House, London, November 9, 1940

Time and Money

Time and money are largely interchangeable terms.

Commons, July 19, 1926

Times, The

The Times is speechless, and takes three columns to express its speechlessness. [Over Irish Home Rule.]

Kinnaird Hall, Dundee, May 14, 1908

Tito

I am the earliest outside supporter of Marshal Tito. It is more than a year since in this House I extolled his guerilla virtues to the world. Some of my best friends and the Hon and gallant Member for Preston [The Prime Minister's son, Major Churchill] are there with him or his forces now. I earnestly hope he may prove to be the saviour and the unifier of his country, as he is undoubtedly at this time its undisputed master.

Commons, January 18, 1942

Tobruk

Historians may explain Tobruk. The Eighth Army has done better; it has avenged it.

Commons, November 11, 1942

It was in this House that I got the news of the fall of Tobruk. I don't think any Englishman in the United States has ever been so unhappy as I was that day; certainly no Englishman since General Burgoyne surrendered at Saratoga.

Washington, DC, May 25, 1943

Tojo, Admiral

The reverberations of the events in Japan, the sense of growing weakness on the sea and in the air, the sense of the vain dispersal of their forces and of economic tribulation at home, have produced the fall of Admiral Tojo, the chief war leader of Japan, whose accomplice and close colleague, Admiral Yamamoto, declared at one time that he would dictate his terms of peace to the United States in Washington. It is not easy for us here to measure the character of the seismic forces which have produced this remarkable political and military convulsion in Japan, but it can hardly arise from a conviction among the Japanese that Admiral Yamamoto's programme is being realized as fully as he and Admiral Tojo had expected. I must repeat that I am increasingly led to believe that the interval between the defeat of Hitler and the defeat of Japan will be shorter – perhaps much shorter – than I at one time had supposed.

Commons, August 2, 1944

Too late

Two years ago it was safe [to stand up to the dictators], three years ago it was easy, and four years ago a mere dispatch might have rectified the position. But where shall we be a year hence? Where shall we be in 1940?

Commons, March 24, 1938

Tools for the Job

We shall not fail or falter. We shall not weaken or tire. Neither the sudden shock of battle, nor the long-drawn trials of vigilance and exertion will wear us down. Give us the tools, and we will finish the job.

London, February 9, 1941

Total War

Harsh as it may seem to say, a terrible thing to say in dealing with our own precious flesh and blood, it is our interest and the American interest that the whole western front, and the air everywhere at all possible flying times, should be in continuous action against the enemy, burning and bleeding his strength away at every opportunity and on all occasions, if we are to bring this horror to an end.

Commons, January 18, 1945.

Trade Overseas

Exports are only the steam over the boiling water in the kettle. They are only that part of the iceberg that glitters above the surface of the ocean.

Commons, October 28, 1947

Trade Unions

The trade unions of this country have made an outstanding contribution to the war effort.

London, February 6, 1945

I have always been a firm supporter of British trade unionism. I believe it to be the only foundation upon which the relations of employers and employed can be harmoniously adjusted.

Woodford Green, July 10, 1948

Tradition

I confess myself to be a great admirer of tradition. The longer you can look back, the farther you can look forward. This is not a philosophical or political argument – any oculist will tell you this is true. The wider the span, the longer the continuity, the greater is the sense of duty in individual men and women, each contributing their brief life's work to the preservation and progress of the land in which they live, the society of which they are members, and the world of which they are the servants.

Royal College of Physicians, March 2, 1944

Tragedy averted

The long and terrible march which the rescuing Powers are making is being accomplished stage by stage, and we can now say, not only with hope but with reason, that we shall reach the end of our journey in good order, and that the tragedy which threatened the whole world and might have put out all its lights and left our children and descendants in darkness and bondage – perhaps for centuries – that tragedy will not come to pass.

London, March 26, 1944

Trinity Sunday

Today is Trinity Sunday. Centuries ago words were written to be a call and a spur to the faithful servants of Truth and Justice: "Arm yourselves, and be ye men of valour, and be in readiness for the conflict; for it is better for us to perish in battle than to look upon the outrage of our nation and our altar. As the Will of God is in Heaven, even so let it be."

London, May 19, 1940

Trouble

If we proceed to argue on lines which have no connection with reality, we shall get into trouble.

Commons, March 14, 1933

Truth

This truth is incontrovertible. Panic may resent it; ignorance may deride it; malice may distort it; but there it is.

Commons, May 17, 1915

Tunis, Battle of

It is, indeed, quite remarkable that the Germans should have shown themselves ready to run the risk and pay the price required of them by their struggle to hold the Tunisian tip. While I always hesitate to say anything which might afterwards look like over-confidence, I cannot resist the remark that one seems to discern in this policy the touch of the master hand, the same master hand that planned the attack on Stalingrad, and that has brought upon the German armies the greatest disaster they have ever suffered in all their military history.

Commons, February 11, 1943

Tyranny

> Tyranny presents itself in various forms but it is always the same, whatever slogans it utters, whatever name it calls itself by, whatever liveries it wears. It is always the same and makes a demand on all free men to risk and do all in their power to withstand it.
>
> *Amsterdam, May 9, 1948*

We do not war primarily with races as such. Tyranny is our foe: whatever trappings or disguise it wears, whatever language it speaks, be it external or internal, we must forever be on our guard, ever mobilized, ever vigilant, always ready to spring at its throat. In all this we march together. Not only do we march and strive shoulder to shoulder at this moment under the fire of the enemy on the fields of war or in the air, but also in those realms of thought which are consecrated to the rights and the dignity of man.

Harvard University, September 6, 1943

ONE FAULT, ONE CRIME, AND ONE CRIME ONLY,

can rob the United Nations and the British people of the victory upon which their lives and honour depend.

A weakening in our purpose and therefore in our unity – that is the mortal crime.

London, February 15, 1942

U-boat Peril

Owing to past neglect in the face of the plainest warnings, we have now entered upon a period of danger greater than has befallen Britain since the U-boat campaign was crushed; perhaps, indeed, it is a more grievous period than that, because at that time at least we were possessed of the means of securing ourselves and of defeating that campaign. Now we have no such assurance.

Commons, November 12, 1936

'The first of all our dangers is the U-boat peril. Our food, our means of making war, our life, all depend upon the passage of ships across the sea'

The first of all our dangers is the U-boat peril. That is a very great danger. Our food, our means of making war, our life, all depend upon the passage of ships across the sea. The whole power of the United States to manifest itself in this war depends upon the power to move ships across the sea. Their mighty power is restricted, it is restricted by those very oceans which have protected them. The oceans which were their shield have now become a bar, a prison house, through which they are struggling to bring armies, fleets, and air forces to bear upon the great common problems we have to face. Now we see our way through. I say that with all solemnity and sobriety: we see our way through. Although it is true that there will be many more U-boats working next year than there are now, and there may be 300 to 400 at work now, yet we have a vast construction of escort vessels, submarine-hunting vessels, afloat, as well as replacements of merchant ships; in the United States, which has resources in steel far greater than ours and which is not so closely and deeply involved at present, a programme on astronomical lines has been developed and is being carried forward in the construction both of escort vessels and of merchant ships. But what a terrible waste it is to think of all these great ships that are sunk, full of priceless cargoes, and how necessary it is to make that extra intensification of effort which will enable us to get ahead and to establish more complete mastery and to save these ships from being sunk, as well as to add new ones to the fleet, by which alone the victory of the good cause can be achieved.

Westminster Central Hall, London, October 31, 1942

The Royal Navy has immediately attacked the U-boats, and is hunting them night and day – I will not say without mercy, because God forbid we should ever part company with that, but at any rate with zeal and not altogether without relish.

BBC, October 1, 1939.

Ulterior Motives

There was a custom in ancient China that everyone who wished to criticize the Government had the right to memorialize the Emperor, and provided he followed that up by committing suicide, very great respect was paid to his words, and no ulterior motive was assigned. That seems to me to have been, from many points of view, a wise custom, but I certainly would be the last to suggest that it should be made retrospective.

Commons, November 12, 1941.

Unanimity

Parliament does not rest on unanimity. Democratic assemblies do not act on unanimity. They act by majorities.

Commons, September 21, 1945

Unconditional Surrender

It was only after full and cold, sober, and mature consideration of all these facts, on which our lives and liberties certainly depend, that the President, with my full concurrence as agent of the War Cabinet, decided that the note of the Casablanca Conference should be the unconditional surrender of all our foes. Our inflexible insistence upon unconditional surrender does not mean that we shall stain our victorious arms by any cruel treatment of whole populations. But justice must be done upon the wicked and the guilty, and within her proper bounds, justice must be stern and implacable.

Commons, February 11, 1943

Peace, though based on unconditional surrender, will bring to Germany and Japan an immense, immediate amelioration of the suffering and agony which now lie before them. We, the allies, are no monsters, but faithful men trying to carry forward the light of the world, trying to raise, from the bloody welter and confusion in which mankind is now plunged, a structure of peace, of freedom, of justice, and of law, which system shall be an abiding and lasting shelter for all.

Commons, January 18, 1945

The policy of unconditional surrender does not exclude unconditional surrender piecemeal. It does not necessarily apply wholesale.

Commons, April 12, 1945

I am not of the opinion that a demand for unconditional surrender will prolong the war. Anyhow, the war will be prolonged until unconditional surrender has been obtained.

Commons, January 16, 1945

Understatement

It is always, I think, true to say that one of the main foundations of the British sense of humour is understatement.

Commons, July 27, 1950

Uneasiness

I was asked last week whether I was aware of some uneasiness which it

'Victory is traditionally elusive. Accidents happen. Mistakes are made. War is very difficult, especially to those who are taking part in it or conducting it'

was said existed in the country on account of the gravity, as it was described, of the war situation. So I thought it would be a good thing to go and see for myself what this "uneasiness" amounted to, and I went to some of our great cities and seaports which had been most heavily bombed, and to some of the places where the poorest people had got it worst. I have come back not only reassured, but refreshed. To leave the offices in Whitehall with their ceaseless hum of activity and stress, and to go out to the front, by which I mean the streets and wharves of London and Liverpool, Manchester, Cardiff, Swansea or Bristol, is like going out of a hothouse on to the bridge of a fighting ship. It is a tonic, which I should recommend any who are suffering from fretfulness to take in strong doses when they have need of it.

London, April 27, 1941

Unemployment

The best way to insure against unemployment is to have no unemployment.

London, March 21, 1943

Unexpected, The

Very few set-piece battles that have to be prepared over a long period of time work out in the way they are planned and imagined beforehand. The unexpected intervenes at every stage. The will-power of the enemy impinges itself upon the prescribed or hoped-for course of events. Victory is traditionally elusive. Accidents happen. Mistakes are made. Sometimes right things turn out wrong, and quite often wrong things turn out right. War is very difficult, especially to those who are taking part in it or conducting it.

Commons, December 11, 1941

United Nations

One fault, one crime, and one crime only, can rob the United Nations and the British people, upon whose constancy this grand alliance came into being, of the victory upon which their lives and honour depend. A weakening in our purpose and therefore in our unity – that is the mortal crime. Whoever is guilty of that crime, or of bringing it about in others, of him let it be said that it were better for him that a millstone were hanged about his neck and he were cast into the sea.

London, February 15, 1942

United States

During the last year we have gained by our bearing and conduct a potent hold upon the sentiments of the people of the United States. Never, never in our history, have we been held in such admiration and regard across the Atlantic Ocean. In that great Republic, now in much travail and stress of soul, it is customary to use all the many valid, solid arguments about American interests and American safety, which depend upon the destruction of Hitler and his foul gang and even fouler doctrines. But in the long run – believe me, for I know – the action of the United States will be dictated, not by methodical calculations of profit and loss, but by moral sentiment, and by that gleaming flash of resolve which lifts the

'The workshop and the fighting line are one. All may fall, all will stand together. We must aid each other, we must stand by each other'

hearts of men and nations, and springs from the spiritual foundations of human life itself.

London, April 27, 1941

The United States have an immense interest in the prosperity of Great Britain and of the British Empire, and their own prosperity could not survive for many years in the midst of a ruined world or in the presence of a ruined and broken Britain. It is in the working of these practical forces that we must put our trust for the future, and I am sure that it is along such paths, and through such influences, that a happy outcome will eventually be reached. United, these two countries can, without the slightest injury to other nations or to themselves, almost double each other's power and safety.

Commons, December 6, 1945

The people of the United States cannot escape world responsibility. Although we live in a period so tumultuous that little can be predicted, we may be quite sure that this process will be intensified with every forward step the United States make in wealth and in power. Not only are the responsibilities of this great Republic growing, but the world over which they range is itself contracting in relation to our powers of locomotion at a positively alarming rate.

Harvard University, September 6, 1943

Unity

This is a very hard war. Its numerous and fearful problems reach down to the very foundations of human society. Its scope is world wide, and it involves all nations and every man, woman and child in them. Strategy and economics are interwoven. Sea, land and air are but a single service. The latest refinements of science are linked with the cruelties of the Stone Age. The workshop and the fighting line are one. All may fall, all will stand together. We must aid each other, we must stand by each other.

Caxton Hall, London, March 26, 1942

Unknown, The

I know of nothing more remarkable in our long history than the willingness to encounter the unknown, and to face and endure whatever might be coming to us, which was shown in September by the whole mass of the people of this island in the discharge of what they felt sure was their duty. There never was a war which seemed so likely to carry its terrors at once into every home, and there never was a war to which the whole people entered with the same united conviction that, God helping, they could do no other.

Free Trade Hall, Manchester, January 27, 1940

USE

We must build a kind of United States of Europe.

Zürich, September 19, 1946

Utopia, Communist

In the Communist sect it is a matter of religion to sacrifice one's native land for the sake of the Communist Utopia. People who, in ordinary life, would behave in a quite honourable manner, if they are infected with the disease of the mind, will not hesitate a moment to betray their country or its secrets.

Commons, June 5, 1946

YOU ASK, WHAT IS OUR AIM?

I can answer in one word: Victory – victory at all costs, victory in spite of all terror,

victory however long and hard the road may be; for without victory there is no survival.

Commons, May 13, 1940

Vegetarians

Everyone knows the distinguished talents which the Right Hon Gentleman [Sir Stafford Cripps] brings unstintedly to the services of his fellow countrymen. No one has made more sustained exertions to contribute to the common pot and few take less out of it than he does. I have got my vegetarian too, my honoured friend Lord Cherwell. These etheral beings certainly do produce a very high level and a very great volume of intellectual output, with the minimum of working costs in fuel.

Commons, December 6, 1945

Vengeance

Nothing is more costly, nothing is more sterile, than vengeance.

Commons, June 5, 1946

Verdict

We shall not be judged by the criticisms of our opponents but by the consequences of our acts.

Commons, April 22, 1926

Veto in the UN

It was never contemplated at any time that the veto should be used in the abrupt, arbitrary and almost continuous manner that we have seen it used, but that it should be reserved as a last assurance to a great power that they would not be voted down on a matter about which they are prepared to fight.

Commons, October 23, 1946

Vices and Virtues

The inherent vice of Capitalism is the unequal sharing of blessings; the inherent virtue of Socialism is the equal sharing of miseries.

Commons, October 22, 1945

Vichy France

I never had the slightest doubt myself that Hitler would break the

Armistice, overrun all France and try to capture the French fleet at Toulon; such developments were to be welcome by the United Nations, because they entailed the extinction for all practical purposes of the sorry farce and fraud of the Vichy Government. This was a necessary prelude to that reunion of France without which French resurrection is impossible. We have taken a long step towards that unity. The artificial division between occupied and unoccupied territory has been swept away. In France all Frenchmen are equally under the German yoke, and will learn to hate it with equal intensity. Abroad, all Frenchmen will fire at the common foe. We may be sure that, after what has happened, the ideals and the spirit of what we have called Fighting France will exercise a dominating influence upon the whole French nation.

London, November 29, 1942

Victors Vanquished

Now the victors are the vanquished, and those who threw down their arms in the field and sued for an armistice are striding on to world mastery.

Commons, March 24, 1938

Victory

I have never promised anything but blood, tears, toil, and sweat. Now, however, we have a new experience. We have victory – a remarkable and definite victory. The bright gleam has caught the helmets of our soldiers, and warmed and cheered all our hearts.

Mansion House, London, November 10, 1942

Let us be of good cheer. Both in the west and in the east overwhelming forces are ranged on our side. Military victory may be distant, it will certainly be costly, but it is no longer in doubt. The physical and scientific force which our foes hurled upon us in the early years has changed sides, and the British Commonwealth, the United States and the Soviet Union undoubtedly possess the power to beat down to the ground, in dust and ashes, the prodigious might of the war-making nations and the conspiracies which assailed us. But, as the sense of mortal peril has passed from our side to that of our cruel foes, they gain the stimulus of despair, and we tend to lose the bond of combined self-preservation, or are in danger of losing it.

Commons, January 18, 1945

We have before us an ordeal of the most grievous kind. We have before us many, many long months of struggle and of suffering. You ask, what is our policy? I will say: It is to wage war, by sea, land and air, with all our might and with all the strength that God can give us: to wage war against a monstrous tyranny, never surpassed in the dark, lamentable catalogue of human crime. That is our policy. You ask, what is our aim? I can answer in one word: Victory – victory at all costs, victory in spite of all terror, victory however long and hard the road may be; for without victory there is no survival.

Commons, May 13, 1940

There are two maxims which should always be acted upon in the hour of victory. All history, all experience, all the fruits of reasoning alike enjoin them upon us. They are almost truisms. They are so obvious that I hardly dare to mention them to the House. But here they are. The first is, "Do not be carried away by success into demanding more than is right or prudent." The second is, "Do not disband your army until you have got your terms."

Commons, March 3, 1919

Vigour

We should lay aside every hindrance; and endeavour, by uniting the whole force and spirit of our people, to raise again a great British nation standing up before all the world. For such a nation, rising in its ancient vigour, can even at this hour save civilization.

Commons, March 24, 1938

THEN HITLER MADE HIS SECOND BLUNDER.

He forgot about the winter.

Hitler forgot about this Russian winter. He must have been very loosely educated. I have never made such a bad mistake as that.

London, May 10, 1942

War

In the main, war consists of the same tunes, played through the ages, though sometimes only on a reed flute or a bagpipe and sometimes through a full modern orchestra.

London, July 4, 1950

War Aims

Thoughtless, dilettante, or purblind wordlings sometimes ask us: "What is it that Britain and France are fighting for?" To this I answer: "If we left off fighting you would soon find out."

BBC, March 30, 1940

I have, as the House knows, hitherto consistently deprecated the formulation of peace aims or war aims – however you put it – by His Majesty's Government, at this stage. I deprecate it at this time, when the end of the war is not in sight, when the conflict sways to and fro with alternating fortunes, and when conditions and associations at the end of the war are unforeseeable.

Commons, September 9, 1941

We seek no profit, we covet no territory or aggrandizement. We expect no reward and we will accept no compromise. It is on that footing that we wish to be judged, first in our own consciences and afterwards by posterity.

Commons, June 8, 1943

There is only one thing certain about war, that it is full of disappointments and also full of mistakes.

London, April 27, 1941

War is very cruel. It goes on for so long.

Commons, April 14, 1937

> # War never pays its dividends in cash on the money it costs.
>
> *Commons, July 17, 1901*

Twice the United States has had to send several millions of its young men across the Atlantic to find the war; but now war can find any nation, wherever it may dwell, between dusk and dawn.

Westminster College, Fulton, Missouri, March 5, 1946

War is a hard school, but the British, once compelled to go there, are attentive pupils.

Commons, August 2, 1944

Wars come very suddenly. I have lived through a period when one looked forward, as we do now, with anxiety and uncertainty to what would happen in the future. Suddenly something did happen – tremendous, swift, over-powering, irresistible.

Commons, February 7, 1934

War Casualties

In the last war [1914–1918] millions of men fought by hurling enormous masses of steel at one another. "Men and shells" was the cry, and prodigious slaughter was the consequence. In this war nothing of this kind has yet appeared. It is a conflict of strategy, of organization, of technical apparatus, of science, mechanics, and morale. The British casualties in the first 12 months of the Great War amounted to 365,000. In this war, I am thankful to say, British killed, wounded, prisoners and missing, including civilians, do not exceed 92,000, and of these a large proportion are alive as prisoners of war. Looking more widely around, one may say that throughout Europe for one man killed or wounded in the first year perhaps five were killed or wounded in 1914–1915.

Commons, August 20, 1940

War Cemeteries

There is really no limitation to the number of different ways in which the desire to show reverence and affection to the memory of the fallen, and to preserve that memory, have manifested themselves. But the great mass of those who fell could not indulge in expensive monuments, and the thing that is deeply ingrained in soldierly breasts is that all should be treated alike, general and private, prince and peasant, all who lie there in common honour, and that the wealthy should forgo in this matter that which their wealth would enable them to obtain.

Commons, December 17, 1919

War Debts

I have always held the view that these war debts and reparations have been a great curse.

Commons, July 11, 1932

War, Duration of

Directions have been given by the Government to prepare for a war of at least three years. That does not mean that victory may not be gained in a shorter time. How soon it will be gained depends upon how long Herr Hitler and his group of wicked men, whose hands are stained with blood and soiled with corruption, can keep their grip upon the docile, unhappy German people. It was for Hitler to say when the war would begin; but it is not for him or for his successors to say when it will end.

Commons, October 1, 1939

War, Fruits of

I do not believe that Soviet Russia desires war. What they desire is the fruits of war and the indefinite expansion of their power and doctrines.

Westminster College, Fulton, Missouri, March 5, 1946

'Safety will be the sturdy child of terror, and survival the twin brother of annihilation'

War of the Future

It may well be that we shall by a process of sublime irony have reached a stage in this story where safety will be the sturdy child of terror, and survival the twin brother of annihilation.

Commons, March 1, 1955

War Propaganda

When Herr Goebbels's Nazi propaganda blares and blethers upon the ether that Britain and France have lost the capacity to make war if it is forced upon them, we do not get angry because we know it is not true. We know that our sufferings will be very hard and we are determined not to be guilty of bringing about a crash, the consequences of which no man can measure. We know also that we could only throw ourselves into such a struggle if our consciences were clear.

City Carlton Club, London, June 28, 1939

War Machine

Hitler is a monster of wickedness, insatiable in his lust for blood and plunder. Not content with having all Europe under his heel, or else terrorized into various forms of abject submission, he must now carry his work of butchery and desolation among the vast multitudes of Russia and of Asia. The terrible military machine, which we and the rest of the civilized world so foolishly, so supinely, so insensately, allowed the Nazi gangsters to build up year by year from almost nothing, cannot stand idle lest it rust or fall to pieces. It must be in continual motion, grinding up human lives and trampling down the homes and the rights of hundreds of millions of men. Moreover it must be fed, not only with flesh but with oil.

London, June 22, 1941

War Office

I am going to do something that has never been done before, and I hope the House will not be shocked at the breach of precedent. I am going to make public a word of praise for the War Office. In all the forty years I have served in this House I have heard that Department steadily abused before, during, and after our various wars. And if my memory serves me aright I have frequently taken part in the well-merited criticism which was their lot.

Commons, August 2, 1944

War Policy

I say, let pre-war feuds die; let personal quarrels be forgotten, and let us keep our hatreds for the common enemy. Let Party interest be ignored, let all our energies be harnessed, let the whole ability and forces of the nation be hurled into the struggle, and let all the strong horses be pulling on the collar. At no time in the last war were we in greater peril than we are now, and I urge the House strongly to deal with these matters not in a precipitate vote, ill debated and on a widely discursive field, but in grave time and due time in accordance with the dignity of Parliament.

Commons, May 5, 1940

Wartime Press

I sympathize very much, as an old former journalist and war correspondent, with the many able representatives of the Press who waited here from day to day, but I know they understood. All these matters have to be secret, and there cannot be any detailed information given here from day to day, or even at the end of the proceedings. The enemy will learn soon enough, in due course, all that we have decided here. I think we said this last year, now I come to think of it – almost these very words. Well, they have learned. What was then secret is now public. What was then concealed is now apparent. What was then in egg is now afoot. What was then a tender sprout has become a gigantic forest tree. What was then a design has become a blow, a mortal blow to the greatest of the military powers which have ranged themselves up against civilization and the progress of the world.

The Citadel, Quebec, September 16, 1944

'There never was a war easier to prevent by timely action than the one which has just desolated such great areas of the globe'

War, Prevention of

Up till the year 1933 or even 1935, Germany might have been saved from the awful fate which has overtaken her, and we might all have been spared the miseries Hitler let loose upon mankind. There never was a war in all history easier to prevent by timely action than the one which has just desolated such great areas of the globe. It could have been prevented, in my belief, without the firing of a single shot, and Germany might be powerful, prosperous and honoured today; but no one would listen and one by one we were all sucked into the awful whirlpool.

Westminster College, Fulton, Missouri, March 5, 1946

War, Shortening the

To shorten the war by a year, if that can be done, would in itself be a boon greater than many important acts of legislation. To shorten this war, to bring it to an end, to bring soldiers home, to give them a roof over their heads, to reestablish the free life of our country, to enable the wheels of commerce to revolve, to get the nations out of their terrible frenzy of hate, to build up something like a human world and a humane world – it is that that makes it so indispensable for us to struggle to shorten, be it even by a day, the course of this terrible war.

Commons, September 28, 1944

War, Strain of

The strain of protracted war is hard and severe upon the men at the executive summit of great countries, however lightly care may seem to sit upon them. They have need of all the help and comfort their fellow countrymen can give them.

Guildhall, London, June 30, 1943

War, Universal

There is another more obvious difference from 1914. The whole of the warring nations are engaged, not only soldiers, but the entire population, men, women, and children. The fronts are everywhere. The trenches are dug in the towns and streets. Every village is fortified. Every road is barred. The front line runs through the factories. The workmen are soldiers with different weapons but the same courage. These are great and distinctive changes from what many of us saw in the struggle of a quarter of a century ago.

Commons, August 20, 1940

'Every village is fortified. Every road is barred'

War of Unknown Warriors

All depends now upon the whole life-strength of the British race in every part of the world and of all our associated peoples and of all our well-wishers in every land, doing their utmost night and day, giving all, daring all, enduring all – to the utmost – to the end. This is no war of chieftains or of princes, of dynasties or national ambition; it is a war of peoples and of causes. There are vast numbers not only in this island but in every land, who will render faithful service in this war, but whose names will never be known, whose deeds will never be recorded. This is a war of the Unknown Warriors; but let all strive without failing in faith or in duty, and the dark curse of Hitler will be lifted from our age.

Commons, July 14, 1940

War, The Unnecessary

President Roosevelt one day asked what this war should be called. My answer was, "The Unnecessary War". If the United States had taken an active part in the League of Nations, and if the League of Nations had been prepared to use concerted force, even had it only been European force, to prevent the re-armament of Germany, there was no need for further serious bloodshed. If the Allies had resisted Hitler strongly in his early stages, even up to his seizure of the Rhineland in 1936, he would have been forced to recoil, and a chance would have been given to the sane elements in German life, which were very powerful, especially in the High Command, to free Germany of the maniacal government and system into the grip of which she was falling.

Brussels, November 16, 1945

War, Way to Lose a

To hear some people talk, however, one would think that the way to win the war is to make sure that every Power contributing armed forces and branches of these armed forces is represented on all the councils and organizations which have to be set up, and that everybody is fully consulted before anything is done. That is, in fact, the most sure way to lose a war.

Commons, January 27, 1942

Warfare in the Desert

Warfare in the Western Desert or, indeed, in all the deserts which surround Egypt, can only be conducted by comparatively small numbers of highly-equipped troops. Here the fortunes of war are subject to violent oscillation, and mere numbers do not count. On the contrary, the movement in the desert of large numbers would, if things went wrong, lead only to disaster on a larger scale. That is what happened to the Italians.

Commons, May 7, 1941

The desert warfare has to be seen to be believed. Large armies, with their innumerable transport and tiny habitations, are dispersed and scattered as if from a pepper-pot over the vast indeterminate slopes and plains of the desert, broken here and there only by a sandy crease or tuck in the ground or an outcrop of rock. The ground in most places, especially on all commanding eminences, is rock with only an inch or two of sand on the top, and no cover can be obtained for guns or troops except by blasting. Scattered though the troops are, there is an elaborate system of signalling, the enormous development of which is incredible. The more improvements there are in our means of communication, the more people are required to serve the Signal Branch. But owing to this elaborate system of signalling, in which tens of thousands of people are engaged, this army, scattered over the vast areas, can be moved and brought into action with extraordinary rapidity, and enormous distances can be covered by either side in what would have seemed a few years ago to be an incredibly short space of time.

Commons, September 8, 1942

Warfare, Lowest Form of

In the last few weeks the German U-boats, having largely abandoned the gun for the torpedo, have descended from the torpedo to the mine. This is about the lowest form of warfare that can be imagined.

Commons, December 6, 1939

Warsaw

The fall of Warsaw, at a time when Allied Armies are everywhere victorious, and when the final defeat of Germany is in sight, must come as a very bitter blow to all Poles. At such a moment, I wish to express our respect for all those Poles who fell, fought, or suffered at Warsaw, and our sympathy with the Polish nation in this further grievous loss. Our confidence that the days of their tribulation are rapidly drawing to an end is unshakable. When the ultimate allied victory is achieved, the epic of Warsaw will not be forgotten. It will remain a deathless memory for the Poles, and for the friends of freedom all over the world.

Commons, October 5, 1944

I welcome this opportunity of paying tribute to the heroism and tenacity of the Polish Home Army and the population of Warsaw, who, after five years of oppression, have yet fought for nearly two months to contribute all in their power to the expulsion of the Germans from the capital of Poland.

Commons, September 26, 1944

Wealth

What we desire is freedom; what we need is abundance. Freedom and abundance – these must be our aims. The production of new wealth is far more beneficial, and on an incomparably larger scale, than class and Party fights about the liquidation of old wealth. We must try to share blessings and not miseries.

Commons, August 16, 1945

'New wealth must precede common-wealth, otherwise there will only be common poverty'

Wealth, New

The production of new wealth must precede common-wealth, otherwise there will only be common poverty.

Commons, August 16, 1945

Weapons

There is one more general feature which has emerged in the fighting in Normandy to which I must draw the attention of the House. No new tank weapon or type of ammunition has been employed by the enemy. They have brought out nothing new so far, whereas we have put into operation for the first time in these operations the Sherman tank mounting the 17-pounder, the latest Churchill tank, and the new Cromwell tank, and we have also a number of interesting variants of very great ingenuity, which I cannot tell the House about today, because we do not know whether the enemy have had an opportunity of testing them and tasting them. It is only when I know they know that the secrets can be unfolded. One has to be very careful, because people object very much indeed if anything is revealed which seems to take away any chance that our troops may enjoy in this country and with our Allies.

Commons, August 2, 1944

We must not in any circumstances allow these favourable tendencies to weaken our efforts or lead us to suppose that our dangers are past or that the war is coming to an end. On the contrary, we must expect that the terrible foe we are smiting so heavily will make frenzied efforts to retaliate. The speeches of the German leaders, from Hitler downwards, contain mysterious allusions to new methods and new weapons which will presently be tried against us. It would, of course, be natural for the enemy to spread such rumours in order to encourage his own people, but there is probably more in it than that.

Commons, September 21, 1943

'Between 100 and 150 flying bombs, each weighing about one ton, are being discharged daily from the firing-points in France'

To the blood-curdling threats which German propaganda has been making in order to keep up the spirit of their people and of their satellites, there have been added the most absurd claims about the results of the first use of the secret weapon. I minimize nothing, I assure the House, but I think it right to correct those absurdities by giving some actual facts and figures, knowledge of which, although they may not be known to the enemy, will do him very little good, in my opinion and in the opinion of my advisers. Between 100 and 150 flying bombs, each weighing about one ton, are being discharged daily, and have been so discharged for the last fortnight or so, from the firing-points in France. Considering the modest weight and small penetration-power of these bombs, the damage they have done by blast effect has been extensive. It cannot at all be compared with the terrific destruction by fire and high explosives with which we have been assaulting Berlin, Hamburg, Cologne, and scores of other German cities and other war-manufacturing points in Germany.

Commons, July 6, 1944

Weather in War

The great episode seemed to everyone to be the crossing of the Channel, with its stormy waters, swift currents, and 18-foot rise and fall of the tide, and above all the changes of weather, which when an operation as big as this has to be undertaken might easily cut a portion of the Army off upon the shore for several days without anyone being able to get to them to reinforce them or even to withdraw them, and thus leave them at the mercy of a superior enemy. That was the element, this possible change in the weather, which certainly hung like a vulture poised in the sky over the thoughts of the most sanguine.

Commons, August 2, 1944

Weitzmann, Dr Chaim

Those of us who have been Zionists since the days of the Balfour Declaration know what a heavy loss Israel has sustained in the death of its President, Dr Chaim Weitzmann. Here was a man whose fame and fidelity were respected throughout the free world, whose son was killed fighting for us in the late war, and who, it may be rightly claimed, led his people back into their promised land, where we have seen them invincibly established as a free and sovereign State.

Guildhall, London, November 10, 1952

Win or Lose

If we win, nobody will care. If we lose, there will be nobody to care.

Commons, June 25, 1941

Winant, John G

It is a great pleasure to see Mr Winant among us. He gives the feeling that all President Roosevelt's men give me, that they would be shot stone dead rather than see this cause let down.

London, March 27, 1941

"Winter, General"

Then Hitler made his second blunder. He forgot about the winter. There is a winter, you know, in Russia. For a good many months the temperature is apt to fall very low. There is snow, there is frost, and all that. Hitler forgot about this Russian winter. He must have been very loosely educated. We all heard about it at school; but he forgot it. I have never made such a bad mistake as that.

London, May 10, 1942

Wisdom

I have an invincible confidence in the genius of Britain. I believe in the instinctive wisdom of our well-tried democracy. I am sure they will speak now in ringing tones, and that their decision will vindicate the hopes of our friends in every land and will enable us to march in the vanguard of the United Nations in majestic enjoyment of our fame and power.

London, June 30, 1945

I have always been astonished, having seen the end of these two wars, how difficult it is to make people understand Roman wisdom, "Spare the conquered and war down the proud." I think I will go so far as to say it in the original: *Parcere subjectis, et debellare superbos.* The modern practice has too often been, punish the defeated and grovel to the strong.

Commons, December 14, 1950

Wisdom, Spread of

It would be a great reform in politics if wisdom could be made to spread as easily and as rapidly as folly.

Guildhall, London, September 10, 1947

Wishful Thinking

There is danger in wishful thinking that victory will come by internal collapse of the Axis. Victory depends on force of arms. I stand pat on a knock-out, but any windfalls in the way of internal collapse will be gratefully accepted.

Washington, DC, May 25, 1943

Woe

I never take pleasure in human woe.

Glasgow, April 17, 1953

Women

The war effort could not have been achieved if the women had not marched forward in millions and undertaken all kinds of tasks and work for which any other generation but our own – unless you go back to the

Stone Age – would have considered them unfitted; work in the fields, heavy work in the foundries and in the shops, very refined work on radio and precision instruments, work in the hospitals, responsible clerical work of all kinds, work throughout the munitions factories, work in the mixed batteries – I take a special interest in those most remarkable societies where there are more women than men and where the weapons are handled with the utmost skill and proficiency. These mixed batteries have saved scores of thousands of strong men from static employment, and set them free for the field armies and the mobile batteries. Nothing has been grudged and the bounds of women's activities have been definitely, vastly, and permanently enlarged.

The Royal Albert Hall, London, September 29, 1943

Words

Words, which are on proper occasions, the most powerful engine, lose their weight and power and value when they are not backed by fact or winged by truth, when they are obviously the expression of a strong feeling, and are not related in any way to the actual facts of the situation.

Commons, April 22, 1926

Words, Short

> Short words are best and the old words when short are best of all.
>
> *London, November 2, 1949*

Personally, I like short words and vulgar fractions.

Margate, October 10, 1953

Workmen, British

The average British workman in good health, in full employment at standard rates of wages, does not regard himself and his family as objects for compassion.

Commons, April 28, 1925

World Destruction

What is Herr Hitler going to do? Is he going to try to blow up the world or not? The world is a very heavy thing to blow up. An extraordinary man at a pinnacle of power may create a great explosion, and yet the civilized world may remain unshaken. The enormous fragments and splinters of the explosion may clatter down upon his own head and destroy him and all who stand around him, but the world will go on. Civilization will not succumb; the working people in the free countries will not be enslaved again.

City Carlton Club, London, June 28, 1939

There is a general opinion which I have noticed, that it would be a serious disaster if the particular minor planet which we inhabit blew itself to pieces, or if all human life were extinguished upon its surface, apart, that is to say, from fierce beings, armed with obsolescent firearms, dwelling in the caverns of the Stone Age. There is a general feeling that that would be a regrettable event. Perhaps, however, we flatter ourselves. Perhaps we are biased: but everyone realizes how far scientific knowledge has outstripped human virtue. We all hope that men are better, wiser, more merciful than they were 10,000 years ago. There is certainly a great atmosphere of comprehension. There is a growing factor which one may call world public opinion, most powerful, most persuasive, most valuable. We understand our unhappy lot, even if we have no power to control it.

Commons, November 7, 1945

World, Future of the

The future of the world is to the highly-educated races who alone can handle the scientific apparatus necessary for pre-eminence in peace or survival in war.

London, March 21, 1943

'We intend to set up a world order and organization to prevent the breaking-out of future wars, or the long planning of them in advance by restless and ambitious nations'

World Order, New

Scarred and armed with experience, we intend to take better measures this time than could ever previously have been conceived in order to prevent a renewal, in the lifetime of our children or our grandchildren at least, of the horrible destruction of human values which has marked the last and the present world wars. We intend to set up a world order and organization, equipped with all the necessary attributes of power, in order to prevent the breaking-out of future wars, or the long planning of them in advance by restless and ambitious nations.

Commons, May 24, 1944

Worry

Worry has been defined by some nerve-specialists as a "spasm of the imagination". The mind, it is said, seizes hold of something and simply cannot let it go. Reason, argument, threats, are useless. The grip becomes all the more convulsive. But if you could introduce some new theme, in this case the practical effect of a common purpose and of co-operation for a common end, then indeed it might be that these clenched fists would relax into open hands, that the reign of peace and freedom might begin, and that science, instead of being a shameful prisoner in the galleys of slaughter, might pour her wealth abounding into the cottage homes of every land.

Commons, April 14, 1937

Worst of Both Worlds

There is something to be said for isolation; there is something to be said for alliances. But there is nothing to be said for weakening the Power on the Continent with whom you would be in alliance, and then involving yourself further in Continental tangles in order to make it up to them. In that way you have neither one thing nor the other; you have the worst of both worlds.

Commons, March 14, 1934

Wrong-Doing

It is always very difficult to know, when you embark on the path of wrong-doing, exactly where to stop.

Commons, February 22, 1911

TO THE YOUTH OF AMERICA I SAY: "YOU CANNOT STOP."

There is no halting place at this point.

There can be no pause. We must go on. It must be world anarchy or world order.

Harvard University, September 6, 1943

Yalta

I am not prepared to say that everything discussed at Yalta could be made the subject of a verbatim report.

Commons, June 7, 1945

Yalta Agreement

The Agreement which was made at Yalta, to which I was a party, was extremely favourable to Soviet Russia, but it was made at a time when no one could say that the German war might not extend all through the summer and autumn of 1945, and when the Japanese war was expected to last for a further eighteen months from the end of the German war.

Westminster College, Fulton, Missouri, March 5, 1946

Yalta and Polish Frontiers

Broadly speaking, at Yalta we reached an agreement about the eastern frontiers of Poland on the basis of full Polish independence. We did not reach the point of deciding what compensation should be given to Poland for the changes on her eastern frontiers in favour of Russia – what compensation should be given her at the expense of Germany – but there had been some talk, during the days of Teheran, about the line of the Oder.

Commons, January 23, 1948

You never can tell

There are times when so many things happen, and happen so quickly, and time seems to pass in such a way that you can neither say it is long or short, that it is easy to forget what you have said three months before. You may fail to connect it with what you are advocating at the particular moment. Throughout a long and variegated Parliamentary life this consideration has led me to try to keep a watchful eye on that danger myself. You never can tell. There are also people who talk and bear themselves as if they had prepared for this war with great armaments and long careful preparation. But that is not true. In two and a half years of fighting we have only just managed to keep our heads above water.

Commons, January 27, 1942

Youth

You young men here may be in the battle, in the fields or in the high air.

Others will be the heirs to the victory your elders or your parents have gained, and it will be for you to ensure that what is achieved is not cast away, either by violence of passion or by sheer stupidity. But let keen vision, courage and humanity guide our steps, so that it can be said of us that not only did our country do its duty in the war, but afterwards in the years of peace it showed wisdom, poise and sincerity, which contributed in no small degree to bind up the frightful wounds caused by the struggle.

Harrow School, Harrow, November 5, 1943

Youth cannot stop

To the youth of America, as to the youth of Britain, I say: "You cannot stop." There is no halting place at this point. We have now reached a stage in the journey where there can be no pause. We must go on. It must be world anarchy or world order. Throughout all this ordeal and struggle which is characteristic of our age, you will find in the British Commonwealth and Empire good comrades to whom you are united by other ties besides those of State policy and public need. To a large extent, they are the ties of blood and history. Naturally I, a child of both worlds, am conscious of these.

Harvard University, September 6, 1943

Yugoslavia

This valiant, steadfast people, whose history for centuries has been to struggle for life, and who owe their survival to their mountains and to their fighting qualities, made every endeavour to placate the Nazi monster. If they had made common cause with the Greeks when the Greeks, having been attacked by Italy, hurled back the invaders, the complete destruction of the Italian armies in Albania could certainly and swiftly have been achieved long before the German forces could have reached the theatre of war. And even in January and February of this year, this extraordinary military opportunity was still open. But the Government of Prince Paul, untaught by the fate of so many of the smaller countries of Europe, not only observed the strictest neutrality and refused even to enter into effective Staff conversations with Greece or with Turkey or with us, but hugged the delusion that they could preserve their independence by patching up some sort of pact or compromise with Hitler. Once again we saw the odious German poisoning technique employed. In this case,

however, it was to the Government rather than to the nation that the doses
and the inoculation were administered.

Commons, April 9, 1941

Yugoslavia, Attack on

A boa constrictor, who had already covered his prey with his foul saliva
and then had it suddenly wrested from his coils, would be in an amiable
mood compared with Hitler, Goering, Ribbentrop and the rest of the
Nazi gang when they experienced this bitter disappointment. A frightful
vengeance was vowed against the Southern Slavs. Rapid, perhaps
hurried, redispositions were made of the German forces and German
diplomacy. Hungary was offered large territorial gains to become the
accomplice in the assault upon a friendly neighbour with whom she had
just signed a solemn pact of friendship and non-aggression. Count
Teleki preferred to take his own life rather than to join in such a deed of
shame. A heavy forward movement of the German armies already
gathered in and dominating Austria was set in motion through Hungary
to the northern frontier of Yugoslavia. A ferocious howl of hatred from
the supreme miscreant was the signal for the actual invasion. The open
city of Belgrade was laid in ashes, and at the same time a tremendous
drive by the German armoured forces which had been so improvidently
allowed to gather in Bulgaria was launched westward into Southern
Serbia. And as it was no longer worth while to keep up the farce of love
for Greece, other powerful forces rolled forward into Greece, where they
were at once unflinchingly encountered, and have already sustained
more than one bloody repulse at the hands of that heroic army. The
British and Imperial troops have not, up to the present, been engaged.
Further than this I cannot attempt to carry the tale.

Commons, April 9, 1941

Yugoslavia in Revolt

Early this morning the Yugoslav nation found its soul. A revolution has
taken place in Belgrade and the Ministers who but yesterday signed away
the honour and freedom of the country are reported to be under arrest.
This patriotic movement arises from the wrath of a valiant and warlike
race at the betrayal of their country by the weakness of their rulers and the
foul intrigues of the Axis Powers.

London, March 27, 1941

THERE IS NO ROOM NOW FOR THE DILETTANTE, THE WEAKLING,

for the shirker, or the sluggard.

From the highest to the humblest tasks, all are of equal honour; all have their part to play.

Canadian Senate and Commons, Ottawa, December 30, 1941

Zeal, Unrelenting

According to my sense of proportion, this is no time to speak of the hopes of the future or the broader world which lies beyond our struggles and our victory. We have to win that world for our children. We have to win it by our sacrifices. We have not won it yet. The crisis is upon us. The power of the enemy is immense. If we were in any way to underrate the strength, the resources, or the ruthless savagery of that enemy, we should jeopardize, not only our lives, for they will be offered freely, but the cause of human freedom and progress to which we have vowed ourselves and all we have. We cannot for a moment afford to relax. On the contrary, we must drive ourselves forward with unrelenting zeal. In this strange terrible world war there is a place for everyone, man and woman, old and young, hale and halt; service in a thousand forms is open. There is no room now for the dilettante, the weakling, for the shirker, or the sluggard. The mine, the factory, the dockyard, the salt sea waves, the fields to till, the home, the hospital, the chair of the scientist, the pulpit of the preacher – from the highest to the humblest tasks, all are of equal honour; all have their part to play.

Canadian Senate and Commons, Ottawa, December 30, 1941

Zeppelins

No responsible officer at the War Office or at the Admiralty whom I ever met before the war anticipated that Zeppelins would be used to drop bombs indiscriminately on undefended towns and the countryside. This was not because of any extravagant belief in human virtue in general, or in German virtue in particular, but because it is reasonable to assume that your enemy will be governed by good sense and by a lively regard for his own interests.

Commons, May 17, 1916

Zionism

If our dreams for Zionism are to end in the smoke of assassins' pistols, and our labours for its future to produce only a new set of gangsters worthy of Nazi Germany, many like myself will have to reconsider the position we have maintained so consistently and so long. [Ref. to the assassination of Lord Moyne.]

Commons, November 17, 1944

TIMELINE

OF THE MORE IMPORTANT EVENTS IN THE
LIFE OF SIR WINSTON CHURCHILL

1874

- Winston Leonard Spencer Churchill, son of Lord and Lady Randolph Churchill, is born prematurely at Blenheim Palace (November 30th).

1888

- Enters Harrow in the bottom form (April).

1892

- Leaves Harrow (December) and is seriously injured in an accident.

1893

- Enters the Royal Military College, Sandhurst, as a cavalry cadet (June 28th).

1894

- Prepared, but not required, to make a speech on behalf of the Entertainments Protection League.
- Passes out of Sandhurst (December).

1895

- His father dies (January 24th).
- Gazetted to the 4th Hussars (April 1st).
- Visits Cuba to study the fighting there (November). He writes his first article, a descriptive letter to the *Daily Graphic* (published December 6th).

1896

- Leaves for India with the 4th Hussars, takes up polo and discovers Gibbon and Macaulay.

1897

- During leave, accompanies the Malakand Field Force against the Pathans as a war correspondent.

1898

- Takes part in the Battle of Omdurman, at his own expense (September 2nd).
- Sails to India to rejoin his regiment (December 1st).
- Published: *The Malakand Field Force*.

1899

- Leaves the Army.
- Fights his first by-election, unsuccessfully, at Oldham (July).
- Sent to South Africa as a war correspondent by the *Morning Post* (October).
- Captured by the Boers (November 15th), but escapes (December 13th).
- A reward of £25 is offered for his recapture.
- Published: *The River War.*

1900

- Accepts a commission in the South African Light Horse.
- One of the first to enter captured Pretoria (June 5th).
- Returns to England (July).
- Elected Conservative Member of Parliament for Oldham in a General Election (October 1st).
- Gives the first lecture of an American tour in New York, with Mark Twain in the chair (December 16th).
- Published: *Savrola, London to Ladysmith via Pretoria, Ian Hamilton's March.*

1901

- Takes his seat in Parliament (January).
- Makes his maiden speech (February).
- Attacks the Estimates (May 13th).

1903

- Attacks Joseph Chamberlain's policy of Protection (May 28th).
- Published: *Mr. Brodrick's Army.*

1904

- A large number of Unionists leaves the chamber of the House when he rises to speak (March 21st).
- Forced to abandon his speech on the Trades Disputes Bill when his memory fails (April 22nd).
- Crosses the floor of the House to sit with the Liberal Party (May 31st).

1906

- Is elected Liberal Member of Parliament for North-West Manchester in General Election.
- Joins the Government as Under-Secretary for the Colonies.
- Published: *Lord Randolph Churchill.*

1907

- Made a Privy Councillor.

1908

- Appointed President of the Board of Trade with a seat in the Cabinet and therefore has to seek re-election. He is defeated at Manchester (April 24th) but elected to represent Dundee (May 23rd).
- Marries Miss Clementine Hozier at St Margaret's Church, Westminster (September 12th).
- Published: *My African Journey.*

1909

- Instrumental in the setting up of Labour Exchanges.
- His daughter Diana is born.

1910

- Becomes Home Secretary and introduces the Mines Accidents Act.
- Attends manoeuvres of the German Army near Wurzburg.

1911

- Present at the "siege of Sidney Street" (January 3rd).
- Calls out the military on the occasion of a railway strike (August).
- Becomes a member of the Committee of Imperial Defence and circulates to the Cabinet (August 13th) a memorandum on *Military Aspects of the Continental Problem.*
- Becomes First Lord of the Admiralty (October 25th) and appoints a new Admiralty Board (November 28th).
- His son Randolph is born (May 28th).

1912

- Raises the rate of battleship construction from two to four a year, although urging Germany to agree to a "shipbuilding holiday".

1913

- Becomes an Elder Brother of Trinity House.

1914

- Secures Parliamentary approval of a plan for buying control of a Persian oilfield to secure supplies for naval ships newly converted to oil burning (June 17th).

- Orders a mobilization exercise for the fleet, which does not disperse when the exercise ends (July).
- Orders full naval mobilization (August 2nd).
- Organizes the defence of Antwerp during the Battle of Ypres (October 2nd).
- His daughter Sarah is born (October).
- Elected Lord Rector of Aberdeen University.

1915

- Proposes a joint naval and military attack on the Dardanelles at a meeting of the War Council (January 3rd).
- Removed from the Admiralty in the new Coalition Government and appointed Chancellor of the Duchy of Lancaster (May 28th).
- Experiments with his children's paintboxes and takes up oil painting as a hobby.
- Resigns from the Cabinet, returns to the Army and leaves for France (November 19th) with the 6th Royal Scots Fusiliers.

1916

- Returns to political life in London (May).

1917

- Becomes Minister of Munitions in Lloyd George's Government (July 16th).

1918

- Visits France to survey the position for Lloyd George (March).
- Becomes Secretary of State for War and Minister for Air (December).

1921

- Succeeds Lord Milner as Colonial Secretary and attends a Middle Eastern Conference at Cairo (March).
- Assists Lloyd George in negotiations with Sinn Fein leaders.
- Appeals to the Dominions for support against the threatened Turkish invasion of Thrace.
- His mother dies.

1922

- Resigns the post of Colonial Secretary after his defeat at Dundee in the General Election: during his campaign his appendix is removed.
- Becomes a Companion of Honour.

1923

- Stands at an election for West Leicester as a Liberal Free Trader and is defeated.
- Published: *The World Crisis* (Six volumes, 1923–31).

1924

- Breaks with the Liberal Party (February) and stands as a Constitutionalist for the Abbey Division of Westminster in a by-election, but is defeated (March 20th).
- Wins a libel case against Lord Alfred Douglas.

- In a General Election is elected Member of Parliament for Epping as a Constitutionalist and Anti-Socialist, with Conservative support.
- Becomes Chancellor of the Exchequer in Stanley Baldwin's Government (November).

1925

- Introduces his first Budget and announces the decision to return to the Gold Standard (April 28th).
- Receives the honorary degree of DCL from Oxford University.

1926

- Organizes and edits the *British Gazette* during the General Strike (May).

1928

- Takes up brick-laying as a hobby and joins the Amalgamated Union of Building Workers.

1929

- Loses office when Baldwin resigns after his Party's defeat in the General Election (May).
- Elected Lord Rector of Edinburgh University.

1930

- Resigns from the Conservative "Shadow Cabinet" after a disagreement with Baldwin on policy in India (January).
- Becomes Chancellor of Bristol University (January).
- Resigns from the chairmanship of

the Conservative Finance Committee (April).

- At Oxford, delivers the Romanes lecture, on Party Government and the Economic Problem.
- Published: *My Early Life.*

1931

- Is a member of the Conservative majority supporting the Government, but without office (August).

1932

- Published: *Thoughts and Adventures.*

1933

- Published: *Marlborough, Volume I.*

1934

- Published: *Marlborough, Volume II.*

1936

- Attempts, unsuccessfully, to prevent the abdication of King Edward VIII.
- Published: *Marlborough, Volume III.*

1937

- Exclusion from office is continued when Neville Chamberlain succeeds Baldwin.
- Published: *Great Contemporaries.*

1938

- Protests against Chamberlain's policy of "buying a few years of peace" (April).
- Attacks the Munich agreement as

"a total and unmitigated defeat" (September).

- Published: *Marlborough, Volume IV.*

1939

- Joins Chamberlain's Cabinet as First Lord of the Admiralty (September) and sets the convoy system in operation.
- Urges the creation of an all-party Government.
- Published: *Step By Step.*

1940

- Gives direct orders for the boarding of the *Altmark* and rescue of British prisoners (February 16th).
- Appointed head of the Committee of Service Ministers (April).
- Makes a statement on naval operations after the first battle of Narvik (April 11).
- Succeeds Chamberlain as Prime Minister, forming a Coalition Government to include the Labour and Liberal Parties (May 10th).
- In his first speech as Prime Minister he offers the House of Commons nothing but "blood, toil, tears and sweat" (May 13th).
- In his first broadcast as Prime Minister he warns the nation of the coming "battle for our island" (May 19th).
- Reports to the House of Commons the news of Dunkirk and determination not to surrender (June 4th).
- Invites France to join Great Britain in a Federal Union (June 16th).
- Makes a statement on the

possibilities of invasion
(June 18th).

- Makes a statement on Oran where a British fleet has caused great damage to French ships which refused either to join the British or to allow themselves to be interned (July 4th).
- In the House of Commons he pays tribute to the gallantry of fighter pilots (August 20th).
- Makes a statement on German invasion preparations to the House of Commons (September 17th).
- Elected leader of the Conservative Party (October 9th).
- Attends the christening of his grandson, Winston (December 1st).

1941

- Becomes Lord Warden of the Cinque Ports.
- Answers critics of the Crete campaign in the House of Commons (June 10th).
- When Russia is invaded, he broadcasts an assurance of help (June 22nd).
- At sea, he signs the Atlantic Charter with President Roosevelt (August 9th).
- Visits Iceland (August 17th).
- Concludes the Anglo-American Agreement (September).
- Introduces a new National Service Bill, which includes provisions for the conscription of women (December 2nd).
- Addresses a joint meeting of both Houses of Congress in Washington

(December 26th).
- Addresses the Canadian Legislature at Ottawa (December 30th).

1942

- Broadcasts on the occasion of the fall of Singapore (February 15th).
- Announces the mission of Sir Stafford Cripps to India offering Dominion status (March 11).
- Flies to the United States to discuss the proposed invasion of North Africa with President Roosevelt (June 18th).
- After visiting Cairo, El Alamein and Teheran, arrives in Moscow (August 12th).

1943

- Attends the Allied Conference at Casablanca, agreeing that peace must come only by the unconditional surrender of the Axis Powers (January 14th).
- Holds discussions with the President of Turkey at Adana (January 30th).
- Elected an Honorary Academician Extraordinary of the Royal Academy.
- Addresses US Congress (May 19th).
- Visits North Africa to consult with Generals de Gaulle and Giraud (May 30th).
- In a speech at the Guildhall, he gives a pledge to crush Japan after Germany (June 30th).
- Arrives in Canada for further conferences with President Roosevelt (August 10th).

- In a speech at Harvard, he advocates the world teaching of Basic English (September).
- Attends a conference of the Allied leaders in Cairo, followed by another in Teheran where he and President Roosevelt are joined by Marshal Stalin. Returns to Cairo for discussions with the President of Turkey (November).
- Falls ill with pneumonia, but is saved by a new drug, M and B 693. He goes to Marrakesh for his convalescence (December).

1944
- Arrives back in London (January).
- Opens the conference of Commonwealth Prime Ministers in London (May 1st).
- Six days after D-Day he tours the battle-front in France (June 12th).
- Arrives in Italy to meet the Pope and Yugoslav representatives (August 11th).
- Confers with President Roosevelt in Quebec (September 10th).
- Confers with Marshal Stalin in Moscow (October 9th).
- At the time of the invitation to France to become a member of the European Advisory Commission, he visits Paris (November 10th).
- Arrives for a conference with Greek political representatives in Athens (December 25th).

1945
- Meets President Roosevelt at Malta (February 2nd).

- He and President Roosevelt join Marshal Stalin at Yalta (February 4th).
- Confers with rulers of Middle Eastern states in Cairo (February 16th).
- Broadcasts the news of the unconditional surrender of all German fighting forces (May 8th).
- Resigns the Premiership and is invited to form a new administration (May 23rd).
- Attends a Three-Power Conference at Potsdam (July 17th).
- Resigns the Premiership when the Conservative Party is defeated in a General Election (July 26th).

1946
- Awarded the Order of Merit (January 8th).
- Delivers a speech in Fulton, Missouri, coining the phrase "the Iron Curtain" and advocating "fraternal association of the English-speaking peoples" (March 5th).
- Published: *Victory.*

1947
- Advocates the European Movement in a speech at the Royal Albert Hall, London (May 14th).
- Exhibits at the Royal Academy.

1948
- Addresses the Congress of Europe at The Hague (May).
- Published: *Painting as a Pastime, The Gathering Storm.*

1949

- Awarded the Grotius Medal (February 3rd).
- Addresses Massachusetts Institute of Technology (March 31st).
- Addresses, discouragingly, the first meeting of the Council of Europe at Strasbourg (August 9th).
- Published: *Their Finest Hour.*

1950

- At a meeting of the Council of Europe he advocates a European Army (August).
- Visits Denmark and receives a prize from the Sonning Foundation (October 9th).
- Published: *The Grand Alliance.*

1951

- Following a Conservative victory in a General Election, he becomes Prime Minister again (October 26th).
- Published: *The Hinge of Fate.*

1952

- The *Daily Mirror* publishes a full apology for the story headlined "Whose finger on the trigger?" (May 24th).
- Published: *Closing the Ring.*

1953

- Made a Knight of the Garter (April 24th).
- Awarded the Nobel Prize for Literature (October 15th).
- Attends a conference at Bermuda with the US President and the French Prime Minister (December).

1954

- Visits Washington for discussions with President Eisenhower (June).
- Supports the Nine-Power Conference in London (September).
- In a speech at his constituency of Woodford, he starts a controversy with the mention of a telegram sent to Field-Marshal Montgomery on the subject of German arms (November 23rd).
- To celebrate his 80th birthday, he is presented by both Houses of Parliament with his portrait painted by Graham Sutherland (November 30th).
- Published: *Triumph and Tragedy.*

1955

- Resigns the Premiership and Leadership of the Conservative Party (April 5th).
- Accepts the Freedom Award (October 9th) and the Williamsburg Award (October 16th).

1956

- Receives the Benjamin Franklin Medal (January 11th).
- Published: *History of the English-Speaking Peoples, Vol. 1.*

1965

- Dies and is given state funeral.